EMINENT DISTORIANS

Advance Praise

'History is not a science. It is an interpretation, a narrative, based on facts and scientific evidence gathered at that point of time. Oftentimes, historical narratives have been challenged. Sometimes because new facts and scientific evidence have emerged; at other times because the earlier historians had their own biases and even incapabilities. Whatever the reasons be, the challenging of the establishment norms is a rich Indian tradition. And there is no doubt that the historical interpretations handed down to us by the British Raj and the establishment historians need to be challenged, and even decolonized. Utpal Kumar does this simply and well. With the skills of a history connoisseur and the light-touch readability of a journalist. Do read this book!'

Amish Tripathi, author and former director,
Nehru Centre, London

'The history of a country is usually written by its own people steeped in its own culture. The history of India, however, as we read it today, was reconstructed by Western scholars during colonial times and was then narrated during the post-independent period through the lens of partisan ideological interests by its own eminent historians. This book sets out to correct this distorted version for the general reader and accomplishes its goal so successfully that it was unputdownable once I started reading it.'

Arvind Sharma, Birks Professor in comparative religion,
McGill University, Montreal

'This important book by noted author Utpal Kumar, with clarity, depth and detail, exposes the massive distortion of India's history perpetrated by Marxists and the Nehruvian left, which they built on colonial and missionary prejudices and were used by the Congress party to cement its dynastic control over the idea of India. Such so-called eminent historians were deceptive anti-Hindu propagandists who betrayed the Indian independence movement, which was built on honouring India's civilizational history by great gurus like Sri Aurobindo, Rabindranath Tagore and Lokmanya Tilak. This insightful book should be introduced into classes on India's history and its views integrated into India's history textbooks to remove these harmful distortions and help India/Bharat reclaim its past, identity, dignity and future as the oldest, most enduring and profound nation and civilization in the world.'

David Frawley, author and director,
American Institute of Vedic Studies

'*Eminent Distorians* is a masterful deconstruction of previous colonialist and Marxist narratives that dominated the history of India. The fast-paced discussion tells the history of India from the perspective of the residents of India rather than the outsider perspective as was the case previously. Analyzing major aspects of each historical era addressing the major qualities while also taking the previous distorted narratives to the Laundromat, *Eminent Historians* makes an important contribution to the history of India. The slanted and opinionated writings of Marxist historians are barred from dispelling the misunderstandings of the Vedas, Harappan civilization and historical achievements of early history while continuing with the analysis of the destructions of invaders including forest clearances of Islamic rulers in addition to the destruction of civilizational centres like cities, temples and *viswavidyalayas* like Nalanda by the exploitative British rule, and independence struggles and post-independence erasure of the sacrifices of revolutionary leaders. This well-researched book highlights the previously missing information in addition to overruling the misunderstandings promoted by the previously distorted historical narratives. For understanding the true history of India, *Eminent Distorians* is the necessary refresher.'

Lavanya Vemsani, Board of Trustees Distinguished University Professor, Shawnee State University; honorary visiting professor, Jawaharlal Nehru University; and former president, Ohio Academy of History

'This is a history of what became the official history of India after independence. In his fast-paced style, Utpal Kumar recounts the twists that led to a particular twisted narrative, the characters and their shadowy motivations, and finally how Indian history is being clawed back from colonial, Marxist and Nehruvian biases.'

Sanjeev Sanyal,
bestselling writer and acclaimed economist

'Bharat's history written from Bharat's perspective, *Eminent Distorians* has its heart in the right place as it deals with some of the most pressing and contentious issues of Indian history. Whether it's the myth of the Aryan invasion/migration theory or the invented greatness of the so-called Mughals or even the over-glorification of the role of Mahatma Gandhi in the country's freedom struggle, Utpal Kumar doesn't shy away from calling a spade a spade. And in the process, he exposes the monumental hypocrisy of our eminent historians ... err distorians. The book's sweeping and thought-provoking revision of the conventional colonialist view of Bharat's history should be a mandatory reading for all.'

Subhash Kak, Regents Professor,
Oklahoma State University

EMINENT DISTORIANS

Twists and Truths in Bharat's History

Utpal Kumar

ink | OCCAM

ISBN: 978-93-6547-718-4

First published in India 2025
This edition published 2025

BluOne Ink Pvt. Ltd
A-76, 2nd Floor, Sector 136, Noida
Uttar Pradesh 201301
www.bluone.ink
publisher@bluone.ink

Printed and bound in India by Thomson Press India Ltd.

Kali and Occam are imprints of BluOne Ink

ink | OCCAM

For
my elder brothers
Pranav Kumar
and
Ajit Pragya Kumar

For

my elder brothers

Pranav Kumar

and

[illegible] Kumar

CONTENTS

CONTENTS

Acknowledgements

The year was 1995. I had just passed my board exams. My family was badly divided over my decision to take the arts stream; for some of them, only mediocre students take that path. But my parents stood by me; they, in fact, thought I was doing the right thing.

A few months later, I received a registered post from Guwahati. My eldest brother, Pranav Kumar, who was pursuing his engineering course there, had sent it. When I opened the parcel, I was pleasantly surprised by its content: two books with simple but beautiful covers. The first was Romila Thapar's *History of India* (volume 1) and the second, *India's Struggle for Independence*, was written by Bipan Chandra, Mridula Mukherjee, Aditya Mukherjee, Sucheta Mahajan and K.N. Panikkar.

My 'historical' journey had just taken off. Over the next few years, the works of other historians such as R.C. Majumdar, Jadunath Sarkar, A.L. Basham, R.S. Sharma, D.N. Jha, Irfan Habib, Sumit Sarkar, among others, joined my bookshelves. It all went well for the next 4–5 years when my father, Braj Bihari Kumar, introduced me to Sita Ram Goel and his publication, Voice of India. If ever a single individual had moved the intellectual mountain in the left-gripped Bharat, it was Sita Ram Goel. He, under the guidance of Ram Swarup, took the entrenched 'eminent historians' by the horns, exposing their distortions, often deliberate and mischievous, by bringing out books written by the likes of

Koenraad Elst, Subhash Kak, David Frawley, Shrikant Talageri, N.S. Rajaram, among others.

Since I had read leftist historians extensively—and also intensively, often reading the same book several times—the Voice of India books jolted me out of my leftist slumber. Earlier, while reading Thapar and company, I used to feel that something was missing. Then, of course, came Arun Shourie who, with his stylish, fact-oriented writing, dismantled the intellectual halo around leftism. In that sense, this book is a tribute to Shourie and his *Eminent Historians*, and to all those people I met in the last 30 years, including eminent distorians, for informing, enlightening and even provoking me. *Eminent Historians* has had a splendid 30-year run; with its publication, it has finally reached home.

I am indebted to Amish Tripathi, Prof. Arvind Sharma, David Frawley, Prof. Lavanya Vemsani, Sanjeev Sanyal and Prof. Subhash Kak for taking time out of their busy schedules to read the book's manuscript and sharing their views on it. I am also grateful to Abhijit Majumder for inspiring me to write this book and to Shishir Tripathi for being a positive influence all through the journey. Above all, the book is the physical manifestation of unwavering faith shown by my publisher, BluOne Ink, especially Anirudh Chakravartty and Praveen Tiwari. I still remember the day they asked me over coffee if I would be interested in writing a book on Bharat's history. In fact, they had reached out to me even before they published my first book, *Bharat Rising: Dharma, Democracy, Diplomacy*. I am also thankful to Thanglenhao Haokip and Aditi Chopra for editing this book.

Finally, my wife, Chandra, and son, Ahaan, deserve a special thank-you note. It was their time that I took away to write this book—mostly after coming from office in the evening and over the weekends. Thank you!

Introduction
History Hijacked

Time to retell Bharat's story from its own perspective

I

There is something called 'time capsule'. For this, all you need is to get a historian to write a 'history' of your choice, and you bury it somewhere safe. Several prominent individuals and families have done this in the past. Even certain nations have gotten their history 'time-capsuled'! The United States, we are told, did the same in the early 20th century.

Modern Bharat, too, has a 'time capsule' story to tell. This was no ordinary time capsule, but the one that saw the then prime minister, Mrs Indira Gandhi, reach the Red Fort on 15 August 1973—another version that says it was done in 1975—and bury it with her own hands. Then, as fate would have it, Mrs Gandhi's Congress, for the first time since Independence, was routed in the 1977 general elections. And, on 8 December that very year, this time capsule was reportedly dug out in the presence of the then education minister, Pratap Chandra Chunder.

The incident was widely discussed and debated then, but today it has become a sort of urban legend. No one is sure if it at all took place. There is no official information about it. In fact, in 2013, when an academician-cum-activist sought the information about the capsule, the prime minister's office claimed it had no record at its disposal. She also reached out to the education ministry and then to other ministries; in one voice they all denied having any record related to the project.[1]

So comprehensive has been the blackout that one finds the mention of this incident in just two books—one in Hindi and another in English. The Hindi book, *Aisa Bhi Socha Jata Hai*,[2] written by Harishankar Parsai, a noted litterateur, is currently out of print, while Shankar Sharan is the author of the English book, *Marxism and the Writing of Indian History*.[3]

Parsai writes,

> Indira Gandhi lost the 1977 election. The Janata Party formed the government. It was then rumoured that the madam (Indira Gandhi) got the Time Capsule buried to make herself immortal in history. It must be a sheer eulogy of the Nehru family. The Janata Party government exhumed the Time Capsule. It contained the history of our times in just 3,000 words. There were no other names in it—not even the name of Mahatma Gandhi. It was said that the writer was paid three to four lakh rupees… He wrote whatever he was told to write. The history was all about Nehru, Nehru, Nehru, Indira, Indira, Indira.[4]

He continues,

> Later, an article by that writer (the author of the Time Capsule), who was a professor from Madras, was published. He wrote that Dr S. Gopal called him to Delhi and entrusted him with that task. He said that he was paid very little and had to spend from his own pocket for his stay in Delhi. 'What to talk of lakhs, I was not paid a single penny,' he added.[5]

Sharan brings out an unscrupulous side of Prof. Gopal as he quotes a detailed interview the 'eminent historians' aka distorians had given to the leftist weekly, *Link,* on 25 December 1977, soon after Indira Gandhi's Emergency regime was over. 'It was as ridiculous to dig up the time capsule as it was to bury it', Gopal said, adding, 'It is tragic that we have replaced a Right-wing fascist dictatorship with a Right-wing communal reactionary government.'[6]

In other words, Prof. Gopal, in a truly eating-the-cake-and-having-it-too style, 'showered some of the choicest abuses from the Marxist lexicon on the two governments, one led by Mrs India Gandhi and the other which replaced it'.

Sharan raises a few pertinent questions. 'Does it all go well with Prof. Gopal's scholarly abilities or moral norms that, first, he got a distorted version of history written for a government and, then, condemned the same government as 'right-wing' and 'fascist'?'[7]

Prof. Gopal's duplicity, personal as well as academic, did not stop here. He had been a known Nehru–Gandhi family lackey who would openly and viciously target those opposing the first prime minister and his daughter. In his three-volume Nehru biography, he would call Subhas Chandra Bose 'impatient, wilful and endlessly ambitious', besides being an 'egotistic, complicated, (and) ill-fated being' who was 'incapable of the wider view'.[8]

He was equally scathing in his assessment of other rivals of Nehru. He, for instance, saw Rajendra Prasad as 'the meek follower of Gandhi' who was 'untouched in any real sense by the spirit of Gandhi's teachings'—a 'loyal party man but of inferior intellectual quality and with a social outlook which belonged to the eighteenth century'. At another place in the book, he found the president to be 'prominent in the ranks of medievalism'.[9]

Prof. Gopal, as Sharan writes, 'was earlier an officer in the Ministry of Foreign Affairs and later was made a Professor of History in the Jawaharlal Nehru University (JNU), New Delhi. When the Time Capsule was removed Prof. Gopal was the chairman of the Centre of Historical Studies in JNU.' He, thus, owed a great deal to Jawaharlal Nehru and Indira Gandhi, but when the family's political fortune dipped post-1977, it didn't take Prof. Gopal a second to call the previous Congress regime 'a right-wing fascist dictatorship'![10]

Interestingly, the Gopal saga reminds one of what Raj Thapar, wife of Romesh Thapar—the two, in the 1970s, were an inalienable part of Mrs Indira Gandhi's 'kitchen cabinet'—has to say about Dr S. Radhakrishnan, father of Prof. Gopal and the second president of India. In her seminal memoirs, *All These Years*, Raj Thapar writes:

> Radhakrishnan finally dies and was given a state funeral. To me he was and will remain a wily Brahmin, keeping himself covered from all angles, sitting comfortably away during the freedom movement but making noises that could be tuned into at some late date as proof of his commitment, entertaining thoughts of a position even higher than that of presidentship, collecting feathers from wherever they fell to make the nest cushier… I was quite startled that so many thousands lined the roads for Radhakrishnan's funeral procession. Somehow, he never struck me as a man of the people, any people, but I was obviously wrong. As someone said, 'At least he didn't make money through corrupt practices.'[11]

Coming back to Prof. Gopal, when he made those comments he was accompanied by Prof. Bipan Chandra—another eminent distorian who owed so much to the Nehru–Gandhi family and had even defended Indira Gandhi's Emergency! In *India After Independence 1947–2000*, which he wrote with Mridula Mukherjee and Aditya Mukherjee, Chandra wrote, '[N]either JP nor Indira Gandhi chose the democratic way out of the crisis.' The larger narrative coming out of the book, however, was that Indira Gandhi was pushed to act undemocratically by the 'extra-constitutional and undemocratic... agitational methods adopted and propagated by the JP Movement'.[12]

Prof. Chandra wrote:

> The situation that was being created by the JP Movement was that of insurrection without revolution. The tactics it evolved over time amounted to a revolution. But this was to be a revolution without a revolutionary party, organisation, ideology or programme to give it direction and leadership. In fact, it was to be a revolution to be made with reliance on a mix of ideology-less cadre of the Chhatra Vahini, the conservative cadre of Congress (O), BKD and Swatantra Party and the communal neo-fascist cadre of RSS-Jan Sangh.[13]

Prof. Chandra's defence of Indira Gandhi didn't stop even when the Emergency was imposed. He wrote how 'a large number of people were impressed by the positive outcome of some of the well-publicised Emergency measures'; that 'apart from the arrest of the Opposition leaders, the repressive measures were almost entirely directed either against anti-social elements or against extreme communal Right or the minuscule far-Left'; and that the 'number of persons arrested in the first few days in the entire country was less than 10,000'.[14]

According to Prof. Chandra, it was only from the beginning of 1976 that the Emergency started becoming unpopular. 'Why was this delayed reaction? For one, the people had no experience in recent memory, that is since Independence, of an authoritarian rule. There was bewilderment as also personal fear of the unknown.'[15]

So, the Emergency backlash was the result of the 'fear of the unknown', as per Prof. Chandra! And, incredibly, he was by the side of Prof. Gopal when the latter charged the Indira Gandhi government of being 'a Right-wing fascist dictatorship'!

Prof. Gopal and Prof. Chandra, however, weren't the only distorians indulging in Orwellian doublethink and doublespeak!

II

The year was 2003. Romila Thapar, professor emeritus at Delhi's Jawaharlal Nehru University (JNU) and author of several books on ancient Indian history, was appointed the first holder of Kluge Chair in 'Countries and Cultures of the South' at the US Library of Congress. Established in 2000, the aim of the Kluge chairs was to 'facilitate discourse among top academics and political leaders' based in the US. It so happened that one Brannon Parker, who called himself a 'friend of India', sent a petition calling Thapar's selection a 'travesty' and 'wastage of our American resources on a Marxist ideological assault on Hindu civilisation'. Given Thapar's 'Euro-centric worldview', he wondered how her selection would bring true understanding of Hindu civilisation in the US.[16]

Parker passionately raised the issue, but he found himself dismissed as a right-wing agent. However, as one looks at Bharat's leftist historians led by Romila Thapar, their role in subverting the minds of people, turning them rootless and apologetic about their past, and also projecting a negative image of civilizational Bharat globally, it becomes difficult to ignore these charges. If the West today looks at Bharat as a land bereft of any intrinsic democratic, liberal values of its own, it's primarily the result of their mischief. For, according to them, Bharat is an artificial construct made of borrowed men and minds. It is seen as a landmass rich in natural resources but with no indigenous population of its own—the subcontinent is projected more like a railway platform where people of different racial profiles, from so-called Aryans to Muslims and Europeans, deboarded at various intervals to populate this landmass. And if Hinduism is projected as a religion that promotes superstition, gender violence, caste atrocities, and even religious fanaticism, the blame primarily lies with these distorians.

Leading the pack of these surveyors of Bharat's history is the 93-year-old Romila Thapar, about whom the citation of the Kluge Prize, awarded to her in 2008 by the Library of Congress, says: 'Her research has profoundly changed the way India's past is understood both at home and across the world'.[17]

And it did.

While reviewing Thapar's *Early India* in May 2003 for London's *Financial Times*, Edward Luce wrote:

> Romila Thapar's masterful recent book, Early India, ends before the Islamic era, but it makes it plain that the destruction of temples—a highly combustible issue in today's India—was also the normal thing for incoming Hindu dynasties to do… Well before Islam appeared in India, Hindu dynasties had erased almost all the Buddhist and Jainist temples of early dynasties.[18]

This narrative still finds itself deeply entrenched in certain quarters of the mainstream academia. So much so that when Prime Minister Narendra Modi, at the inauguration of the new campus of Nalanda University in June 2024, said that the university, in its ancient avatar, was burnt by foreign invaders in the 12th century, he was accused of 'parroting the popular perception that Bakhtiyar Khilji, the courtier of Mahmud Ghori, had burnt it', as one writer-cum-activist wrote in an article.[19]

It is believed that Nalanda Mahavihara was founded in the 5th century AD, more than 500 years before Oxford University came into existence. Regarded as the world's first residential university, it attracted 10,000 students and 3,000 teachers from across the world, including Eastern and Central Asia. Like today's elite universities, admission to Nalanda was quite tough. Aspiring students had to face a rigorous oral interview with the institution's top professors. Its library had nine million handwritten, palm-leaf manuscripts, and as per legends, when Bakhtiyar Khilji burnt this university in 1197 AD, the fire in the library raged for months.

Defying the historical consensus, a section of the academia ran a social media campaign—just when Prime Minister Modi was gearing up to inaugurate a new campus at Nalanda—saying Brahmins had destroyed the ancient Nalanda university. The inspiration, obviously, came from eminent distorians such as D.N. Jha, who had not very long ago provided legitimacy to such conspiracy theories by collecting dubious and unreliable records to put the blame on Brahmins for the Nalanda destruction. In the process, he, along with many other distorians—and activists—discounted the contemporary historical evidence such as the writings of Minhaj al-Siraj, a 13th-century Persian historian.

Minhaj writes,

> The greater number of the inhabitants of that place were Brahmans, and the whole of those Brahmans had their heads shaven; and they were all slain. There were a great number of books there; and, when all these books came under the observation of the Musalmans, they summoned a number of Hindus that they might give them information respecting the import of those books; but the whole of the Hindus had been killed. On becoming acquainted (with the contents of

> those books), it was found that the whole of that fortress and city was a college.[20]

Minhaj might have confused Brahmins with Buddhists—and it's understandable given his alien background—but what's irrefutable is the identity of the perpetrators. The likes of D.N. Jha turn such contemporary evidence upside down by taking recourse to not just dubious texts but also records that were written hundreds of years after the destruction of Nalanda.

In his 2004 presidential address in the Indian History Congress, Prof. Jha, for instance, talked about the destruction of Buddhist viharas, particularly the Nalanda Mahavihara. 'A Tibetan tradition has it that the Kalachuri King Karna (11th century) destroyed many Buddhist temples and monasteries in Magadha, and the Tibetan text *Pag Sam Jon Zang* refers to the burning of the library of Nalanda by some Hindu fanatics.' Interestingly, Jha took the help of an 18th-century text to vindicate his 'Hindu fanatics' charge. The author of *Pag Sam Jon Zang*, Sumpa Khan-Po Yece Pal Jor, lived in 1704–88 AD. Also, in his ideological excitement, Jha used a 20th-century expression of 'Hindu fanatics' for a 19th-century text![21]

Jha, however, was simply following the sacred Marxist manual of history writing. The notion of Hindu intolerance, after all, had made a subtle appearance as far back as in 1969, in the booklet, *Communalism and the Writing of Indian History*, written jointly by Romila Thapar, Harbans Mukhia and Bipan Chandra. In this 60-odd-page booklet, Thapar questions the 'assumption' that 'only a Muslim would despoil temples and break idols since the Islamic religion is opposed to idol worship'. She writes:

> Mahmud of Ghazni is primarily associated in most standard histories as the despoiler of temples and the breaker of

> idols. The explanation for this activity is readily provided by the fact that he was a Muslim—the assumption being that only a Muslim would despoil temples and break idols since the Islamic religion is opposed to idol worship. There is the further assumption in this that all Muslim rulers could be potential idol-breakers unless some other factors prevented them from doing so. Little attempt is made to search for further explanations regarding Mahmud's behaviour. Other reasons can be found when one turns to the tradition of Hindu kings and enquires whether any of them were despoilers of temples and idol-breakers: Here we come across the case of Harsha, an eleventh century king of Kashmir, for whom the despoiling of temples was an organised, institutionalised activity. Kalhana informs us in the *Rajatarangini* that Harsha appointed a special officer, the 'devotpatananayaka' (literally, the officer appointed for the uprooting of the gods) whose special job it was to plunder the temples. Here clearly the explanation cannot be that he was a religious iconoclast but that he plundered temples for their wealth which wealth he used for other purposes.[22]

The basic premise was: if Muslim rulers destroyed temples, so did Hindus!

If one thought, given the audacity of communist imagination to bracket Hinduism with Islam, there would be a plethora of evidence supporting the case of Hindu violence and vandalism, the story of Y.C. Rosser would give us a reality check. The American researcher, in the early 2000s, after reading about Hindu rulers' propensity to destroy their own temples and also decimate Buddhist viharas, reached out to the proponents of the theory. Rosser first met Harbans Mukhia, who 'has mentioned the destruction of temples by Hindus' in an article in the *Hindustan Times* (19 March 2000). 'I asked him what documents on the subject he had in possession. He told me that Prof. Romila Thapar has some information to support the proposition.' After some days, Rosser met Thapar and told her about the Mukhia conversation. 'She (Thapar) said she has not written anything but an American research scholar, Richard Eaton, has written something recently about it in the preface to his new book'.[23]

Now, that's the Marxist style of making a claim first and searching for evidence thereafter. Also, the incident shows how our leftist historians have their own time machine: Look how Thapar, in 1969, made an assumption of Hindus being idol-breakers too, and in early 2000, more than three decades later, she claimed she had no evidence with her.

To unearth a Hindu hand in temple-vihara destruction is a sinister lie. Such narratives are actually based on half-a-dozen stories of dubious origins—of Kalinga King Kharvela, Pallava King Narasimhavarman, King Harsha of Kashmir, Kalachuri King Karna and King Shashank of Gauda. (One can also add the names of Pushyamitra Sunga and a Pandya ruler to the list, but their sources are so compromised that even leftist historians use them with a pinch of salt.)

In *Flight of Deities and Rebirth of Temples*, historian Meenakshi Jain talks about Kharavela and Narasimhavarman to demolish the myth. 'Almost without exception, Hindu rulers honoured the images they acquired, thereby reaffirming a shared sense of the sacred. In the Islamic case, seizure of an image entailed its very dismemberment', Jain writes as she explains how Kharavela (2nd–1st century BC) and Narasimhavarman (7th century AD), after vanquishing their adversaries, took the '*murtis*' of a Jaina tirthankar and Lord Ganesh, respectively, and placed them with honour in a shrine in their kingdoms.[24]

As per the *Purva Karana Agama*, the victorious king was supposed to bring deities from the vanquished kingdom and arrange for their worship in an appropriate manner. This will not just divest the defeated ruler of divine protection but also ensure that the idols remain under veneration. Also, it was obligatory for the vanquished king to try and retrieve the images within a span of three years. This explains the so-called 'iconoclastic' tendencies of Hindu rulers. Worse, only a prejudiced mind would think of comparing the acts of Mahmud of Ghazni and Aurangzeb with those of Kharavela and Narasimhavarman.

As for King Shashank of Gauda, he has been accused of persecuting Buddhists, destroying their places of worship, and even cutting the sacred Bodhi tree. But the evidence presented against him must be accepted with 'a great deal of reserve'.[25]

The most interesting case of Hindu iconoclasm is presented by Kalhana's *Rajatarangini,* which mentions that King Harsha of Kashmir plundered Hindu and Buddhist temples. Again, what our eminent distorians deliberately downplay is Kalhaṇa's comment that by indulging in temple destruction and loot, Harsha 'acted like a Turushka (Muslim)' and was 'prompted by the Turushkas in his employ'.

Sir Marc Aurel Stein explains this further in his book, *Kalhana's Rajtarangini*:

> Extravagant expenditure on the troops and senseless indulgence in costly pleasures gradually involved Harsha in grave financial troubles. From these he endeavoured to free himself by ruthless spoliation of sacred shrines. Kalhana relates with some humour how the incidental discovery of the treasures hoarded at the temple of King Bhima Shahi had turned the king's attention to this method of replenishing his exchequer. After the temple treasuries had been ransacked, Harsha proceeded to the still more revolutionary measure of confiscating divine images in order to possess himself of the valuable metal of which they were made. Kalhana records the strange fact that as a preliminary step the sacred images were systematically defiled through outcast mendicants. As Kalhana is particular to specify the few metal statues of gods throughout Kashmir which escaped Harsha's

> clutches, we cannot doubt the extent and thoroughness of Harsha's iconoclasm. Can the latter have been instigated or encouraged somehow by the steady advance of Muhammadanism in the neighbouring territories? Kalhana, when relating these shameful confiscations, gives to Harsha the epithet 'Turushka', i.e., Muhammadan, and later on makes a reference to Turuska captains being employed in his army and enjoying his favour.[26]

This one statement made it clear that '*murti*' desecration was not an Indic phenomenon, and even if someone like King Harsha of Kashmir indulged in it under the Islamic influence, it was severely censored as a Turushka-like act!

The invention of Hindu intolerance was an afterthought. It came into usage when our distorians realized their failure in suppressing the record of Islamist violence and vandalism in mediaeval times. After all, if you cannot sanitise the crimes of Aurangzeb and Mahmud of Ghazni, then create their Hindu equivalents!

III

There has been a dominant school of historical thought that propounds the theory that the 'Delhi Sultanate was no more "Muslim" than the British Empire has been "Christian"'.[27]

The idea was to tell that there was no compulsion in matters of religion and that the Ghaznavid and other Turkish invaders brought the philosophy of 'the brotherhood of a classless society', which the lower classes among the Hindus lapped up at the first given opportunity.

Mohammad Habib explains,

> The essence of the social question was this: Face to face with the social and economic provision of the 'Shariat' and the Hindu 'Smritis' as practical alternatives, the Indian city-worker preferred the Shariat. And the decision of the

> city-worker was decisive for it is in the cities and not in the countryside that governments and empires are made and pulled down.[28]

He elaborates,

> The invasion of the Ghorian Turks brought about this great social and economic revolution because the industrial and social forces in the country had been prepared for it for centuries, but their path had been barred by the ideology of the caste-system and the Thakur-military regime. External pressure broke this regime, and then with remarkable rapidity in the course of half a generation the country settled on new lines. Everyone, except the top-most Rais and their immediate followers, accepted the now social order.[29]

Interestingly, Habib dedicates this book to 'Premier Jawahar Lal Nehru, the guarantee of India's security and the sheet-anchor of her hopes'![30]

K.A. Nizami, a fellow distorian, takes the argument forward when he writes: 'Had the Indian masses resisted the establishment of the Turkish rule in India, the Ghurids would not have been able to retain even an inch of the Indian territory'.[31]

R.C. Majumdar gives a strong and convincing rebuttal to the 'universal brotherhood' lobby as he writes how it's farcical to say that the notion of Islamic brotherhood is universal in nature, and if at all any religion and philosophy that talks about universal brotherhood, then it's Vedanta. He writes:

> It is, however, to be pointed out that the brotherhood of Islam did not extend beyond its own fold and can, by no stretch of imagination, be regarded as universal, if we accept the ordinary meaning of the word. According to Muslim tenets, the non-believers or Kafirs occupied a distinctly inferior

> position. Theoretically speaking, no religion or philosophy preached the universal brotherhood of man more eloquently than the Vedanta, which placed it on the fundamental basis of the identity of all individual souls, all being identical with Brahman. Of course, there was no practical application of this doctrine in social life. But neither the theory of Islam, nor its practice, as regards the Hindus, could appeal to the latter as bringing a new message of equality of men. The Hindus of the medieval age could be under no illusion on this point when they were forbidden to perform their own religious rites in public, denied political and civic rights on equal terms, and when Islam, as the State religion, could impose its legal system upon them. It would be idle to pretend, therefore, that the equality or brotherhood of Islam could have any other effect than a willing conversion to that faith in order to escape the rigorous distinctions of Hindu society and religion.[32]

The claims that the lower classes among Hindus were excited about Islam's 'universal brotherhood' are equally mischievous. In fact, 'an early report, quoted by a 10th-century geographer, complains that Islam had not made a single convert in India'.[33] Also, Hindu doors were not closed to those who were forcibly converted, as we see in the case of Sukhapala, son of Hindu Shahi ruler Anandapala. Sukhapala was forcefully converted by Mahmud of Ghazni to Islam under the name of Nawasa Shah, but he returned to the Hindu fold at the first opportunity.

Against this backdrop, it's extraordinary to see Hinduism survive more than 1,400 years of assault, first on its body (through Muslim invaders) and then its mind (through Christian missionaries and eminent distorians). When many other civilizations perished without any trace in the mounds of history, Hinduism kept standing, though not without some serious physical and mental injuries.

Hinduism survived precisely because of the reasons it is ridiculed for today: its untidy decentralization and infinite sub-identities. It turned Hinduism into a hydra-headed institution where each head was as important as the other, thus escaping complete annihilation. This may explain why Swami Vivekananda and Sri Aurobindo—the masters of Bharatiya Darshan—desisted from outright criticism of caste institutions while working towards building a more equitable, harmonious society. They could see how these institutions, howsoever regressive they might appear today, actually provided beleaguered Hindus the much-needed straw to hang on to at a time when their world was falling apart like a pack of cards.

And above all, Hinduism could survive because of the contributions of Dalits and outcastes, and not despite them. Alberuni, who visited Bharat during Mahmud of Ghazni's time, spoke of the four traditional castes and eight sections of Antyajas (outcastes).[34] Historian K.S. Lal writes, 'In his (Alberuni's) time, their number in Hindustan was obviously not large. But their numbers and nomenclatures increased with the passage of time.'[35]

Prof. Lal adds,

> It was during the medieval period under Muslim rule—712 to 1707 CE—that many castes and sub-castes of SCs, STs and OBCs came into being, to become more than 2,330 enumerated today. For sure, tribal population increased rapidly under Muslim rule to become the 70-million strong tribal community of India today. It is the largest population of this kind in the world.[36]

Amid Muslim invasions, plunders and killings, the proliferation of castes can be seen as chemotherapy aimed at fighting the cancerous alien attack. Historically, wherever the caste system was strong, conversion into Islam or any other religion had been significantly less. This flies in the face of those intellectuals and historians who say that lower castes welcomed the invaders with open arms and converted to Islam in large numbers.

So, how did lower castes react to the arrival of Arabs, Afghans and Turks? The reality is far from what the likes of Mohammad Habib have tried projecting to us.

In 712 AD, when Mohammed bin Qasim invaded Sindh, the Jats and Meds did join him. The Sammas, another tribal people, welcomed Qasim 'with frolics and merriment'. What our eminent distorians didn't tell us was that the moment these people realized that Qasim was unlike the invaders of the past, they changed their stance. They became inimical to the Arabs after the latter destroyed the temple of Debal and other venerated shrines in Sindh, forcibly converted people to Islam, and imposed *jizya* on the people.

Later events showed that the lower-caste people either sided with their upper-caste co-religionists against the Muslim invaders, as in the case of the Bhils who fought alongside Maharana Pratap against Akbar's army. Or, like the Satnamis, Jats and Marathas, they challenged the Mughals (Timurids) head-on. Shivaji himself had a lower-caste origin, yet he dedicated his life for the cause of 'Hindu Pad-Padshahi'.

Interestingly, Prof. Lal debunks the theory that lower-caste people converted to Islam in large numbers. He cites the example of Uttar Pradesh where the population of Chamars (15.1 per cent) is quite high. This, he says, signifies a low conversion rate among them.

Prof. Lal writes,

> The upper castes might have sometimes submitted to force or temptation, but not the Chamars. For example, in Muzaffarnagar district there were 29,000 Hindu Rajputs and 24,000 Muslim Rajputs according to the 1901 Census. Similarly, there were Hindu Rajputs and Muslim Rajputs

> in almost equal numbers in many western districts of UP. In eastern UP, there were Muslim Pathans and converted Rajputs, as for instance 34,000 each in Basti district. The reason for this phenomenon was that some Rajputs who loved their religion more than their land fought against Muslim invaders to the last. Many perished in the encounters. Those who survived, survived as Hindu Rajputs. Those who loved their land more than their religion converted to Islam to retain their lands and kingdoms… They debunk the theory that low caste people converted to Islam more easily than the high castes.[37]

But then, what explains the rise in Scheduled Caste/Scheduled Tribe (SC/ST) populations in the mediaeval era? According to Prof. Lal, this can be explained by the two ways in which upper-class people drifted into lower classes.

> One way was war, which was of perennial occurrence under Muslim rule. Generally speaking, cultivators who stayed on as Hindus on their land after defeat drifted into Scheduled or other backward castes, whether they were enslaved or just made to work for the conquerors on sundry duties. Those who did not surrender and took to flight and established themselves in inaccessible jungles or mountain recesses became Scheduled Tribes, etc., generally speaking.[38]

The other way, writes Prof. Lal, was the oppressive tax burden that compelled people to abandon their lands and seek shelter in jungles. He states,

> Those who fought in the wars and fled were comparatively few. The largest number was of the oppressed peasants, artisans and labourers who drifted from the good and peaceful agrarian life towards low caste or tribal status. With long and permanent stay in forests or in hiding, many

> of these communities got new nomenclatures and their numbers multiplied.[39]

Babur writes in his memoirs, *Baburnama*, how 'sometimes it rains 10, 15 or 20 times a day, torrents pour down all at once and rivers flow where no water had been'.[40] This weather system helped raise jungles in no time. And these forests gave shelter to Hindus who refused to give in to Muslim suzerainty and its rigid religious and taxation policies. One can gauge the severity of the taxation system from the fact that even during Akbar's 'benign' rule, Todar Mal's revenue, which was later enhanced by successive governments in Bengal, in 1582 AD was as high as four times that of 1901 AD.

Forests, thus, became the last citadel of Hindu resistance. This explains why Muslim rulers—from Balban and Alauddin Khilji to Akbar and Aurangzeb—placed so much importance on the clearance of forests. We are often told how the forest-clearance exercise was aimed at curbing the terror of bandits and robbers beyond the periphery of cities and towns. What these eminent distorians don't tell us was that these bandits were Hindus who were either part of the displaced ruling class that refused to surrender, or were those who were engaged in farming and other economic activities in the previous dispensation.

Ibn Battuta writes how the *kafirs* took refuge in these jungles, and these forests became like ramparts (or forts) for them.[41] But as people vanished in forests for long, they couldn't pursue mandatory caste rituals, and over time found themselves degraded in the social hierarchy.

It was the British who waponized the caste system to divide Hinduism to their advantage. Dharampal's *The Beautiful Tree* further punctures the Dalit-versus-the-rest discourse, as he extensively quotes three reports commissioned and prepared by the British administration for the provinces of Bengal

(1835–38), Madras (1822–26), and Punjab (1882). As per the Bengal report, there existed about 1,00,000 village schools in Bengal and Bihar around the 1830s. Similar statements were made for the Bombay Presidency 'where every village had a school'. Observations made by Dr G.W. Leitner in 1882 show that the spread of education in Punjab around 1850 was to a similar extent. But as the British tightened their grip over the country, one witnessed 'neglect and decay in the field of education'.[42]

The caste composition of the education system in early 19th-century India is equally enlightening. As Dharampal notes, 'It is true that the greater proportion of the teachers came from the Kayasthas, Brahmins, Sadgop and Aguri castes. Yet, quite a number came from 30 other caste groups also, and even the Chandals had six teachers.'[43]

As for the elementary school students, they throw an even greater variety, and every caste group seems to have been represented in the student population, with the Brahmins and Kayasthas nowhere forming more than 40 per cent of the total. 'In the two Bihar districts, together they (Brahmins and Kayasthas) formed no more than 15–16 per cent. The more surprising figure is the 61 Dom and 61 Chandal school students in the district of Burdwan, nearly equal to the number of Vaidya students, 126, in that district.[44]

While Burdwan had 13 missionary schools, the number of Dom and Chandal scholars in them was only four. As British administrator William Adam mentioned, only 86 of the 'scholars belonging to 16 of the lowest castes' were in the missionary schools, while 674 scholars from these castes were in the 'native schools'.[45]

Against this backdrop, it won't be an exaggeration to say that caste divide and discrimination in Hinduism might have been a reality in the ancient past, but its extreme and loathsome face emerged during the British era. In many ways, this can be regarded as the product of colonial afterthought, which missionaries, Marxists and eminent distorians added to their respective toolkits for obvious gains.

Also, if Hinduism is surviving today, a lot of credit should go to the sacrifices made by the so-called lower castes. If Brahmins were the mind of Hinduism, Kshatriyas its arms, and Vaishyas its thighs, then Shudras and outcastes were definitely the feet that enabled the whole body to stand. Hinduism wouldn't have ever walked without those strong feet!

Here, the feet analogy is deliberate, for our eminent distorians have often misused a similar example given in the *Rig Veda*'s Purusha Sukta to claim victimhood for Shudras. Oh, look, Shudras are compared with feet... dirty feet, we are told. But even a cursory understanding of Indic tradition would expose this as a clear case of coloniality, if not deliberate distortion. For, in Indic traditions, as Prof. Arvind Sharma brings out with so many examples in his book, *The Ruler's Gaze*, how 'some of the poignant cultural gestures within Hinduism have to do with the feet'. He reminds us how one touches the feet of the elders. 'One even drinks the water in which the feet of a worthy person have been washed'.[46]

IV

More than seven decades since Independence, Bharat is still struggling to rewrite its history from its own perspective. Ironically, at the time of Independence, the country had historians such as Sir Jadunath Sarkar who, as Dipesh Chakrabarty writes in *The Calling of History*, considered 'accuracy' a 'virtue'. In those days, 'the idea of historical truth made sense to historians, who presumably, on their part, combated their own biases and perspectives to get to the "truth"'.[47]

Soon after Independence, Sarkar and others like him, including the much venerable R.C. Majumdar, were pushed to the margins of Indian history and history writing, though the bandwagon of 'progressive', ideology-loaded historiography had already made significant headway by the 1920s. By the 1970s, Sarkar, Majumdar and others like them were all but forgotten.

About Sarkar, Dipesh Chakrabarty writes:

> Immediately after Sarkar's death, the eminent Bengali historian, Prof NK Sinha, prophesised: 'It is not likely that Sir Jadunath Sarkar will ever be displaced. His wonderful accuracy will secure to him immunity from the common lot of historical workers. So far as we can visualise, in the near future, in his chosen field, there will be only scanty gleaners after his copious harvest.' So probably it seemed in Calcutta in 1958. But even as Prof Sinha was writing these lines, a group of younger scholars at Allahabad, Aligarh and Oxford were conducting research that would ensure that by the time someone like me came into the world of South Asian history as a young novice in Calcutta in the early 1970s, Jadunath Sarkar's name would be all but forgotten among the prominent historians of India... Sarkar's approach to history had been discredited. Our teachers did not do emperors, battles and the character of kings anymore. Unlike Sir Jadunath Sarkar and other historians of his time, they did not believe in the role of heroes in history. Heroes had been replaced by 'causes'. As Satish Chandra said, '(Sir Jadunath)... projected Aurangzeb's struggle to conquer the south as a Greek tragedy... (but) the search for causal relationships cannot be given up by historians.[48]

Why was Sarkar treated so disdainfully? T.C.A. Raghavan, in *History Men,* explains the reason. 'At a time when being politically correct in writing academic history was gaining in importance, Sarkar's assessment of, and emphasis on, Aurangzeb's orthodoxy was viewed by many as divisive and negative.'[49]

Raghavan quotes historian A.L. Srivastava to bolster his claim:

> The so-called Allahabad school of medieval Indian history, torn between 'academic rectitude' and 'civic duty', blames Jadunath for not omitting offensive details of temple destruction and putting down of Hinduism by force from his works. It feels that the mere mention of such facts of history is repugnant to Muslim feelings and drives a wedge between the two communities.[50]

It is this newfound sense of political correctness and ideological obsession that turned a giant of a historian into the 'high priest of communal historiography in India', as D.N. Jha derisively describes Sarkar.[51] But was Sarkar's historiography communal? Did he selectively paint a particular community in darker shades? The fact of the matter is that if Sarkar's work on Aurangzeb made him a 'communal' historian among certain left-'liberal' and pseudo-secular sections, his less than charitable portrait of Shivaji incensed several Hindu elements, especially in Maharashtra.[52]

Similarly, Sarkar had nothing but contempt for 'false' patriotism in Bengal. He, as a historian, saw it as his duty to fight such myth-making endeavours. 'The height of absurdity is reached', he wrote in *History of Bengal*, 'when our dramatists call Pratapaditya of Jessore... the counterpart of Maharana Pratap Singh of Mewar'.

Sarkar writes,

> The height of absurdity is reached when our dramatists call Pratapaditya of Jessor as the counterpart of Maharana Pratap Singh of Mewar. It is, therefore, necessary to debunk the Bengali 'hero' by turning the dry light of history on him. His father was Srihari, a Kayastha writer in theial service of Daud Karrani, who rose to be that chief's confidant after the murder of the worthy wazir Ludi Khan. On the fall of Daud, Srihari fled away with his own wealth and the government treasure in his custody, and set up for himself in the extreme

> south of the Khulna district—to which the sea was very much closer then than now. In this marshy land intersected by a maze of channels, he built a home for his family and a safe refuge for fugitives from the advancing tide of invasion. The ex-amla took the grandiloquent title of the Indian Charlemagne—Maharaj Vikramaditya, and could give his son and heir a no lesser title than Pratipaditya—reminiscent of the official designations of the great Gupta emperors of antiquity. Pratapaditya never once defeated any Mughal army in pitched battle; his son and general Udayaditya took to flight at the first sign of a losing naval battle (at Sulka), and Pratapaditya himself tamely submitted to the Mughal general without holding out till he was assured of safety to life and honour.[53]

Sarkar wrote what he thought was right. In fact, in his letter to fellow historian G.S. Sardesai on 19 June 1946, he wrote, 'True, interpretation must differ according to (the) writer's personality; but the basis of the conclusions must be unquestionable facts (as established by latest research) and not mere conjecture. Moreover, the interpretation must be such as to convince an impartial observer.'[54]

He explained this further in his 1915 speech, wherein he said: 'I would not care whether truth is pleasant or unpleasant, and in consonance with or opposed to current views. I would not mind in the least whether truth is or not a blow to the glory of my country.'[55]

Even a year before his death in 1958, Sarkar wrote a letter to Rajendra Prasad, the then president of India, saying:

> National history must be comprehensive, true, accurate and impartial… It will be national not in the sense that it will try to suppress or whitewash everything in our country's past that is disgraceful, but because it will admit them and at the

> same time point out that there were also other and nobler aspects in the stages of our nation's evolution.[56]

Sarkar paid dearly for pursuing non-communal, non-partisan, non-ideological historiography. In July 1954, Rajendra Prasad, as the president of India, forwarded to the then prime minister, Jawaharlal Nehru, a recommendation that Sarkar be awarded the Padma Vibhushan—independent India's second highest civilian award. The recommendation had originally come from the then governor of Madras, Sri Prakasa, who had, in fact, sought the Bharat Ratna, the highest civilian award, for him.

Rajendra Prasad forwarded the recommendation for the Padma Vibhushan because 'no formal recommendation for the grant of this (Bharat Ratna) is to be made by a state government as the award is to be made by you (Nehru) alone'.[57] Two years later, the president sent another recommendation, this time for the Padma Bhushan, the third highest civilian honour, but again to no avail.

Ironically, Sarkar remained largely ignored, even as his juniors and those who could balance the political requirements made big headway. Both history and historians saw a massive change. New heroes were discovered, and old villains given a new leash of life. Indian historiography became a sort of a rope trick where Mahmud of Ghazni was transformed into a secular icon who, with his raids, was destroying the edifice of oppression and superstition in Somnath! Alauddin Khilji became a great economist who introduced a series of reforms. And the Mughals (Timurids) were projected as the repository of the Ganga–Jamuni tehzeeb.

But no one polarizes Indian historiography more intensely than Aurangzeb. Sarkar's attempt to project him as a 'religious fanatic' and his Islamic state as a place where 'religious toleration was an impossibility' turned him into a pariah. Prof. Satish Chandra, in his article, 'Mythifying History', at the height of the Rama Janmabhoomi movement in 1989, explained the changed scenario as he wrote how Aurangzeb was 'neither a hero nor a villain' but someone representing an old order that failed to 'recognize… the stirrings and incipient growth of a new socio-economic system'.[58]

Still, defending Aurangzeb is a tough job. One has to be incredibly ignorant, ideologically jaundiced, or, worse, zealously fundamentalist to do so. For there is more than enough evidence left by the Mughals (Timurids) themselves, proudly proclaiming their acts of violence and vandalism. They thought they were fulfilling their 'sacred duty' as devout Muslims to convert *kafirs* and destroy Hindu temples, which for them were 'institutions of ignorance and darkness'. So much so that Aurangzeb would duly sign and affix the royal insignia each time his *firmans* announced such acts of terrorism!

Despite such obvious handicaps, Aurangzeb has become a 'hero' for a substantial section of left-'liberal' historians. Leading the race today is Audrey Truschke, Professor of South Asian history, Rutgers University, Newark. In her 189-page tome, *Aurangzeb: The Man and the Myth*, she finds Aurangzeb a 'secular' ruler. The primary reason that provoked her to say so was that Aurangzeb employed a large number of Hindus in his durbar.[59]

Prof. Truschke writes,

> Under Akbar, for example, Hindus constituted 22.5 per cent of all Mughal nobles. …in the first 21 years of Aurangzeb's reign (1658-79), it stayed level at 21.6 per cent. But between 1679 and 1707 Aurangzeb increased Hindu participation at the elite levels of the Mughal state by nearly 50 per cent. Hindus rose to 31.6 per cent of the Mughal nobility.[60]

This argument reminded one of American historian Bryan Rigg's book, *Hitler's Jewish Soldiers*, wherein the author writes how 'thousands of men of Jewish descent and hundreds of what the Nazis called "full Jews" served in the military with Hitler's knowledge'. Rigg adds, 'The Nazis allowed these men to serve but at the same time exterminated their families.'[61]

It would, thus, be simplistic to connect the presence of Hindus in Mughal (Timurid) nobility with Aurangzeb pursuing a tolerant policy. Instead, one should look at it as a pragmatic policy of divide and rule, which the British perfected a century later. Aurangzeb used Hindu generals to either fight his Hindu enemies (like Marathas) or to win over the empire's most treacherous terrains (Afghanistan, for example). One should look at the fate of Raja Jai Singh and Raja Jaswant Singh to know the real intent behind Aurangzeb's move.

Also, Truschke, more often than not, is seen putting the cart before the horse. She, for instance, claims that Aurangzeb attacked Mathura and destroyed the Keshav Deo temple because of the Jat rebellions. The fact is that the Jats—historically the defenders of Hinduism—rebelled as a result of Aurangzeb's growing intolerance vis-à-vis Hindus. Truschke's desperate attempt to look for political reasons for temple destruction is the 21st-century version of Mohammad Habib's attempt to turn Mahmud of Ghazni's raids into an economic exercise aimed at plundering India's disproportionately rich temples. Worse, she even quotes dubious records to accuse the victims (Brahmins) themselves of forcing Aurangzeb to act against them. Brahmins, after all, 'in Thatta, Multan and especially at Benaras… were teaching false books at their established schools'. Aurangzeb, thus, writes Truschke, 'evinced concern with elite Brahmins deceiving common Hindus about their own religion and was perhaps especially alarmed that Muslims were falling prey to charlatans. Brahmins may even have profited financially from such ventures.'[62]

The defenders of Aurangzeb and other Islamist tyrants, especially those who wear liberalism on their sleeves, need to realize that truth and reconciliation—and not duplicity and deception—are the first steps towards amicable relations between Hindus and Muslims. Also, by clubbing Aurangzeb and his ilk with today's Muslims, they are casting aspersions on the community as a whole.

The story of Bharat needs to be rewritten and told from Bharat's perspective. The country's history cannot be just about invasions and invaders, about defeats and submissions, about vices and atrocities. And, more importantly, we have to stop being obsessed with Delhi-centric historiography. For, in the Indic scheme of things, the Mauryas and the Mughals (Timurids) are as mainstream as the Cholas, the Karkotas and the Ahoms.

This book is an earnest attempt to correct this anomaly.

1

Saraswati Sutra

How Harappan and Vedic Cultures Are Two Sides of the Same Coin

I

Nirad C. Choudhuri, in his book *The Continent of Circe*, brought out an inherent contradiction in the working of Bharat's ruling class soon after Independence. He wrote:

> There is nothing which frightens the present Indian ruling class more than the idea of doing anything without the advice and help of White experts. So, we have them, and they range from specialists who advise us about taxation and contraception, to those who build our dams and steel plants. Even a Japanese gardener was brought over to convert a public park, which was being grossly neglected by the Delhi Municipality, into a Japanese garden.[1]

Choudhuri informed us how, among all these foreign experts, the economists were the most sought-after:

> There is no other country in the world in which the tribe of pundits called economists are held in greater honour… So

> India has become an El Dorado for every kind of economist from every part of the world.[2]

Ironically, Bharat, despite being 'an El Dorado for every kind of economist from every part of the world', missed the bus to economic prosperity. By the mid-1960s, it was obvious that Bharat's economy was faltering, but our famed economists used this to further increase the doses of moribund statism, as one saw in a series of nationalisation drives initiated by the then prime minister, Indira Gandhi.

If economists were much in demand post-Independence, historians were not far behind either. Incidentally, these historians too looked Westward for ideas and inspirations, and like their economic counterparts, they also grew in importance and influence in the late 1960s when Mrs Gandhi became the prime minister.

Over the years, as in the economic arena, extreme leftism has hit Bharat's historiography hard. While one has seen statist economists making a retreat since 1991, no such development has taken place in history writing per se. Most current-day history books continue to resemble the textbooks of yore. They still begin with the Harappan civilization, to be followed by the much-maligned Aryans—even when there is ample evidence suggesting that Harappan and Vedic civilizations were the same; that they were the two sides of the same coin; that the Rig Vedic period preceded the Harappan; and that the Harappan civilization flourished as much, if not more, on the banks of the Saraswati river as on the Indus.

However, truth invariably finds its way out of the closet, howsoever well-locked it is. In May 2022, archaeologists discovered a 5,000-year-old jewellery factory in Haryana's Rakhigarhi village and ruled out external attacks as the reason for the abandonment of this Harappan settlement. The fact that Rakhigarhi, currently the biggest Harappan site excavated so far, bigger than Mohenjodaro, wasn't found along the Indus or its tributaries but on the dried tracks of the Saraswati, has the potential to upend Bharat's history, as we know it today.

Of course, our eminent distorians have already made a beguiling shift from the Aryan invasion theory to the Aryan migration theory, as new discoveries, including the one at Rakhigarhi, showed no signs of external aggression. However, the truth is that apart from the terminological modification—making a shift from 'invasion' to 'migration'—there has been no change in the way the country's 'official/mainstream' history is being written and taught today. But the discovery of the biggest of the Harappan sites on the course of the Saraswati, which recent studies suggest dried up by 1900 BC—almost 500 years before the Vedic people were said to have set foot on the subcontinent, as per the Aryan invasion/migration theory—threatens to turn the leftist historical applecart upside down.

In contrast to the Aryan invasion theory, the migration theory—aimed at withstanding the new archaeological revelations—is placed on an even more slippery slope. It defies a basic understanding of human society and languages. How could, for instance, 'small-scale migrations'—as the proponents of the migration theory argue to deal with the overwhelming archaeological evidence that negates any large-scale migration into the subcontinent in the second millennium BC—push aside so easily a society that was more populous, materially more prosperous and scientifically more advanced? And even if they managed to do so, how could the more refined and urbane Harappans leave their own language in favour of the one being spoken by largely illiterate nomads?

Historically, languages have been the stickiest part of a culture/civilization. The inhabitants of Bengal, for instance, converted in large numbers to Islam, but they continued to speak Bengali. As David Frawley writes in *The Myth of Aryan Invasion in India*,

> If such a migration was so small and did not have any great impact on existing populations or leave any archaeological record, as is the case, it could not have changed the region on the level of language either, which to reiterate is the hardest and slowest part of culture to change.[3]

The irony of the Aryan invasion/migration theory is that it propounds a theory where an urban civilization that excelled in meticulous town planning and indulged in vibrant commercial activities was bereft of any literature, while illiterate nomadic people possessed one of the world's most profound literary works. It ignores the obvious indications in the Vedas regarding the expansion of the Vedic civilization from East to West. Even the Nadistuti Sukta of the *Rig Veda*, which invokes 19 rivers, begins with Ganga and Yamuna. Saraswati finds itself in the third position in the list.

Moreover, there's great affinity and reverence while mentioning these rivers. The *Rig Veda* addresses them as 'my Ganga, my Yamuna, my Saraswati', and so on. An outsider would never care to address a river so endearingly. Saraswati, often dismissed as a mythical river by a number of left-leaning historians, has been profusely praised in the *Rig Veda* as 'the greatest of mothers, greatest of rivers, greatest of goddesses'.

The Vedas specifically locate the Saraswati to the west of Yamuna and east of Sutlej. Still some of our eminent distorians want us to believe that Saraswati was actually the Helmand river in south Afghanistan. Michel Danino, in *The Lost River*, gives a strong rebuttal to this as he writes:

> If the migrating Aryans were so attached to a Sarasvati left behind in Afghanistan, it is unclear what prevented

> them from transferring its name to the Indus—the first river they encountered after descending into its vast plains—or to any of its respectable tributaries, from the Jhelum to the Sutlej… It stretches the imagination to picture them having a sudden afterthought some 200 or 300 years after they left Afghanistan, and lauding the bygone Sarasvati by transferring its hallowed name to a petty seasonal stream.[4]

Saraswati finds a detailed mention in the Mahabharata as well. Danino states how 'the *Mahabharata* doesn't miss the opportunity to weave a few legends around the theme of the Sarasvati's disappearance'. In fact, there is a detailed account of Balarama, the elder brother of Krishna, going on a pilgrimage along the banks of the Saraswati. Writes Danino:

> At length, Balarama reached a spot where 'although the Sarasvati seems to be lost, yet persons crowned with ascetic success… and owing also to the coolness of the herbs and of the land there, know that the river has an invisible current through the bowels of the earth'.[5]

So, is it all over for the Aryan invasion/migration theory?[6] Far from it! For every 'revelation', there's a 'counter-revelation', howsoever implausible it may appear. The latest is Tony Joseph's *Early Indians* (2018), which takes the recourse of genetics to salvage the theory well past its expiry date. Analysed closely, as Shrikant G. Talageri has done in *Genetics and the Aryan Debate,*[7] it's another leftist rope trick at work by 'falling back on a totally new field of study: Genetics', after 'Linguistics, Archaeology and Textual/Inscriptional Data' failed to salvage the Aryan invasion/migration theory. It's an old but hardly redundant tactic: When in danger of getting exposed, change the goalpost. If nothing else, it would buy you some time for another trick!

Talageri sums up the new genetic theory as such:

> The genetic data definitely doesn't prove any immigration of 'Aryans' into India after 2000 BC. The joint testimony of the chronological and geographical data in the *Rig Veda* and the Mitanni-related documents (and also *Avesta*), on the other hand, proves that the Indo-European languages were already in India from long before 3000 BCE.[8]

It's time we discarded the Aryan invasion/migration theory. But this seems far-fetched, given the 'maybe, perhaps, probably, mostly… therefore' methodology used by left-leaning historians to get the desired result. The above term was used by Arun Shourie in *Eminent Historians* to explain the leftist tendency of first making a pompous historical claim with a 'maybe' and then using it to reach the desired 'therefore' conclusion.[9]

II

Recent archaeological and scientific studies indicate what Vedic literature had been saying all along: That the inhabitants of this landmass didn't come from outside. Instead, there are numerous records, literary and otherwise, suggesting an out-of-Bharat migration. But, yes, very long ago, the subcontinental landmass did make a long, solitary journey of thousands of miles to reach where it is today after being separated from Madagascar around 90 million years ago. Initially, it wasn't a solitary journey: It is believed that Bharat had the company of Antarctica and Madagascar when it first started moving away from Africa around 158 million years ago. They travelled together for a while till Bharat and Madagascar parted ways with Antarctica around 130 million years ago.

Until about 100 years ago, one thought the landmasses on the earth were static and stationary. But in 1912, geologist Alfred Wegener came up with the theory of continental drift, according to which the Earth had a series of cycles of coming together into one supercontinent and then breaking up into different continents.[10] Pangea was the last supercontinent before our times that existed between 335 and 175 million years ago. And it began to break up around 175 million years ago. It was first divided between a northern continent, called Laurasia, consisting of Asia, Europe and North America, and a southern continent, named Gondwana, comprising Africa, South America, Australia, Antarctica, and Bharat.

Around 55–60 million years ago, the plate carrying Bharat's landmass, long after parting ways with Madagascar, collided with the Eurasian plate. The Himalayas, a relatively recent physical phenomenon in the history of the Earth, were formed after the collision of the two plates. The process is still on going and this explains why the Himalayas are still rising by about 5mm every year, though the simultaneous erosion must have reduced the actual increase in height.

Earth, formed about 4.5 billion years ago, has seen life come into existence about 3.8 billion years ago when 'certain molecules combined to form particularly large and intricate structures called organism'.[12] Just as Newtonian determinism once set the narrative of the universe's evolution but later gave way to Einsteinian relativity, with science shedding its overbearing and unbending rigidity, the 'evolutionary shrub of humankind', as per Adam Rutherford, has become so 'murky' and 'messier' that 'researchers have told me of their reluctance to publish new findings for the fear of them being superseded not within years or months, but within weeks and day'.[12]

Not too long ago, it was commonly believed that there was just one human species, *Homo sapiens*, which came into existence about 3 lakh years ago in East and North Africa. It was, in a way, to give a unique status to humanity. 'We are used to thinking about ourselves as the only humans', to use Yuval Noah Harari's words, 'because for the last 10,000 years, our species has been the only human species around'. But we now know that 'not only do we possess abundance of uncivilised cousins, once upon a time we had quite a few brothers and sisters as well'.[13] As per the last count, there were more than half a dozen human species—at one and the same time.

The story thus far known to us is that humans first evolved in Africa about 2.5 million years ago from an earlier genus of apes called *Australopithecus*, meaning 'Southern Ape'. About 2 million years ago, some of these archaic men and women left Africa for Asia and Europe. Those who migrated to Europe and western Asia evolved to become Neanderthals. They were physically stronger than other human species, given the cold climatic habitat they adopted. The eastern regions of Asia were populated by *Homo erectus*, who survived the longest—for about two million years.

Over a decade ago, in 2010, the world came to know about another human species while scientists were excavating the Denisova Cave in Siberia. Named Denisovans, they are extinct today, but their genetic influence can be found in people currently living in East Asia.

In an Indonesian island of Flores, another human species was found; they were unique in the sense that they were dwarf beings, reaching a maximum height of one metre and weighed no more than 25 kg. It is assumed that when humans first reached Flores, the sea level, given the Ice Age, was low—what is an island today was vastly accessible from the mainland then. But when the sea level rose, these people were trapped on the resource-starved island. This ensured that over generations, humans evolved into dwarfs.

With the 'evolutionary shrub of humankind' becoming 'murky' and 'messier', it is anybody's guess as to how many more cousins and relatives of *Homo sapiens* are waiting to be discovered. The last word on the subject hasn't been written yet.

III

Writing, which is believed to have emerged some 6,000 years ago, is what divides history from prehistory. Another milestone moment that changed the course of human history was the Agricultural Revolution that took place around 12,000 years ago. It was this revolution that transformed the pastoral, foraging nature of human life into a sedentary one.[14] It is on the back of this revolution that the world saw the coming up of the first of human civilizations. One such civilization emerged in Bharat's northwestern region.[15]

In 1856, British engineer William Brunton, while laying a Lahore–Multan railway line, found thousands of uniformly shaped kiln-fired bricks in a series of mounds in a small village of Harappa. They were in such good condition that people then thought they were of recent origins. But further digging brought out the truth: These bricks belonged to a much older era. Alexander Cunningham (1814–93), the founder of the Archaeological Survey of India (ASI), did an extensive survey of the region in 1873 and came to the conclusion that these were the remains of a Greek settlement left behind by Alexander's army in the fourth century BC. He found a few seals having the image of a bull with no hump and also an alien script, making him believe that these seals originally came from elsewhere.

There was a lull for about four decades when Harappa came back in the limelight with a vengeance, turning the entire historiography upside down. It all began with archaeologist Daya Ram Sahni, under the direction of Sir John Marshall, the then ASI chief, initiating a comprehensive excavation of Harappa in 1921. In the meantime, R.D. Banerji was excavating another site along the Indus in Sind province—Mohenjodaro. By the mid-1920s, Marshall was convinced about the antiquity of the new findings and concluded that Mohenjodaro was 'the largest Bronze Age city in the world'.

Soon, more sites with Harappan features began to appear. Over the decades, the extent of the Indus valley civilization exceeded way beyond Punjab and Sind to stretch from Sutkagendor on the Makran coast near Gwadar, close to the Iranian border, to Alamgirpur in western Uttar Pradesh, and from Manda in Jammu district to Bhagatrav in southern Gujarat. It covers an area of about 13 lakh square kilometres, making it bigger than the mighty civilizations of Egypt and Mesopotamia combined.

Given its large geographical stretch, it would be erroneous to call it the Indus valley civilization, though it can still be named after Harappa as it was first discovered in this Punjab village. 'If we limit ourselves to the mature phase, Baluchistan alone has 129 sites against 108 in Sind, where Mohenjodaro is located. Gujarat has 300, while the Sarasvati basin has 360,' Danino writes.[16] Given the presence of the maximum number of Harappan sites, including the largest one in Rakhigarhi, along the now-dried tracks of the Saraswati river, many historians have begun calling it the Saraswati or the Indus–Saraswati civilization.

The Harappan sites might not have grand, majestic buildings unlike their Egyptian counterparts, but the former had something that the world could not emulate for the next two millennia at least: meticulous town planning, impressive urban design, and efficient municipal management. One finds the streets and lanes laid out according to a set plan: the main road running from north to south and the cross-streets and lanes running at right angles to them. These sites also had an excellent water management system. While Mohenjodaro alone had 600–700 wells, Dholavira had its waters 'diverted from two neighbouring streams into a series of dams and preserved in a complex system of reservoirs'.[17] They have a covered drainage system connected to most houses, including modest ones, and each of them had their own bathrooms and toilets.

IV

The discovery of Harappa caused havoc in Bharat's historiography, which till then saw the Vedic civilization as the oldest one in the country. The Aryans, we were told, came to the subcontinent from somewhere in Central Asia sometime in 1500 BC. Suddenly, with Harappa's discovery, Bharat's history went back by at least 2,000 years. The Harappan civilization, after all, grew up in three phases: Early (3300–2600 BC), Mature (2600–1900), and Late (1900–1300).

Interestingly, this challenge was dealt with leftist sleight of hand. The Aryans were suddenly transformed into invaders who destroyed the Harappan civilization. Mortimer Wheeler, while digging in the late 1930s, discovered 37 skeletons in Mohenjodaro. Since he was well acquainted with Max Mueller's commentaries on the *Rig Veda*, he manipulated the Vedic text to show how Aryan god Indra destroyed citadels (*puras*). 'Where are—or were—these citadels?' Wheeler wondered. The answer, he thought, could be found at Mohenjodaro.

This claim, despite being based on dubious archaeological and literary records, remained in currency till the 1990s when it began crumbling under the weight of new archaeological findings. However, the proponents of the Aryan invasion theory were ready with another trick: they turned their invasion theory into a migration one. But then there was no archaeological evidence of any large-scale migration in the second millennium BC. Thus was added another rider to the already untenable hypothesis: the migrating population was too minuscule in number to leave any archaeological record behind.

Despite fundamental challenges, Romila Thapar, as recently as in 2019, refused to give up the theory as she wrote in *Which of Us Are Aryans?*: 'There may have been small-scale migrations motivated by pastoralism and incipient trade, both of which were well-established activities from earlier times.'[18]

The Aryan invasion/migration theory is undoubtedly a product of a great leftist rope trick. Our eminent distorians—first with colonial backing, followed by Marxist orientation—came up with this theory despite no literary support to back it; if anything, Vedic texts talked of out-of-Bharat migrations. And there was no archaeological evidence either. One may say there are philological arguments supporting the case, but its limitations have been conceded by none other than Michael Witzel. He writes,

> Theoretically, a scenario of IE (Indo-European) emigration from the Panjab is of course possible—the direction of the spread of languages and linguistic innovations cannot easily be determined, unless we have written materials (preferably inscriptions).[19]

Interestingly, a closer philological analysis too suggests a westward movement, rather than the east. Around 1500 BC, there was a Mitanni kingdom in West Asia. Its rulers signed a treaty with a rival king in 1380 BC, which named Indra, Varuna, Mitra and the Nasatyas (Ashvins) as divine witnesses for the Mitannis. The Indo-Aryan identity of the long-known Mitanni kings was discovered only in the early 20th century after the decipherment and detailed study of documents and inscriptions in West Asia. The discovery sent the Indologists into a tizzy, with the emergence of a dilemma: How could the Vedic Indo-Aryan speakers be present in West Asia at the same time they were reportedly entering the subcontinent and were yet to compose the *Rig Veda*? Indologists resolved this riddle by declaring the Mitannis as a pre-Rig Vedic group that split from the other Indo-Aryans in Central Asia itself.

The *Rig Veda*, comprising 10 mandalas (books) and 1,028 suktas (hymns), is unanimously believed to be divided into Old Rig Veda (2–7) and New Rig Veda (1, 8, 9, 10). If the

Mitanni culture exhibited a pre-Rig Vedic phase, then the words commonly used there should be found in the Old Rig Veda. The evidence suggests otherwise. 'There is no word in the Mitanni records which is found in the Old Rig Veda and becomes rare or extinct later', writes Shrikant G. Talageri in *Genetics and the Aryan Debate*. He explains:

> Of the three Mitanni words for the horse colours, paprunnu (brown), paritannu (grey) and ninkarannu (reddish brown), the first Vedic word babhru is a common Rig Vedic as well as a common IE word found in all the other IE branches as well as in all post-Rig Vedic and Sanskrit literature; the second, palita, is found five times in the *Rig Veda* (in I.144.1; 164.1; II.55.9; X.4.5: 55.5), although mostly in the New Rig Veda; and the third, pingala, is not found in the *Rig Veda* at all, but is found once in the Atharva Veda and commonly after that in later texts. However, this may not be evidence in any direction. The same is the case with most other common words: the four Rig Vedic Gods named in a Mitanni treaty are found named together in the RV in that same order only in one verse, X.125.1, which verse happens to be found in a hymn in the chronologically latest part of the New Rig Veda. But this also may not be very significant in itself.
>
> There is only one very significant word of cultural significance, and this gives a preview of what follows: Mitanni word mani-nnu (Vedic mani, bead/ gemstone/ ornament) is a very late Vedic word, found only twice and only in late parts of the New Rig Veda (in I.33.8; 122. 14) but more than a hundred times in the Atharva Veda, and a common word in later Vedic texts, in Classical Sanskrit, and in all later and modern Indo-Aryan languages and in other non-Indo-European languages which have borrowed from Sanskrit.
>
> Now we come to the main evidence: the 'large array of personal names adopted by the ruling class' (Witzel; 2005: 361). These common personal names consist of names having the following prefixes and suffixes: -aśva, -ratha,-Sena,

> -bandhu, -uta, Vasu-, rta-, priya-, and (as per the analysis of the Indologist PE Dumont), also brhad-, sapta-, abhi-, uru-, citra-, -kṣatra, yam/yami-.
>
> The evidence is devastating: These names are not found in the names of composers in a single hymn in the Old Rig Veda, or in a single hymn or verse in the Old Rig Veda. But they are found in the names of composers in 108 hymns spread out over all the five books of the New Rig Veda, and in 77 hymns, 126 verses, 129 references again spread out over all five books of the New Rig Veda.[20]

There are also fundamental flaws in the philological arguments put forward by historians. First, as David Frawley brings out in *Gods, Sages and Kings*, 'in the primitive state of culture, the rule is a situation of language diversity not one of language uniformity, with languages changing quickly from region to region, often over short distances'. Second, Frawley says, 'in the primitive state of culture, languages change quickly over time, lacking a sophisticated culture of written tradition to sustain any uniformity'.[21] This goes against the very grain of the country's historiography where the Vedic people are projected as primitive and pastoral—and if they were so, they could not have come up with such a resilient and sophisticated language system as Sanskrit.

Is it any surprise that eminent distorians are now slowly shunning the philological argument too, and have started taking refuge in genetics? Another classic example of shifting goalposts.

V

The Vedic texts talk about battles and wars, the most prominent being the Battle of the Ten Kings (Dasarajana Yuddha), but these are not racial in nature, as Sri Aurobindo writes in *The Secret of Vedas*. 'The distinction between Aryan and non-Aryan', writes Aurobindo, 'on which so much has been built, seems on the mass of the evidence to indicate a cultural rather than a racial difference'. He continues,

> There is nothing in the Veda, as there is nothing in the ethnological features of the country to prove that this descent took place near to the time of the Vedic hymns or was the slow penetration of a small body of fair-skinned barbarians into a civilised Dravidian peninsula.[22]

Interestingly, in all this Sri Aurobindo finds support from an unexpected quarter. At a time when even a hard-core nationalist like Lokmanya Bal Gangadhar Tilak couldn't completely disown the Aryan invasion/migration theory, B.R. Ambedkar called the Aryan–Dravidian divide bluff. 'Whether a tribe or family was racially Aryan or Dravidian was a question which never troubled the people of India until foreign scholars came in and began to draw the line', Babasaheb wrote in a paper published in 1918.[23]

In *Who Were the Shudras?*,[24] Ambedkar states quite categorically that the 'Shudras were Aryans'. He cites several instances where the *rishis* of the *Yajur Veda* and the *Atharva Veda* wished glory to Shudras, and on several occasions, a Shudra became the king himself.

Ambedkar reaches a similar conclusion vis-à-vis outcastes. In *The Untouchables: Who Were They and Why They Became Untouchables?*,[25] he quotes two studies, 'one in Maharashtra by (British administrator HH) Risley and another in Punjab by Mr Rose, and the results flatly contradict the theory that the untouchables are racially different from the Aryans and the Dravidians'. Ambedkar later quotes the *Narada Smriti* to show that 'the Aryans did not at all mind engaging themselves in filthy occupations. If scavenging was not loathsome to an Aryan, how can it be said that engaging in filthy occupations was the cause of Untouchability.'[26]

The proponents of the Aryan invasion/migration theory often cite the absence of horses in pre-Vedic (meaning Harappan) times as evidence of this animal arriving with the invading/migrating people from Central Asia. But the *Rig Veda* categorically says that horses were one of the objects that the Aryans won from Dasyus. In fact, a horse, as described in the Asvamedha Yajna (horse sacrifice) of the *Rig Veda*, had 34 ribs—16 each for the right and the left sides, respectively—thus proving their South Asian origins rather than the Central Asian (36 ribs). Also, to say that invading/migrating Aryans introduced chariots to this landmass defies logic as chariots are neither the vehicles of nomadic people, nor do they function well in hilly/desert regions. Chariots are primarily the vehicles of the rich, urbane populace. But then the spoked wheel, mentioned in the *Rig Veda*, makes its first appearance in Mesopotamia in the middle of the second millennium BC. But once we turn to the 'out of Bharat' theory, everything falls in place. Also, more importantly, archaeologists haven't discovered any dramatic increase in the number of horses in the country in the middle of the second millennium BC.

There is, thus, more than enough evidence suggesting Harappan and Vedic cultures were two sides of the same coin. The moment one sees it through this prism, one finds the answer to the riddle of illiterate, pastoral Aryans producing one of the most profound texts in human history, with the urbane, sophisticated Harappans ending up without having any literature of their own! The *Rig Veda*, for instance, talks of places with a thousand doors and a thousand pillars. As Subhash Kak writes, 'Some take the description of the thousand-pillar palace to be metaphorical; however, such a plausible explanation doesn't work for the reference of other large palaces in RV 2.41.5, 5.62.6, 7.88.5.'[27]

The *Rig Veda* talks of oceans[28] and is well aware of settled agriculture and urban life. A study of the text makes it obvious that it doesn't belong to nomadic tribes. Yes, the Vedas don't give a glimpse of planned city life, but then they are religious texts. To look for such things in the Vedas is like searching for Chanakya's mandala theory in Vatsyayana's *Kama Sutra*!

Our eminent distorians still invoke the horse to differentiate the Harappans from the Vedic Aryans. While the horse is not depicted in any of the seals, there are at least two terracotta figurines that showcase a horse-like animal. The set of 'chessmen' found in Lothal, too, has a specimen that appears like a horse's torso. Be that as it may, it is highly unlikely to expect the Harappans to be unaware of the existence of a horse despite indulging in intense trading activities with the Sumerians. The Harappans, after all, had a trading outpost on the Amu Darya in Central Asia. Interestingly, the Stone Age rock paintings of Bhimbetka showcase horses. Even the Neolithic site of Mahagara in Prayagraj, eastern Uttar Pradesh, has yielded horse bones. Horses, thus, were not alien to Bharat, though the best breed would still be imported from Central Asia, as was the case in mediaeval times.

Similarly, the new information coming from genetics suggests that the cow found in the subcontinent is an indigenously evolved breed going back thousands of years. It is not an of the Central/West Asian cow, thus negating the theory of them coming to Bharat with the invading/migrating Aryans.

More importantly, an examination of human skeletal remains does not show any perceptible racial change in the second millennium BC—the phase when the Aryans supposedly made their entry into the subcontinent either by invading or migrating. In fact, a study in 2006 came up with the conclusion that Bharat's population mix has been broadly stable for a very long time and that there has been no major injection of Central Asian genes for over 10,000 years. This means, as Sanjeev Sanyal writes in *Land of the Seven Rivers*, that 'even if there had been a large-scale influx of so-called Indo-Europeans, it would have taken place more than 10,000 years ago, long before iron weapons and the domestication of horses'.[29]

VI

Historians from different ideological orientations now agree that the Harappan civilization declined around 1900 BC—the decline was slow but steady. There is also near consensus that it was not invaded and decimated by any invasion or migration from the West; even those who believe in the Central Asian origins of the Vedic people now downplay, if not completely deny, Wheeler's enthusiastic claims of finding Harappa's decimation in the Rig Vedic hymns, crediting Indra with the destruction of *puras* (citadels).

Historians have now mostly concluded that Harappa's decline is linked to nature's fury. Floods, drought and earthquakes may all have joined hands to bring this great urban civilization to an end in circa 1900 BC. Around 2200 BC, Bharat's northwest began witnessing a distinct weakening in rainfall, thus the advent of prolonged droughts. Archaeological findings also show Harappan cities witnessing a series of ups and downs, caused primarily by floods, but they would often rise phoenix-like, many times over the debris of the old site.

However, something incredibly devastating happened in 1900 BC to finally force the Harappans to leave the cities once and for all. The Saraswati river, on the banks of which the maximum number of Harappan sites have of late been unearthed, dried up around 1900 BC.

Survey and satellite photographs confirm that Saraswati was once a great river—the *Rig Veda* calls it the mother of all rivers, emerging from the Himalayas and running through the Thar–Cholistan desert of Rajasthan and eastern Sindh, flowing through the Rann of Kutch in Gujarat to finally drain into the Arabian Sea. Satellite images show that both the Sutlej and Yamuna were once the tributaries of Saraswati before joining the Indus and Ganga, respectively. Around 1900 BC, due to tectonic shifts, the Saraswati, besides parting ways with the two rivers, also seemed to have lost its glacial connection with the Himalayas, thus becoming a rain-fed seasonal river. This marked the drying up of the mighty Saraswati, and with it ended the Harappan civilization. This would have been a double whammy for the Harappans, already facing tough times due to the weakening monsoon in the region, forcing them to migrate both westward and eastward.

Navaratna S. Rajaram and David Frawley write:

> Most of the movements of the people from the prehistoric to early historic periods were from east to west. The Hittites, the Mitannis, the Kassites, and before them, the Druhyus, the Alinas and others were eastern people who were forced to move west. How do we account for this? Overpopulation? Or could it be due to the loss of water in the previously hospitable regions of north India? We do know that the desert regions of Sind and Rajasthan at one time were moister and could support larger populations. The gradual desiccation of these regions could have forced these people to move on putting pressure on the heartland, the Sapta Sindhu region or the Punjab.[30]

The Battle of the Ten Kings, an important historical event mentioned in various hymns of the *Rig Veda*, too talks about the westward migration from Bharat. Sudas was a Bharata king of the Tritsu family. At first Vishwamitra was the priest of Sudas, but later he was dismissed and Vasishtha was appointed as his priest. 'Thereupon a long and bitter rivalry ensued between the two priests, and in revenge Vishwamitra led a tribal confederacy of ten kings against the Bharatas, the federation consisting of the five well-known tribes Puru, Yadu,

Turvasha, Anu, and Druhyu, along with five of little note, viz. Alina, Paktha, Bhalanas, Siva and Vishanin. In the bloody and decisive struggle on the Parushni, the Bharatas emerged victorious, defeating the confederacy, of whom the Anu and Druhyu kings were drowned, and Purukutsa of the Purus met his death.'[31] Some of the defeated tribes such as Anus, Druhyus, Pakthas, etc, migrated westward after the war.

Interestingly, the *Avesta* looks eastward for the original homeland of Iranians. It refers to 'Airayana Vajjo' (*Aryavarta*) as their homeland. This stands in sharp contrast to Vedic and Puranic traditions that unanimously call Bharat their home. A closer look at the *Avesta*, however, suggests that their movement out of Bharat may have happened much before 2000 BC. It, after all, mentions the Sapta Sindhu region and also the Saraswati river. They may have been the descendants of Parsus, one of the 10 tribes who lost the famous war against the Bharata king Sudas.

P.L. Bhargava, in his book *India in the Vedic Age*, explores the commonalities between the Iranian and later Vedic traditions. He is quite categorical in saying that the Iranian culture is post-Rig Vedic in nature. He writes:

> The evidence of the Avesta makes it clear that sections of these Aryans in the course of time left Sapta Sindhu and settled in Iran. The first chapter of Vendidad of the handbook of the Parsees enumerates 16 holy lands created by Ahura Mazda which were later rendered unfit for residence of man (i.e. the ancestors of the Iranians) on account of different things created by Angra Mainyu, the evil spirit of the Avesta… The first of these lands was of course Airyana Vaejo which was abandoned by the ancestors of the Iranians because of severe winter and snow; of the others, one was Hapta Hindu, i.e. Sapta Sindhu This is clearest proof that the Aryan ancestors of the Iranians were once part and parcel of the Aryans of Sapta Sindhu before they finally settled in Iran.[32]

Here Shrikant G. Talageri makes a pertinent point. In *Aryan Invasion Theory and Indian Nationalism*, he writes:

> The Hapta Hindu mentioned in the Vendidad is obviously the Sapta Sindhu (the Punjab region), and the first land, 'abandoned by the ancestors of the Iranians because of severe winter and snow' before they came to the Sapta Sindhu region and settled down among the Vedic people, is obviously Kashmir. Even today the Dardic languages of the Kashmir region share many features of the Iranian languages.[33]

People who move to other places tend to remember their original homeland. The *Avesta*, for instance, categorically mentions an original Aryan homeland and its people even name the Helmand river in Afghanistan as Harahvaiti, after the Saraswati. In fact, the Persian people insisted on being Aryans and called their country the Land of Aryans or Iran. As is the case with outsiders, they were more conscious about their identity in the new place.

Explaining this phenomenon, author K.D. Sethna quotes well-known Indologist S. Srikanta Sastri as saying: 'Migrating races look back to the land of their origin for centuries. The Parsis of India remember their origin after 800 years. The ancient Egyptians and Phoenicians remembered their respective lands of origin even though they had forgotten their location.' To this Sethna adds that the Parsis' 'memory extends backward actually for more than 1,300 years' as they started coming to India from 639 AD. [34]

The Vedas, in sharp contrast, remember Bharat to be the only homeland of the Vedic people. And if there were migrations, they, along with the Puranas, only talk of westward movements.

2

Epics and Empires

From the Ramayana and Mahabharata to Buddha and Ashoka

I

When horses fail to deliver, then look for lions to come to your rescue! This seems to be the mantra for our eminent distorians when horses couldn't take the Aryan invasion/migration theory to the logical conclusion.

In *Exotic Aliens: The Lion and the Cheetah in India*,[1] Romila Thapar argues that the 'iconic meaning of the lion had clearly not been appropriated by the Harappans'. She then goes on to say that the *Rig Veda*, the first of the Vedic texts, several centuries later, 'refers to the thunderous roar of the lion, *simha*, which lives in the hills and is a beast that kills'. She, however, adds that the *Rig Veda* doesn't know the tiger. 'A possible explanation', Thapar says, 'could be that the geographical context of the earliest hymns of the *Rig Veda* was beyond the far northeast of India and impinges on northeastern Iran and the Oxus valley'.[2]

Interestingly, Thapar, in *Early India: From the Origins to* AD *1300*, emphasized on the 'greater familiarity' of the *Rig Veda* with Punjab and the Indo-Gangetic watershed—the traditional land of tigers. She writes:

> The geographical knowledge of the authors of the Rig-Vedic hymns can be ascertained by their reference to various rivers. The *Rig Veda* shows greater familiarity with eastern Afghanistan, the Swat Valley, Punjab and the Indo-Gangetic watershed—largely what came to be called the Sapta-Sindhu region.[3]

Thapar tries hard to create an imaginary lion–tiger divide to bolster the sagging Aryan invasion/migration theory. But she is well aware that her claims are based more on assumptions than on hard facts. She knows well that it won't be possible to completely deny the presence of lions in ancient Bharat. So, she goes for the typical leftist subterfuge: mentioning the presence of lions in ancient texts, but simultaneously invoking tigers to say that the former were not too common in the subcontinent.

Thapar writes,

> In the Mahabharata, prowess is associated with the tiger and strength with the bull. The hero is frequently referred to as a 'tiger among men' or is compared with the bull rather than the lion; occasionally, the hero is said to have the gait of the lion. The royal seat, however, is the simhasana (the 'lion seat'), as was the case in West Asia. Yet, when the forest on the Yamuna, the Khandava Vana, is set on fire in order to clear it in preparation for constructing the city of Indraprastha, both tigers and lions are said to have died in the conflagration.[4]

To bolster her claim, Thapar quotes a line from the Mahabharata: 'The tiger protects the forest and the forest nurtures the tiger.' She then adds, 'The primary interdependence does not refer to the lion.'[5] What she fails to mention, deliberately or out of ignorance, is that lions, unlike tigers, don't live in dense jungles. They thrive in landscapes ranging from savannah-like grasslands to sparse forests. So, if lions don't live in dense forests, how are they going to protect them?

This basic nature of lions—along with the fact that they live in groups, making them easy to spot—explains why they could have been wiped out in Bharat, currently confined to Gujarat's Gir forest. Records suggest there were hundreds of lions in Bharat till a couple of centuries ago. Even as late as the mid-19th century, one Colonel A. Smith claimed to have shot up to 300 lions around Delhi and Haryana. By 1931, not one lion was found in the given region by one Major Brown, who himself conceded: 'The lion was once very numerous in Haryana but not one (is) to be found'.[6]

Divyabhanusinh Chavda, an authority on Asiatic lions, too concedes the presence of lions across the subcontinent. He claims in *The Story of Asia's Lions* that at one point in history lions were found across the Asian continent 'from Palestine in the west to Palamau in eastern India'.[7]

Interestingly, while the leftist historiography has worked hard to turn lions into an exotic animal, even when there have been numerous instances suggesting to the contrary, it was the Nehruvian ecosystem, under which the Marxist historiography illegitimately usurped a *numero uno* position for themselves, that strived overtime to bring lions to the centre of the nation's imagination—again with some historical distortions of course.

Charles Allen, in his book *Ashoka: The Search for India's Lost Emperor*, reminds the readers about Jawaharlal Nehru's fascination for Ashoka from as early as the 1920s. He writes,

> In 1927, writing from his prison cell to his 14-year-old daughter Indira—whom he had also named Priyadarshini in direct homage to the emperor who liked to be called *Priyadasi*, or 'Beloved-of-the-Gods'—the Harrow-educated secularist Pandit Jawaharlal Nehru put Ashoka on a par with

Jesus Christ as a source of inspiration in his non-violent struggle against the British rulers of India.[8]

Patrick Olivelle, in his book on Ashoka, while quoting Rajeev Bhargava, who, he writes, 'has investigated Ashoka's thought as a political philosophy', provides another reason for Nehru's fascination for the Mauryan emperor: The first prime minister of independent Bharat saw Ashoka's religious policy to be 'the forerunner' of Nehruvian secularism![9]

Prof. Upinder Singh shares an interesting anecdote in *Political Violence in Ancient India* about Nehru, then the prime minister designate, introducing the new national flag to the Constituent Assembly in July 1947. It was a tricolour with three bands of saffron, deep green and white in the middle, with a navy-blue 24-spoked wheel (*chakra*) in the centre. As the debate followed, various members in the assembly interpreted the flag as per their perceived notions. Some, for instance, saw the wheel in the flag as the Gandhian spinning wheel, others regarded it as the sun's rays, while a few thought it was the wheel of time. 'But Nehru was unequivocal that it represented the wheel on the abacus of the Sarnath lion capital of the great Mauryan emperor Ashoka and the teachings of the Buddha,' Singh writes.[10]

A more 'direct, unambiguous and complete incorporation' of an Ashokan symbol took place a few months later, when the capital of the Sarnath Pillar was adopted as the national emblem. The pillar comprises four lions sitting back to back on a circular abacus, which features an elephant, horse, humped bull, and lion carved in high relief.

Interestingly, Chandragupta Maurya, the founder of the Mauryan dynasty, too had a lion connection. Sanjeev Sanyal writes in *Land of the Seven Rivers*:

There is a legend that tells of how Chandragupta had to flee into the forests to escape the Nanda king. Overcome with

> fatigue he collapsed and fell into a deep slumber. However, a lion appeared and licked him clean. Then it stood guard till the future king awoke. When Chandragupta realised what had happened, he saw it as a good omen and renewed his efforts to unseat the Nandas.[11]

It's pertinent to mention here that the Marxist historiography both 'alienized' and 'nationalized' the lion, as and when it suited its agenda. One also wonders if Nehru's fascination for Ashoka had something to do with the former's desire to create a socialistic, *mai–baap* state on the lines of what Ashoka tried creating more than two millennia ago. In the Indic worldview, the role of the state was largely confined to defending borders, maintaining law and order, and providing internal security—more along the lines of what contemporary proponents of economic reforms call: maximum governance, minimum government, of course, with dharma intact. Ashoka endeavoured to change all that to put in place a nanny state, something he openly espoused in his 4th Pillar Edict: 'Just as one entrusts his child to an experienced nurse, and is confident that the experienced nurse is able to care for the child satisfactorily, so my Rajukas have been appointed for the welfare and happiness of the country people'.[12]

The Nehruvian fascination with Ashoka exposes yet another fallacy: tampering with Bharat's history isn't a post-1990s phenomenon, as a dominant academic narrative would want us to believe. It was very much in practice in the initial years of independence: the project was to bolster Ashoka's greatness. So, was Ashoka as great as he was portrayed by many historians? Also, was he as liberal as he is made out to be? A close, critical analysis, sadly, proves otherwise. The Nehruvian lion project to orchestrate Ashoka's greatness was as fake and outlandish as the Marxist-colonial conspiracy to invoke horses to invent an Aryan invasion/migration into Bharat.

II

It's not just the Vedic and Harappan phases that get mixed up by our eminent distorians; even the two great epics aren't left alone. However, it should not come as a surprise to anyone to see our eminent distorians upending the overall consensus regarding the epics: that the events in the Ramayana preceded those mentioned in the Mahabharata. Romila Thapar, for instance, obsessed as she is with the Aryan invasion/migration theory, believes that the 'events described in the Ramayana probably occurred somewhat later, since the scene is set further east than that of the Mahabharata, in eastern Uttar Pradesh'.[13] Thapar hasn't since stopped indulging in 'time travel', and in one of her recent speeches, she was quoted as saying that Yudhishthira, the eldest of the Pandavas, had Ashoka in mind when he wanted to renounce the kingship![14]

If one thought her statement was an accidental slip-up, then think again. All this is a deliberate Marxist toolkit: to create complications, confusion and a sense of doubt by distorting the basic historical timeline; to discredit the two great epics as products of bardic imagination gone wild, as Thapar writes in *Early India*, thus magnifying what was a 'localised feud'.[15] In the end, you are not sure regarding anything about Bharat's civilizational journey.

Coming to the Ramayana, even a cursory look at it would suggest it talks about a more ancient phase than the Mahabharata. Valmiki's Ramayana has extensive geographical details of the subcontinent, but in the Mahabharata, things get both comprehensive and exhaustive. Rama, during his exile in the jungle with his wife Sita and brother Lakshmana, many a time appears to be moving in unfamiliar territories. The epic talks of jungles inhabited by rakshasas. In sharp contrast, in the Mahabharata, Bharat comes across as neatly divided into different kingdoms.

The Ramayana, too, calls the Aryan invasion/migration bluff as it states matter-of-factly that the Rama–Ravana war wasn't racial in nature. Ravana's father Vishwashrawam was a Brahmin, after all. The Kanyakubja Brahmins of Vidisha worship Ravana, calling him one of their own. Yet, Thapar, despite the Ramayana categorically discounting the racial nature of the conflict, explains Rama's 'crossing the peninsula and conquering Ceylon' as 'clearly a representation of Aryan penetration into the peninsula'.[16]

As for the Mahabharata's historicity and ancientness, it needs to be mentioned that some of its characters are mentioned in the later Vedic texts. Krishna, for instance, is mentioned in the *Chandogya Upanishad*. Other Mahabharata characters include Vichitravirya, Shantanu, Dhritarashtra, Janamejeya, and Parikshit.

Traditionally, it is believed that the Kali Age began with the death of Krishna, 35 years after the Kurukshetra war. According to the fifth-century astronomer, Aryabhata, this calendar began in 3102 BC. The Mahabharata war, thus, was believed to have taken place in 3137 BC. Interestingly, the Aihole inscription of 634 AD by Chalukya King Pulakeshin II, too, mentions this traditional date for the Kali calendar.

Subhash Kak makes an interesting observation on this in his book, *The Idea of India: Bharat as a Civilisation*. He writes,

> Modern studies, using software that can reconstruct the ancient skies, indicate that there was actually an approximate conjunction of the planets on February 17, 3102 BC as assumed by Aryabhata, but this could be a coincidence. Even if the Kali calendar is as old as its starting date, its connections with the *Mahabharata* War do not appear to be equally ancient, for there are diverging traditions related to the War.[17]

Kak's observation about the Kali calendar's Kurukshetra war connection seems pertinent as Puranic genealogies give a gap of around 1,000 years between the Mahabharata war and the rule of the Nandas; this means the great war would have taken place around 1400 BC. Noted archaeologist S.R. Rao, while excavating the submerged remains of Dwarka, too reached a similar conclusion for the Mahabharata war.

Both timelines have reasonable merits. What's without doubt is that the core of the Mahabharata belonged to a much older phase. And this again takes Bharat's history back by thousands of years. Kak writes:

> The *Mahabharata* telescopes early genealogical history. The Puranic king-lists provide useful clues to the sequence of events. Some of the main events are: *Generation 45*, Bhagiratha, Ganga changes course; *Generation 65*, Rama Dasarathi, Dvapara begins; *Generation* 94, the Mahabharata War. Given that the *Puranas* speak of the Mahabharata war taking place over a millennium before the Buddha, it is clear that even if we allocate only 20 years to each generation, the Puranic king-lists appear to go back to the fourth millennium BC.[18]

R.C. Majumdar, while accepting the 1400 BC to be the Mahabharata War era, traces back Bharat's history as per the genealogies provided by the Puranas. He writes:

> We may take c. 1400 BC as the provisional date for the Bharata War, and the event must have taken place between this date and 1000 BC in round numbers. Now working backwards from the earlier date, the age of Manu Vaivasvata, who flourished, according to the genealogies prepared on the basis of traditional accounts, 95 generations before the Bharata War, can be put as

> (95 x 18 + 1400 =) 3110 BC, taking one generation to average 18 years (as we have to deal with very long genealogies extending over 90 generations, we would be erring on the side of caution if we assumed 18 years as the average reign). This date, viz. 3110 BC, curiously enough, approaches 3102 BC, which has been taken as the beginning of the hypothetical Kali age for astronomical calculations. There is no doubt that the date 3102 BC signifies some important and epoch-making event in the traditional history of India. If it denotes the period of the beginning of the rule by Manu Vaivasvata, that means that it stands for the date of the Great Flood recorded in the Satapatha Brahmana and other accounts, in which Manu was the saviour of humanity. The devastating flood undoubtedly was the most important landmark in the history of the ancient world, and common flood legends suggest that the same event has been described in Indian, Hebrew and Babylonian accounts. The flood in Mesopotamia is generally held to have occurred about 3100 BC. The flood in India probably also occurred at the same time, and the date 3102 BC, supposed to be the beginning of the Kali era, may, therefore, commemorate this event.[19]

Majumdar takes this accounting further when he places the era of Rama, who 'flourished 65 generations after Manu, i.e., in (3100 - 65 x 18 =) 1930 BC or roughly in 1950 BC, and the famous Dasarajna war, which occurred about three or four generations after Rama, in c. 1900 BC'.[20] Interestingly, this corresponds to the era of the drying up of the Saraswati—and one can understand why the end of the war between the ten kings saw some of the defeated tribes migrate westward out of Bharat.

The Mahabharata war has been seen as a watershed moment in Bharat's civilizational story. It not only marked the arrival of the Kali Yuga (Age of Darkness), but also the perspective of looking at events before and after the big war presented a sharp contrast. John Keay writes in his book, *India: A History*, how 'the language of the Puranas' while mentioning about genealogies underwent 'an unexpected change of tense when they reach the Bharata war'. He explains:

> From one of Sanskrit's innumerable past tenses the verb suddenly switches to the future; in effect, subsequent generations as recorded in these genealogies are being prophesied... the point that the authors of these lists were trying to register was that the Great War marked a watershed in time. It was literally the end of an era... thereafter the dreaded Kali Yuga, the still current 'Black Age', began.[21]

Romila Thapar believes 'the earliest religious ideas of the Aryans' were those of a 'primitive animism' and their 'conception of the universe' to be a 'limited one'.[22] But when analysed closely beyond the literal interpretation of the Vedas, as Sri Aurobindo did, they cease 'to be merely an interesting remnant of barbarism' and take 'rank among the most important of the world's early Scriptures'.[23]

It is in this backdrop that one truly understands and appreciates the meaning of Vedic verses such as the Nasadiya Sukta of the *Rig Veda*:

> Then even nothingness was not, nor existence.
> There was no air then, nor the heavens beyond it.
> Who covered it? Where was it? In whose keeping?
> Was there then cosmic water, in depths unfathomed?...
> But after all, who knows, and who can say,
> Whence it all came, and how creation happened?

> The gods themselves are later than creation,
> So who knows truly whence it has risen?[24]

The later Vedic people took this idea to even greater heights. In the *Chandogya Upanishad*,[25] for instance, there is a discussion between sage Aruni and his son Sevataketu:

> Fetch me a fruit of the banyan tree.
> Here is one, sir.
> Break it.
> I have broken it, sir.
> So, what do you see?
> Very tiny seeds, sir.
> Break one.
> I have broken it, sir.
> Now what do you see?
> Nothing, sir.
> My son, the father said, what you do not perceive is the essence, and in that essence the mighty banyan tree exists. Believe me, my son, in that essence is the Self of all that is. That is the True, that is the Self. And you are that Self, Svetaketu.[26]

There's another discussion between Svetaketu and his father:

> Put this salt in water, and come to me in the morning.
> The son did as he was told. The father said: Fetch the salt.
> The son looked for it, but could not find it, because it had dissolved.
> Taste the water from the top, said the father. How does it taste?
> Of salt, the son replied.
> Taste from the middle. How does it taste?
> Of salt, the son replied.
> Taste from the bottom. How does it taste?
> Of salt, the son replied.

> Then the father said: You don't perceive that the One Reality (sat) exists in your own body, my son, but it is truly there. Everything which is has its being in that subtle essence. That is Reality! And you are that, Svetaketu.[27]

Ananda Coomaraswamy, in *The Dance of Shiva*,[28] writes how the 'essential contribution of India... is simply her Indianness'. Ironically, our eminent distorians have thus far, especially since Independence, regarded this very 'Indianness' as a regressive phenomenon. Anything and everything emerging out in this land is seen to be the result of either an invasion or a migration from the outside world. But the moment a sense of pride is inserted in our 'Indianness', 'the incoherencies of the Vedic texts will at once be explained and disappear', as Aurobindo said. The scripture would stop appearing to be 'confused in thought or primitive in its substance, not a medley of heterogeneous or barbarous elements, but one, complete and self-conscious in its purpose and in its purport'.[29]

III

Around the sixth century BC, Bharat's history emerged, to quote A.L. Basham, 'from legend and dubious tradition'.[30] While one may contest the characterisation of the pre-sixth century BC Indic tradition as 'dubious', what's without doubt is that for the first time, 'we read of great kings, whose historicity is certain and some of whose achievements are known, and from now on the main lines of India's political development are clear'.[31]

It's not that older texts don't talk about the dynasties of the past. The Puranas mention the dynastic rule from the Vedic phase till the post-Mauryan period.[32] In fact, unlike what eminent distorians would say—that 'the focus of civilization'[33] shifted eastward to Uttar Pradesh and Bihar by the sixth century BC—the Puranas have a comprehensive list, though often with different names of kings and dynasties ruling from

Magadha, from the Mahabharata times. Subhash Kak, in *The Idea of India: Bharat as a Civilisation*, after compiling from different Puranas, makes a list of dynasties that had been ruling from Magadha since the Mahabharata war:

- Brihadrathas (32 kings), 967 years
- Pradyotas of Avanti (5 kings), 173 years
- Sisunagas (10 kings), 360 years
- Nandas (Mahapadma + sons), 100 years
- Mauryas (9 kings), 137 years
- Sungas (10 kings), 112 years
- Kanvas (4 kings), 45 years
- Andhras (30 kings), 460 years

Kak's compilation of the Puranic list, incidentally, doesn't mention the Haryanka dynasty, founded by Bimbisara, about whom we will discuss later. There are, however, reasons to believe the overall credibility of the list. Explaining the list of Magadhan dynasties in the Puranas, Kak writes:

> One may question the reliability of the earlier parts of this list since the average span of reign for the pre-Nanda kings is more than twice as much as the post-Nanda ones. The explanation may be that it was during the imperial Maurya age that comprehensive king-lists were made, and consequently, only the better-known names of the earlier period were included… The length of the Brihadratha dynasty may be questioned, but it may represent the cumulative sum of several early dynasties.[34]

Be that as it may, the fact is that there existed 16 states (*mahajanapadas*) in Bharat in the sixth century BC. They were: Gandhara, Kamboja, Assaka, Vatsa, Avanti, Shurasena, Chedi, Malla, Kuru, Panchala, Matsya, Vajji (Vrijji), Anga, Kashi, Kosala, and Magadha.

Of the 16 *mahajanapadas*, Kashi, with its capital in Benares, was the most powerful to begin with. It, however, lost its position and relevance to Kosala and Magadha—the two kingdoms that were vying for supremacy in the sixth century BC when Gautam Buddha and Mahavira came into the scene. Eventually, Magadha emerged victorious, and the centre of political power shifted to modern-day Bihar.

Bimbisara, the founder of the Haryanka dynasty (c. 544–413 BC), was the first important ruler of the sixth-century Magadha. He had his capital in Rajagriha, about 60 miles to the southeast of modern Patna. Bimbisara strengthened his position through marriages, first with the royal house of Kosala and then with a princess from Vaishali. Having secured his western and northern frontiers, respectively, he set out to conquer Anga, situated on the borders of modern-day Bengal. Champa, its capital, 'situated on the bank of the river of the same name, was noted for its wealth and commerce'.[35]

Impatient to rule Magadha, Ajatashatru, the son of Bimbisara, murdered his father in about 493 BC. He fortified Rajagriha and built a small fort in Pataligrama, in the vicinity of Ganga, which later became the city of Pataliputra. Ajatashatru resorted to the military route to expand his kingdom. He first attacked Kosala, whose king was his maternal uncle, and then focused on integrating the Vrijji confederacy with Magadha. This endeavour, however, took him 16 years to accomplish. But once done, Magadha became the most powerful kingdom of that time.

Ajatashatru, who died in around 461 BC, was succeeded by five kings who, as per Ceylonese Buddhist chronicle *Mahavamsa*, were all parricides. Finally, the people of Magadha deposed the last of the five in around 413 BC and appointed a viceroy, Shishunag, as king. Shishunag's dynasty lasted to about half a century when Mahapadma Nanda established a new dynasty, which was uprooted in around 321 BC by Chandragupta of the Maurya dynasty under the able guidance of Chanakya.

The Nandas were believed to be of low origin. Some sources say Mahapadma Nanda was the son of a Shudra mother; others believe that he was born of the union of a barber and a courtesan. Be that as it may, the fact is the Nandas took the Magadhan power to new heights. They employed a vast army: even if one quoted the most conservative number given by Greek writers, the Nandas had 20,000 cavalry, 2,00,000 infantry, 2,000 chariots, and 3,000 elephants—an army big enough to dissuade Alexander's troops from crossing the Beas. They had reasons to be wary: If winning against a relatively small army of Porus was an arduous experience for Alexander's troops, what chances they had in taking on such a big army, and that too in an alien, hostile territory?

Interestingly, Alexander's invasion was a marginal story in Bharat and found no direct mention in Indic texts. But the Greeks' arrival was a boon for Bharat's historiography—they left a detailed account of the country of that time. Though aimed primarily at creating a larger-than-life image of Alexander through his military exploits, it did help in giving us detailed information about the state of Bharat's affairs then. More importantly, Alexander's invasion did trigger a chain of events that led to the rise of the Mauryas in 321 BC—the first historically and archaeologically recorded empire that brought the whole of the subcontinent under one flag.

IV

On 14 October 1956, Dr B.R. Ambedkar renounced Hinduism in the presence of about five lakh followers in the city of Nagpur. Many of his followers too decided to convert, making it 'the single largest religious conversion in history'.[36] So much so that in the 1961 Census, 'the number of Buddhists in India had risen by 1,671 per cent in the space of a decade'.[37]

A few years ago, Arundhati Roy came up with a book, *The Doctor and the Saint*, on the lives of Dr Ambedkar and Mahatma Gandhi. In the book, she explains how 'history has been unkind' to Ambedkar. 'It has made him India's Leader of the Untouchables, the King of the Ghetto. It has hidden away his writings. It has stripped away the radical intellect and the searing insolence,' she writes.[38]

History, however, has its own way of taking revenge.

A man who struggled through his life,[39] and post demise was a victim of the Nehruvian plot that conspired to wipe him out of public consciousness, Ambedkar, in 2012, was voted the 'Greatest Indian', ahead of Gandhi, Nehru and Patel, in a poll conducted by two prominent television channels.[40] The dead Ambedkar has become more powerful than when he was alive. The Congress, which denied him a Bharat Ratna for four decades since Independence, no longer leaves any stone unturned to own him up these days. The Marxists now find it fashionable to invoke him, little realizing how they distrusted and detested him when he was alive. The right wing has gone beyond the 'false god'[41] narrative to appropriate him as a worthy pantheon. And the country's left-'liberal' brigade, which until recently could not see beyond the Gandhis and the Nehrus, just can't get enough of him.

Arundhati Roy is no different. She and her ilk have been on the forefront to distort the phenomenon called Ambedkar, opportunistically weaponizing him to target the Indic civilization and its icons. They constantly reminded us of Ambedkar's uncompromising distaste for Hinduism.

Yes, Babasaheb had said that he was born a Hindu but he would never die as one. Yes, he called Hinduism 'a veritable chamber of horrors'.[42] Yes, he also believed that no real reformation was possible in Hinduism, given its obsession with the 'degrading and discriminatory' caste system.[42] 'There cannot be a more degrading system of social organisation than the caste system. It is the system that deafens, paralyses and cripples people from helpful activity,' Ambedkar said.[44]

There's no denying that Ambedkar renounced Hinduism. But for all his anger against Hinduism, he didn't allow himself to be blinded to the realities of the Semitic religions. 'Muslims in India are an exclusive group, and they have a consciousness of kind possessed by a longing to belong to their own group and not to any non-Muslim group,' he wrote.[45]

In fact, his stand on Islam was so stringent that he even pushed for the transfer of population between Bharat and Pakistan, citing the precedent of Turkey, Greece and Bulgaria. He wrote:

> Those, who scoff at the idea of transfer of population, will do well to study the history of the minority problem, as it arose between Turkey, Greece and Bulgaria. If they do, they will find that these countries found that the only effective way of solving the minorities' problem lay in exchange of population.[46]

True, Ambedkar didn't die as a Hindu, as he had prophesied himself. But when it came to looking for a new religion, he chose Buddhism—a religion deeply rooted in Indic ethos, a religion which is 'a kind of Hindu Protestantism'.[47]

Coming to Buddhism, its founder, Gautam Buddha, was born as Siddhartha in the household of a Sakya king in the Nepalese Terai of Lumbini. At the time of his birth, it was prophesied that the child would either become a *chakravartin* king or a renowned monk. His father, King Suddhodana, wanting to see his son become an emperor, ensured he was cut off from worldly miseries. But, as fate would have it, when he grew up, while travelling outside the palace, he encountered human sufferings. Shocked to find misery in life, he left home in search of answers.

Romila Thapar traces his journey thus:

> After an austere six years he decided that asceticism was not the path to salvation and discarded it. He then resolved to discover the means of salvation through meditation, and eventually on the forty-ninth day of his meditation he received enlightenment and understood the cause of suffering in this world. He preached his first sermon at the Deer Park at Sarnath (four miles from Banaras) and gathered his first disciples.
>
> This sermon was called the Turning of the Wheel of Law, and was the nucleus of Buddhist teaching. It incorporated the Four Noble Truths (that is, the world is full of suffering, suffering is caused by human desires, the renunciation of desire is the path to salvation, and this salvation is possible through the Eight-Fold Path), and the Eight-Fold Path which consisted of eight principles of action, leading to a balanced, moderated life (right views, resolves, speech, conduct, livelihood, effort, recollection, and meditation, the combination of which was described as the Middle Way).[48]

For the next 45 years, Buddha was constantly on the move, spreading Buddhist Dharma. For eight months in a year he and his followers would travel from place to place. Only during the four months of the rainy season he would stay at one place.

Buddha died at the age of 80. In the town of Pava in today's eastern Uttar Pradesh, he was attacked by dysentery after eating a meal of pork[49] prepared by a lay disciple, Cunda. But he kept on moving, and in the town of Kusinagara, he breathed his last under a sal tree. His last words were prophetic: 'All composite things decay. Strive diligently!'

Buddhism wasn't the only sect that came into being in that era, though it definitely was the most prominent and over the next few centuries found itself spread well beyond Bharat's territorial boundaries. Among others, Jainism tops the list. Jainism is today primarily associated with Mahavira, though he was the 24th tirthankara. As per the Jaina tradition, Rishabhanatha was the first tirthankara. He is believed to be born in Ayodhya, and the *Yajur Veda* mentions his name along with two other tirthankaras—Ajitanatha and Arishtanemi.

Mahavira, at the age of 30, renounced his family and became an ascetic. For 12 years he kept wandering in the search of truth and enlightenment. Unlike Buddhism, its teaching was mostly confined to the Gangetic valley, though in later centuries Jainism found patronage and followers in the western part of the country. It spread rapidly among the trading community. It was primarily because of Jainism's extreme emphasis on non-violence (ahimsa), thus preventing its spread among communities pursuing farming and crafts.

There has been a tendency to believe that Buddhism and Jainism were antithetical to Hinduism. But the fact is, as Indologist T.W. Rhys-Davids writes in *Buddhism: Being a Sketch of the Life and Teachings of Gautama,* Buddha 'was born and brought up as a Hindu and lived and died as a Hindu'. Rhys-Davids explains:

> I hope, to remove at least one misconception—the prevalent notion that Gautama was an enemy to Hinduism, and that his chief claim on the gratitude of his countrymen lies in his having destroyed a system of iniquity and oppression and fraud. This is not the case. Gautama was born, and brought up, and lived, and died a typical Indian. Hinduism had not yet, in his time, arisen. And he had but little quarrel with the religion that did prevail. His purpose was to build it up, to strengthen it, not to destroy it. He ignored, it is true, the theory, then held by all, that there existed, inside the body, a minute creature, called a soul. But he considered this theory not essential to religion. In replacing the idea of a 'soul' by the doctrine, not of a unity, but of a multitude of mental states, he was far ahead, indeed, of his time. But, apart from

> this, such originality as Gautama possessed lay in the way in which he adopted, enlarged, ennobled, and systematised that which had already been well said by others; in the way in which he carried out to their logical conclusion principles of equity and justice already acknowledged by some of the most prominent earlier thinkers. The difference between him and other teachers lay chiefly in his deep earnestness and in his broad public spirit of philanthropy. Even these differences are probably much more apparent now than they were then, and by no means deprived him of the support and sympathy of the best among the Brahmins. Many of his chief disciples, many of the most distinguished members of his Order, were Brahmins: he always classed them with the Buddhist mendicants as deserving of respect, and he used the name Brahmin as a term of honour for the Buddhist Arahants or saints.[50]

V

Buddhism, born in the fifth century BC, saw its golden phase two centuries later during the Maurya regime, especially when Ashoka was the king. (Ashoka not just pushed Buddhism to a pre-eminent position within the country, but also sent Buddhist emissaries to foreign countries such as Sri Lanka, China, et al.) The story of the Mauryas, however, began with Chandragupta, the grandfather of Ashoka.

At 25, Chandragupta Maurya overthrew Dhana Nanda, the last of the Nanda rulers, in 321 BC. There are several theories about the origins of Chandragupta, but the most commonly accepted is that he belonged to a cattle-rearing tribe called Moriya. The story gets credence from the fact that his mother placed him in the care of a cattle herdman; it was here that Chanakya, also known as Kautilya, first saw him and took him under his wings.

The young Maurya, under Chanakya's guidance, first took control of Punjab and surrounding areas, and from there gradually moved towards the centre, i.e., Pataliputra: Chandragupta, as the story goes, formulated this strategy after seeing a woman scolding her child for eating from the middle of a dish, since the centre was bound to be much hotter than the sides.

After taking over the Gangetic valley from the Nandas, Chandragupta looked to exploit the power vacuum in the northwest created by Alexander's departure. In 303 BC, he defeated Seleucus Nicator, a Greek general and Alexander's successor, forcing him to cede to the Mauryas the provinces of the Trans-Indus, which today would cover parts of Afghanistan. The treaty of 303 BC also included a marriage alliance, of which unfortunately no details are available. Maybe one of the daughters of Seleucus came to the Mauryan court. Also, Scleucus' ambassador Megasthenes lived for many years in Pataliputra and travelled extensively across Bharat. Though his book, *Indica*, no longer survives, it has been quoted in several books, including the ones written by Pliny, Strabo and Arrian.

Towards the end of his life, Chandragupta abdicated his throne in favour of his son, Bindusara, to become a Jaina ascetic. Together with Jaina saint Bhadrabahu, along with many other monks, he went to Shravana Belgola in Karnataka, and ended his life through slow starvation in the orthodox Jaina manner.

Chandragupta was succeeded by his son, Bindusara, in 297 BC. Not much is known about him except that he maintained links with his Greek neighbours. To the Greeks, Bindusara was known as Amitrochates, perhaps a Greek transcription of the Sanskrit *Amitraghata* (the slayer of foes). Interestingly, he had requested Antiochus I to send him some sweet wine, dried figs and a sophist. To this Antiochus said that he could send him all except a sophist, for this was not allowed under the Greek law.

There is a piece of interesting information about Bindusara, though highly unreliable, given that it had been recorded by a 16th-century Tibetan Buddhist monk, Taranatha. It says that the second Mauryan ruler had conquered 'the land between the two seas', meaning the peninsular region of Bharat. Early Tamil literature, too, mentions the Mauryan invasion of the South. It is thus apparent that at the time of Bindusara's death in 272 BC, practically the entire subcontinent had come under Mauryan suzerainty.

It seems unlikely that Bindusara would invade the south but allow the neighbouring Kalinga (Odisha) to remain independent. In fact, the Nandas had brought Kalinga under Magadhan control. It is, therefore, possible that Kalinga might have rebelled and thrown away the Mauryan yoke amid the chaos for the Magadhan throne after the death of Bindusara in 272 BC. We are told that it took Ashoka four years to gain power in Pataliputra. Maybe this is the reason why Ashoka came down so violently in the Kalinga war, in which, as per the Mauryan emperor's own words in the 13th Major Rock Edict, 'a hundred and fifty thousand people were deported, a hundred thousand were killed, and many more died'.[51]

If Buddhist sources are to be believed, Ashoka came to power in 268–69 BC after killing all rival claimants to the throne. Buddhist texts mention that he killed 99 half-brothers and only his full brother, Tissa, was spared. His initial years as king were so violent that Ashoka was given the name 'Chandashoka' (Ashoka the Cruel). In 260–61 BC, Ashoka took to the battlefield one last time to bring Kalinga under his rule. With this, his control over the subcontinent was absolute, except for the small kingdoms in the extreme south.

It is generally believed that Ashoka converted to Buddhism and became a pacifist after witnessing the Kalinga carnage. The truth, however, is that Ashoka was already a Buddhist when he took the war to the Kalingans. Writes Charles Allen in *Ashoka: The Search for India's Lost Emperor*, 'The Minor Rocks inform us that Ashoka became a lay Buddhist in or around 265 BCE, even if by his own confession he did not take this conversion seriously for the first two and a half years'.[52]

The remorse for the Kalinga war, therefore, seems to be an afterthought, much like a public relations exercise. 'The edicts are, after all, what Ashoka wanted us to remember of him. Notice that Ashoka expresses regret but does not offer to free Kalinga and its inhabitants.'[53]

Even more interesting is the fact that the edict showing 'remorse' for the Kalinga cruelties—the 13th Major Rock Edict—is found not in Odisha, but in far-away Kandahar (today's Afghanistan). None of the inscriptions in Odisha express repentance for the Kalinga violence. Even in the inscriptions where he expresses regret, as in the 13th Major Rock Edict, he makes it abundantly clear that 'one who does wrong should be forgiven as far as it is possible to forgive him'. He warns 'the forest tribes of his empire' that 'he has power even in his remorse, and he asks them to repent, lest they be killed'.[54]

Worse, if the Buddhist text *Ashokavadana* is to be believed, 18,000 Ajivikas in Bengal were put to death at Ashoka's orders. It took place many years after he had become a Buddhist. Equally damning is the story of a Jaina painter in Pataliputra who drew a picture of Buddha bowing to a Jain tirthankara. Ashoka didn't just order his men to set alight the painter's house after locking him and his family inside, but also promised to pay a gold coin to everyone who would bring a decapitated head of a Jaina. The slaughter ended only when someone mistakenly killed Ashoka's only surviving brother, Tissa, a Buddhist monk. He had his queen, Tissarakkha, along with other conspirators, thrown into the fire when he heard of their role in the blinding of his son and heir-apparent, Kunala, despite the latter pleading for their mercy.

There are also question marks over Ashoka's administrative skills. Ashoka died around 232 BC, and within half a century the Mauryan empire, which encompassed the entire subcontinent and more, fell like a pack of cards. In 185 BC, Pushyamitra Shunga assassinated Brihadratha, the last Mauryan ruler, at a military parade. The fact that a king was killed in front of his own army showed not just his incompetence but also how aloof and unpopular he had become.

It cannot be said with certainty how the Mauryan empire collapsed, but there are enough records suggesting the decline actually started during Ashoka's later years. There are several stories about intra-family intrigues and rivalries that left Ashoka increasingly powerless. Such had been the internal feud that *Ashokavadana* mentions Ashoka's son and heir-apparent, Kunala, being blinded at the orders of chief queen Tissarakkha.

Ashokavadana shares another story that showcased how things had gone awry even when Ashoka was alive. Thus goes the story:

> Ashoka is said to have donated all his treasure to the monastery of Kukkutarama. He declares the son of Kunala, Samprati, to be the heir-apparent, and the latter is king in all but name. The source suggests that the prince was in the confidence of the ministers and they were all conspiring against Ashoka because they disapproved of the latter's donations to the Buddhist order. One day a bhikkhu comes around asking for alms. The only thing which Ashoka can give to the bhikkhu is his sole possession, half an amla.[55]

Ashoka died a sad and disappointed person.

3

Invasion to Affluence

Bharat in the Post-Maurya and Gupta Periods

I

The period following the Mauryan dynasty is generally portrayed as Bharat's 'Dark Age', given a series of attacks from the nomadic tribes of Central Asia. Events taking place thousands of kilometres to the northwest of Bharat were influencing, if not interrupting, the flow of history in the subcontinent. It so happened that in the first century BC, a severe famine caused by excessive snow affected the area that comprises today's Mongolia.[1]

The area was occupied by nomadic tribes who were believed to be the forerunners of the later-day Mongols. Given the scarcity of food, these tribes would carry incessant raids on Chinese territories, following which Chinese emperor Shi Huang Ti decided to build the Great Wall in the last half of the third century BC. With the Chinese side blocked, these tribes began looking the other way. The first casualty of this shifting gaze had been the Yueh-chih (Kushanas) tribe, who in turn displaced and occupied the land of Scythians (Shakas). The Shakas then moved eastward to displace the Bactrians (Indo-Greeks) and Parthians. One by one, these nomadic tribes were forced to move into the subcontinent.

No doubt, this period was one of political upheaval. New political players entered the subcontinent. But they were not aliens. They, in fact, belonged to the larger Indic ecosystem. Bharat's links with Central Asia-Tarim Basin and the neighbouring Oxus and Badakhshan regions, since antiquity, have been 'deep and multi-faceted'.[2] Noted British historian Arnold Toynbee traces these linkages back to at least 1,700 years before Christ, saying, 'the region belonged to Sanskrit people from 1700 BC to 400 AD'.[3] Similarly, American scholar Ellsworth Huntington points towards their ethnic connections too. He writes:

> Ancient tradition relates that the original inhabitants of the Lop basin, the probable ancestors of the Chentos of today migrated from northern India. The tradition is confirmed by the fact that the earliest specimens of writing found in the ruins of the Takla-Makan desert are in the Kharosthi tongue, a language akin to Sanskrit and spoken in northern India and far from the beginning of the Christian era. Since the Mohammedan invasion of the tenth century, the ancient tongue has been displaced by the Turki language of the conquerors, which is spoken in several primitive dialects.[4]

One is reminded of this connection each time a Hindu takes a *sankalp* during a puja: the puja begins with the mention of Jambudvipa (comprising a large section of Eurasia), followed by Dakshina Parv (southern part of the Jambu-dvipa), Bharata Khand (Greater Bharat), Bharata Varsha (Bharat subcontinent), to the locality the devotee hails from.

The *Brahma Purana* mentions in detail these geographical regions. It says:

> The dvipas are Jambu, Plaksha, Shalmala, Kusha, Krouncha, Shaka, and Pushkara as the seventh… Jambu-dvipa is located right in the middle of these and in the centre is

> Meru, the golden mountain... The earth is like a lotus and the mountain is established like its pericarp… Bharata is said to be the first varsha, and Kimpurusha is the one that comes next. Harivarsha is to the south of Meru. Ramyaka is to the north and Hiranmaya is next to it. O supreme Brahmanas! Uttarkuru is like Bharata. Each of these extends for 9,000 yojanas. Ilavrita is in the centre and the golden mountain of Meru rises up there. O immensely fortunate ones! In four directions from Meru, Ilavrita extends for 9,000 yojanas.[5]

According to the *Markandeya Purana*, the earth in Jambudvipa 'rises up in the middle and slopes downwards to the north and the south'.[6] The elevated land is known as Ilavrita, in whose centre is Mount Meru.

The *Vayu Purana* mentions in detail the mountains, rivers and valleys of Jambudvipa. Prof. S.M. Ali believes the 'geographical section of this (Vayu) Purana is more complete and detailed than that found in any other Puranas'. According to him, the description of the northern regions of Jambudvipa 'covers a very vast area, from the Urals and the Caspian to the Yenisel and from the Turkestan, Tien Shan ranges to the Arctic. It describes the topography of the whole land very accurately and in some cases picturesquely'.[7]

The area across the Himalayas and Hindukush from Pamir up to the Arctic was known as Uttar Kuru. The Arctic was known as Somagiri. There are numerous references to the two regions in Valmiki's Ramayana and Ved Vyasa's Mahabharata. In the Ramayana, for instance, Sugriva, while sending the monkeys to the north in search of Sita, describes the route and the countries in that direction. Among others, he commands them to search Sita in the lands and towns of the Dardas, Kambojas, Yavanas, and Shakas. He describes Uttar Kuru and Somagiri, which he says is situated in the extreme north.

The region, he says, has no national boundaries and is without the sun and yet very much lighted.[8]

According to the Mahabharata, Shaka, Darada, Pahlava, Kirata, and Parada are said to be Kshatriyas of good birth.[9] Invitations were sent to Shaka, Pahlava, Rishik, and Darada kings to participate in the Mahabharata war from the Pandava side.[10] The Tusharas, more popularly known as Yueh-chihs (Kushanas), were also said to have participated in the Mahabharata war from the Kaurava side.[11] The Mahabharata also mentions Arjuna collecting tribute from Uttar Kuru and Nakula defeating Hunas, Pahlavas, Yavanas, and Shakas. [12]

A Puranic tradition has a clue hidden in a story of Vaivasvata Manu, who had nine sons, including Iksvaku, and a daughter named Ila. The descendants of Iksvaku are members of the solar dynasty (Suryavanshi). Rama of the Ramayana is said to be from this line of dynasty. And from Ila emerged the lunar dynasty (Chandravanshi). Pauravas, whose famous story of falling in love with Urvashi finds mention in the *Rig Veda*, hailed from this line of dynasty. His great-grandson was Yayati, who had five sons: Yadu, Turvasa, Druhyu, Anu, and Puru. The Purus, we are told, ruled around Kurukshetra, the Anus to their north, the Druhyus to the west, the Yadus to their south, and the Turvasas to the east of the Yadus.[13]

The *Vayu Purana*, the *Matsya Purana*, the *Brahmanda Purana*, and the *Bhagavata Purana*, they all agree that after the Battle of the Ten Kings between the victorious Bharata king Sudas and a confederacy of ten kings, about which the *Rig Veda* mentions in detail, the vanquished rulers were pushed westward, some of them out of the subcontinent. These defeated kingdoms were Puru, Yadu, Turvasa, Anu, Druhyu, Alina, Paktha, Bhalanas, Siva, and Vishanin.

If Shrikant G. Talageri is to be believed, the Anus were the ancestors of the Iranians and the Druhyus became the forefathers of Greek and European peoples and of the Druids.[14]

The Puranas regard Pahlavas, Kambojas, Sakas, Yavanas, and Paradas as 'Panca-ganah' (five-hordes). These Panca-ganah, under the military alliance of the Haihaya or Taljunga Kshatriyas of the Yadava line, defeated and dethroned King Bahu of Kosala. Later, Sagara, son of King Bahu, was able to defeat the Haihayas along with these five-hordes. Sagara then divested these people of their Kshatriyahood, following which Brahmin priests abandoned them and in due course of time, these Kshatriyas were degraded socially to become Vrishal/Vratya/Shudra/Kshatriya Shudra.[15]

According to the Sagara saga, the Shakas, Yavanas, Kambojas, Pardas, and Pahlavas were part of the Indic ecosystem from time immemorial. The truth is Bharat's ties with Central and West Asia were always deep and intense, with people and ideas moving in both directions all the time. They shared the same socio-cultural and civilizational values.[16] No wonder when these people invaded Bharat after the decline of the Mauryas, one witnessed no clash of civilizations. They were culturally the extension of the Indic civilization, even before they had landed their feet on the subcontinent.

It is this cultural/civilizational affinity that was evident from the life of Kujula Kadphises, the founder of the Kushana empire and the great-grandfather of Kanishka I. Kadphises was the follower of Shiva even when he had not yet reached Bharat. B.B. Kumar explains this further as he writes:

> The figure of Shiva was found on the coins of Gondopheres, Maves and others. It appears on the coins of the Kushana rulers... It needs mention that the Kushana kings were the devotees of Shiva before their arrival in this country. Shiva was worshipped in India and Central Asia along with

> Vishnu and Sun God, as revealed in famous Nicolo seal, noticed by Cunningham and deciphered by Ghirshman; it was originally in Tocharian language and script, the figure of the devotee on the seal is that of a Haephthalite chief. The seal reveals the composite cult of Shiva, Vishnu and Surya (Mihira, Vedic - Mitra, Sun God). This confirms the fact that the religious behaviour operated in the continuum frame, rather than in the dichotomy fame.[17]

One can look at the history of Mongols to see how the Bharat–Central Asia 'religious behaviour operated in the continuum frame, rather than in the dichotomy frame'. Buddhist Mongols, after all, worship Lord Shiva as Mahakala. Here, it needs to be mentioned that Shiva's *trishul* adorned the flag of Chengiz Khan. According to Berthold Laufer, in Mongolian mythology, an inspirational dream featuring Lord Shiva instigated the conversion of Kublai Khan, Chengiz Khan's grandson, to Buddhism.[18]

To this B.B. Kumar adds:

> The other deities worshipped by them (Mongols) were: Yama (the god of dead), Goddess Devi (Lha-mo; the spouse of Shiva), Kartikeya (Cam-Sran; a war god), Vaisravana or Kubera, Brahma, 33 devas, digpalas, 21 Taras, Hevajra, Buddha-kapala, Yamantaka, Hayagriva (a horse-necked god; seems to be connected with Vishnu, rather than Shiva; the protector of horses), etc. Incidentally, it needs mention that trident still adorns the national flag of Kazakhstan.[19]

One can see a similar connection with the persecuted Yazidis, too: the view of Shiva as the highest god in the Shaivite tradition, with the peacock riding Kartikeya (Skanda) as his son, finds a parallel in the Yazidi tradition, where the angel peacock is considered second only to God.[20] Interestingly, the peacock is native to this subcontinent.

So, what does the Bharat–Central Asia saga tell us? That the two regions had deep, interactive relations. That, Hinduism and Buddhism coexisted amicably, and the dichotomy saga was a mischievous colonial-leftist afterthought. Finally, it was Buddhism that mostly followed Hinduism in Central, West, East and Southeast Asia, rather than the other way round.

II

The Shungas, under Pushyamitra, succeeded the illustrious Maurya empire in around 185 BC. The Shungas were believed to be of the Brahmin origin, hailing most likely from the region of Ujjain. This has given certain historians a licence to turn the entire episode into a Brahmanical rebellion against the Buddhist Mauryas, though the same historians would reiterate that the Mauryas, especially Ashoka, followed a reverential policy towards Brahmins. Buddhist literature would be quoted to portray Pushyamitra, the performer of two Ashwamedha sacrifices, as a persecutor of Buddhists and a destroyer of their monasteries. This projection gets a setback when one looks at the Buddhist structure at Bharhut, built during the time of the Shungas.

Pushyamitra died after a reign of 36 years and was succeeded by his son Agnimitra around 150 BC. Interestingly, Agnimitra is the hero of a famous drama, *Malavikagnimitram*, written by Kalidasa. A glance at *Malavikagnimitram,* and the myth of Brahmin (Hindu)–Buddhist conflict gets shattered. Kalidasa, in his drama, weaves a 'fascinating character of Kaushiki, the ascetic nun'. As Srinivas Reddy, the English translator of the play, writes in the introduction to the book, 'He (Kalidasa) refers to her as a *parivrajika*, a female wanderer of an unnamed denomination. Internal references in the text point to a Buddhist affiliation… Kaushiki is accorded great respect by everyone at the court, including the king who addresses her as *pandita* (learned) and *bhagavati* (revered one).'[21]

After Agnimitra, the Sunga dynasty saw a rapid decline, and by the time the Kanva dynasty (73–28 BC) replaced it, the kingdom had been reduced to the confines of Magadha.

At around the same time, Kalinga successfully rose in rebellion under the Chedi dynasty. In 193 BC, this dynasty saw a remarkable ruler called Kharavela, who left behind a lot of information about himself through his inscription at Hathigumpha on the Udayagiri hill. The inscription tells us how Kharvela not only defeated the Satavahanas and the Indo-Greeks, but also took his revenge against Magadha for the Kalinga carnage of Ashoka.

Kharvela tells us proudly that he brought back the Jaina idols that had been taken away to Pataliputra by the Nandas and that he made King Bahasatimitra (either the last Mauryan king Brihadhrata or the Sunga dynasty founder Pushyamitra) bow to him. With the prestige of the Magadhans in tatters, he had his exploits inscribed on a rock on the Udayagiri hill, near Bhubaneswar, from where one can, on a clear, sunny day, see Ashoka's Dhauli edit. 'It is unmistakable how Kharavela had his inscriptions placed directly looking out at those of Ashoka at Dhauli. It is as if to tell Ashoka that he, Kharavela of Kalinga, had sacked Pataliputra and caused the end of Mauryan rule.'[22]

The power of the Chedis, however, declined after Kharvela.

Meanwhile, the Satavahanas rose to power. They seemed to have been from Andhra and called themselves 'Andhra-bhritya' or servants of the Andhras. The founder of the family was Simuka. However, it was Satakarni I, the son or nephew of Simuka, who raised the dynasty to prominence. After his death, the Satavahanas suffered a setback at the hands of the Indo-Greeks and Sakas (Scythians) who had taken over northwestern Bharat and were in serious contention to control the north. An inscription in Nashik tells us of the Satavahana King Gautamiputra Satakarni, who defeated and pushed back the Greeks and Scythians (Shakas).

Rudradaman of the western Shaka dynasty, ruling in the middle of the second century AD, gave his daughter in marriage to a Satavahana king. Rudradaman, however, records how he defeated a Satavahana king twice and yet chose to forgive him because of the matrimonial alliance. By the third century AD, the Satavahana dynasty had declined and disintegrated into much smaller kingdoms—of these, the Pallavas emerged as a major power by the middle of the sixth century AD. We will talk about the Pallavas in the next chapter.

In the mid-third century BC, Diodotus, the governor of Bactria (Balkh), revolted against the Seleucid King Antiochus. When attempts to subjugate Bactria failed, Antiochus III recognized its independence and gave a Seleucid bride to Diodotus' great-grandson, Demetrius, in 200 BC. Demetrius conquered Arachosia and eastern Gedrosia (modern-day southern Afghanistan and the Makran areas). Demetrius II, being more ambitious, invaded Punjab, thus setting up Indo-Greek power in northwestern Bharat. Menander, better known as Milinda, further stabilized Indo-Greek authority in the subcontinent. His coins have been found as far as Kabul in the northwest and Mathura in the southeast.

The decline of the Greek kingdoms in Bharat in the north-west coincided with an attack on Bactria by nomadic tribes from Central Asia. Those who initially attacked Bactria in the late second century BC included the Parthians (Pahlavas) and Scythians (Shakas). By the middle of the first century BC, only a few Greek chiefs ruled in Bharat, and the Shaka power extended as far as Mathura in the east.

The Shakas were driven southwards by the Yueh-chihs (Kushanas). A Chinese source records that one of their chiefs, Kujula Kadphises, united the five tribes of the Yueh-chih, establishing his authority in Bactria and extending his kingdom from Afghanistan to Kashmir. It was, however, under the leadership of his grandson, Kanishka I, that the Kushana dynasty flourished. With his capital in Purushpura (Peshawar), his rule seemed to have extended from the Oxus frontier of Afghanistan in the west and the Xinjiang region of today's China in the north to Varanasi in the east and Sanchi in the south. Tradition further testifies to his conquest of Magadha. Buddhist sources hail him as another Ashoka for his liberal patronage of the Sangh, besides presiding over the fourth Buddhist council. The date of Kanishka I is uncertain, though the majority of historians put it somewhere between 78 and 144 AD. About the middle of the third century AD, Vasudeva, one of Kanishka's successors, was defeated by Shapur I of the new Sasanian dynasty of Persia, and from then on the northwestern region came under Iranian influence.

Around the same time, another Shaka dynasty, generally known as the Western Satraps, took control of Gujarat and Malwa, to extend as far as Sindh and Rajasthan at its apogee. The greatest king of this line was Rudradaman, who left the famous Junagadh inscription with a long panegyric highlighting his military and administrative exploits, including the reconstruction of an artificial lake at Girnar in Saurashtra. The inscription puts the date of Rudradaman's rule around 150 AD.

It was at this time that the history of south Bharat became clearer. Traditionally, the extreme south, comprising today's Tamil Nadu and Kerala, had been divided into three kingdoms—Chola (the Coromandel Coast), Chera (Malabar) and Pandya (the southern tip of the peninsula). These three kingdoms are mentioned in Ashoka's inscriptions as the places of his 'victories of righteousness' beyond his dominions. Even in the earliest Tamil literature, the Sangam, these three kingdoms are shown to be incessantly in warfare among themselves.

Tamils, like the Kalingans in the east, had taken to the sea very early. They had already invaded Ceylon, today's Sri Lanka, in the second century BC. They also had, by then, found their way to Southeast Asia and had close trade ties with Egypt and the Roman Empire.

III

Then came the Guptas, who ruled over much of the subcontinent from roughly 320 to 550 CE. There is not enough evidence regarding their origin and antecedents. Most historians believe that the Guptas were Vaishyas, but a few accord them Brahmin status too.

The dynasty first gained prominence with the accession of Chandra Gupta I around 320 AD. With his base in Magadha (today's Bihar), Chandra Gupta I expanded his territory over a significant part of northern Bharat through a combination of military conquest and strategic alliances. His marriage to a Lichchhavi princess is often cited as a key factor in his rise to power. The Lichchhavis were a powerful clan, and this marriage helped him gain influence and legitimacy. Such was the significance of this matrimonial alliance that their son, Samudra Gupta, in his Prayagraj pillar inscription, calls himself with pride 'Lichchhavi-dauhitra', 'the daughter's son of the Lichchhavi (king)'. The same epithet has been applied to him by his successors in their records.[23]

It was, however, Samudra Gupta, who significantly expanded the Gupta territory. Samudra Gupta's reign (c. 335–375 AD) is noted for his military conquests, which extended the empire across much of northern Bharat and into parts of the Deccan Plateau. His campaigns are documented in the Allahabad pillar inscription, which praises his conquests and achievements. The *prashasti* informs us that Samudra Gupta uprooted Achyuta of Ahichchhatra, Nagasea of Padmavati and Ganapatinaga in Mathura; he also captured the prince of the Kota family ruling the region around today's Bulandshahr.

The *prashasti* mentions Samudra Gupta successfully campaigning in the south as far as Kanchipuram (near today's Chennai). We are told he captured and then released 12 kings of Dakshinapatha: Mahendra of Kosala, Vyaghraraja of Mahakantara, Mantaraja of Kurala, Mahendragiri of Pishtapura, Svamidatta of Kottura, Damana of Erandapalla, Vishnugopa of Kanchi, Nilaraja of Avamukta, Hastivarman of Vehgi, Ugrasena of Palakka, Kubera of Devarashtra, and Dhananjaya of Kusthalapura.

We are also informed how he 'violently exterminated' eight kings of Aryavarta. The rajas of the forest peoples of central Bharat and the Deccan were forced into servitude. Chiefs of five border states and nine tribal republics in Rajasthan were forced to pay tribute and taxes. Even foreign kings such as Devaputra Shahanushahi (most likely a Kushana title), the Shakas, and the ruler of Sinhala (Sri Lanka) paid tribute.

If the Prayagraj *prashati* is to be believed, Samudra Gupta was not just known for his military exploits but also he excelled as a poet, musician and a patron of learning. His literary compositions have not survived, but his love for music is engraved into his gold coins, showing the emperor playing the veena.

Samudra Gupta's territorial and cultural achievements were taken to a higher level by Chandra Gupta II, who ruled from 375 to 415 AD. If Vishakhadatta's[24] *Devichandraguptam* is to be believed, Samudra Gupta was succeeded by Rama Gupta, who was defeated by the Sakas, to whom he agreed to surrender his wife, Dhruvadevi. His younger brother Chandra protested against this and went to the Shaka camp disguised as the queen, killing the Shaka ruler. This created estrangement between Rama Gupta and Chandra. Eventually, as *Devichandraguptam* says, Chandra killed his elder brother and married Dhruvadevi. This story finds credence from the fact that coins of Rama Gupta have been found near Bhilsa, and some inscriptions prove that Dhruvadevi was the wife of Chandra Gupta II.

Like his grandfather, Chandra Gupta II entered into matrimonial alliances with several royal dynasties. He married Kuveranaga of the Naga family and had a daughter, Prabhavati Gupta, who, in turn, was married to Rudrasena II of the Vakataka dynasty, which ruled over the areas that were once the stronghold of the Satavahanas. A while later, Rudrasena died, and Prabhavati ruled the kingdom as regent between 390 and 410 AD. The Vakataka kingdom, thus, was virtually a part of the Gupta empire. Also, Kuntala ruler Kukutsthavarman, ruling over the Konkan region, is said to have given his daughter in marriage to the Guptas.

The period saw advancements in art, science and literature. Notable figures such as the playwright Kalidasa and the mathematician Aryabhata emerged during this time.

Chandra Gupta II was succeeded by Kumara Gupta (415–454 AD). A branch of the Huns from Central Asia occupied Bactria around this time and threatened the Gupta empire. Kumara Gupta's reign, however, remained peaceful, as he managed to successfully hold on to his empire.

His successor, Skanda Gupta, was the last of the great Gupta rulers, though his reign wasn't free from internal rebellions and external wars. One of the major challenges he faced was the invasion of the Huns, who began encroaching upon Gupta territories during his rule. His military efforts were crucial in defending the empire from external threats.

Skanda Gupta ascended the throne around 455 AD. According to the Bhitari pillar inscription, he restored 'the fallen fortunes of his family'. As the inscription states, he had to spend a night on 'bare earth' before defeating his enemies, who had grown wealthy and powerful. The same inscription also states how Skanda Gupta defeated the Huns.

After he died in 467 AD, the central authority of the Guptas declined. A major blow came towards the end of the fifth century AD when Huns succeeded in finding a foothold in the northern part of Bharat. The Hun dominance, however, didn't last long. The first important Hun ruler was Toramana. In 515 AD, he was succeeded by his son, Mihirakula—a successful but tyrannical king who ruled from Sakala (Sialkot). Nothing much was heard about the Huns after him.

The Huns might have hurt the prospect of the Guptas, but ultimately the latter were the victims of the very forces that made them successful in the first place. Unlike the Mauryas with their highly centralized administrative system, the Guptas had a decentralized order that allowed the defeated rajas to retain power at the expense of accepting Gupta suzerainty. Just as the Mauryan centralized system showed signs of disorder and distress under a weak ruler, the decentralized Gupta order saw the subordinated rajas seek independence under incompetent rulers. Similarly, unlike the Mauryans who had a large standing army, the Guptas depended on feudal kings for soldiers. Again, the downside of the two systems was evident in their decline: while the Mauryans retained a strong army till the end but couldn't control it, with the last ruler perishing during a military parade, the Guptas lost a large portion of their armed men and material with deserting feudal kings.

IV

Anyone with a sense of history would understand that all the talk these days about 'Bharat rising' aren't just bunkum. There's a kernel of truth behind these claims, for history suggests that Western dominance is no more than just a blip in the overall human history. For most part of human civilizational history, political power, military might and especially economic heft largely resided in the East, more so in Bharat.[25] It was only after the mid-18th century that scale turned drastically in favour of the West.

At the beginning of the Common Era, according to noted economic historian Angus Maddison, when the world GDP was $102.5 billion, Bharat contributed $33.75 billion, which was almost a third (32.9 per cent) of the total world economy. China's share then was 26.1 per cent. Bharat continued to occupy the *numero uno* position in 1000 AD, with 28.9 per cent of the global economy, followed again by China (22.7 per cent). Even in 1700 AD, despite centuries of attacks from Muslim invaders, Bharat continued to lead at 24.4 per cent, followed by China (22.3 per cent). In 1820, Bharat's share in world GDP went down to 16 per cent to China's 32.9 per cent, Interestingly, Bharat found itself in the second spot just one time before 1820 AD: according to Maddison, in 1600 AD, Bharat stood second behind China, with Bharat at 22.4 per cent and China at 29 per cent.[26]

The Mauryas provided the initial impetus to trade by not just improving internal security and communications but also constructing a royal highway from Pataliputra to Takshashila. Pataliputra was then connected via road to Tamralipti, in today's Bengal, the chief port for ships sailing to Burma and Sri Lanka. In the west, Takshashila was connected by a highway with Kabul, from where roads went to different parts of Central and West Asian regions.

As for the south, Megasthenes, in the third century BC, mentions the Pandya kingdom. Even Ashoka in his famous rock edicts talks about his southern neighbours, such as Cholas and Pandyas, among others. In fact, Kautilya's *Arthashastra* makes it a point to say that north Bharat's most valuable trade partner wasn't Central Asia but south Bharat: the trade via the *Dakshinapatha* (southern route) was the most profitable, besides being much safer, the text says.

It was, however, the maritime trade that saw revolutionary changes during this period. Merchant ships set sail from Satavahana and Kalinga ports, as well as those of the small kingdoms from Tamilakam in the far south to trade as far as Egypt in the west and Vietnam and Cambodia in the east.

Wilfred H. Schoff explains how trade had been carried on between Egypt and Bharat which extended to the Mediterranean region even in the pre-Roman period. This trade was initially controlled by the Arabs and Phoenicians and the 'clothes and precious stones, the timber and spices... particularly cinnamon... were reintroduced at Socotra or Guardafi, and carried to the Nile and Mediterranean'.[27] Even after Rome had replaced Alexandria as the hub of Mediterranean trade, Arabs and Indians still controlled the sea routes. It was only after the 'discovery' of the monsoon wind by Hippalus in 45 AD that the Romans joined the trade race as a big player.

Rome soon became the largest market for products from Bharat. Such was the magnitude of trade that the number of Roman ships increased from 20 in a year to almost a ship a day. Early Tamil literature mentions in detail about Yavana (Roman) ships arriving with their cargoes at ports such as Maziris, and is enthusiastic about the quality of the wine that they bring, not to mention the Roman gold coins to buy local goods.

The *Periplus of the Erythrean Sea* tells us that ships sailing from Berenike, a buried ancient Egyptian port, to Bharat went down the Red Sea to Yemen and then, evading pirates, to the Island of Socotra, whose Indic connection can be ascertained from its name deriving from Sanskrit—Dwipa Sukhadara (Island of Bliss).[28]

According to the *Periplus of the Erythrean Sea*, in the first century AD, 'three types of vessels were found in these waters—country ships trading along the coast; large vessels made of single logs bound together, called *sangara*; and the very large ships called *colandia* which made the voyage to Malaya and north to the Ganga'.[29]

Subhash Kak highlights the sophistication of merchant ships in ancient Bharat, especially in comparison to Roman merchant ships. He writes:

> While in the entire European area the ships only possessed a single mainsail (and at best a fore-and-aft sail) right up to the late Middle Ages, in India two, and later three sails were common. Of course, the home territory of the Indian seafarers was not an inland sea like the Mediterranean, but the Indian Ocean. Hence they developed a sophisticated system of sails which in number of sails was only matched and surpassed by the explorers' ships of the 15th century.[30]

Periplus of the Erythrean Sea, the first-hand account of a person who actually sailed to Bharat and traded there, describes ports on the country's west and east coasts. Ptolemy's *Geography*, written around 125 AD, too, lists ports on both the west and east coasts.

The first Western maritime route to Bharat reached Gujarat, which had several ports, the most important being Barygaza (modern-day Bharuch). Imports to Barygaza, as mentioned in *Periplus*, included metals such as gold and silver, along with perfume and wine. The second route was from Socotra to Muziris on the Kerala coast. Spice trade dominated this route.

Here it needs to be mentioned that the maritime route connecting Bharat with Rome was the main passage of trade between the East and the West—and not the so-called Silk

Road, supposedly connecting China with Europe. A few years ago, at a seminar, Indologist Lokesh Chandra said that the term 'Silk Road' was a misnomer. 'Silk never travelled on this route. The Chinese used silk only as part of political diplomacy; to get horses, they supplied bales of silk,' he added. According to Chandra, the so-called Silk Road was more of a 'Sutra Road' as monks and pilgrims used this route to carry Sanskrit manuscripts and disseminate Hindu–Buddhist knowledge and philosophy. His assertion has been vindicated by the discovery of numerous manuscripts and 'spectacular masterpieces of Buddhist monastic art', as William Dalrymple writes in *The Golden Road*, in caves along the ancient route.[31]

While the Indian influence in the so-called Silk Road region had been intense and overwhelming, the Chinese presence appeared to be cursory, at best. The Chinese, in fact, were late entrants in Central Asia. According to eminent scholar Rahul Sankrityayan, as he writes in *Madhya Asia Ka Itihas* (History of Central Asia), when Chinese envoy Chiang Kyang, sent by Chinese emperor Wi-ti (141–187 BC), came to Central Asia to have first-hand information about the region and to persuade the Tusharas (Yueh-chihs) to return to their original homeland, he found Indian and Chinese goods in Bactria brought by Indian traders.[32] So, till the second century BC, the Chinese were largely clueless about Central Asia, as Indian traders introduced both Indian and Chinese goods to the region.

To this, author Bertil Lintner adds in his book, *The End of the Chinese Century?*, that the 'traders came from a multitude of countries, and very few, if any, would have been Chinese'. Lintner further reminds the readers how the Chinese state during that era had 'dissociated itself with trade, and most trade was conducted in China by private initiative'. In fact, the Tang Code of the Emperor Taizong (627–649 BC) 'viewed commerce as polluting and did not allow officials above the fifth rank (out of nine ranks) to enter marketplaces'.[33]

This explains why Roman coins, found in abundance in western and southern Bharat, are conspicuous by their absence in China. Prof. Valerie Hansen of Yale University, thus, writes in *Silk Road: A New History*:

> The earliest European coins unearthed in China are from Byzantium, not Rome, and date to the 530s and 540s. Vague rumours to the contrary, not a single Roman coin has turned up in China—in contrast to the thousands of Roman gold and silver coins excavated on the south Indian coast, where Roman traders often journeyed.[34]

Prof. Hansen explains how the term 'road' was as misleading as the term 'silk'. While emphasizing that the term 'Silk Road' is a recent invention[35], she writes, 'The peoples living along different trade routes did not use it. They referred to the route as the road to Samarkand (or whatever the next major city was), or sometimes just the "northern" or "southern" routes around the Taklamakan desert.'[36]

She continues,

> From its inception, the Silk Road was shown as relatively straight and well-travelled, but it never was. Over a hundred years of archaeological investigation have revealed no clearly marked, paved route across Eurasia—nothing remotely like the Appian way of Rome—but instead a patchwork of drifting trails and unmarked footpaths.[37]

What further put a question mark on the imagined grandeur of the Silk Road was the fact that the actual volume of trade along this 'patchwork of drifting trails and unmarked footpaths' was small.[38]

With a 5,000-mile coastline, Bharat has always been a maritime, trading nation, and not a land-obsessed civilization, as colonial-Marxist historiography would make us believe. While the Western trade with Bharat had been better documented, the less-talked-about trade towards East and Southeast Asia was equally flourishing. These ships set sail from not just Satavahana and Kalinga ports but also the Tamil region or Tamilakam down south.[39]

Bharat's engagement with the East was so strong that it led to the emergence of several Indic colonies in East and Southeast Asia. In the Mekong delta we witness the establishment of such a kingdom in the first century BC. The Chinese called it the Kingdom of Funan. Sanjeev Sanyal shares an interesting legend on how this kingdom was founded. He writes:

> It is said that an Indian merchant ship was sailing through the (Mekong) region when it was attacked by pirates led by Soma, daughter of the chieftain of the local Naga clan. The Indians fought back and fended off the attackers led by a handsome young Brahmin called Kaundinya. Unfortunately, the ship had been damaged and had to be beached for repairs.
>
> The merchants must have been worried about a second attack but luck turned in their favour. It appears Princess Soma had been impressed by Kaundinya's bravery and had fallen in love! She proposed marriage and the offer was accepted. The union is said to have founded a lineage that ruled Funan for many generations.
>
> So, who was Kaundinya? We know nothing about him except that he was a Brahmin from India, but his name provides a clue. While Kaundinya is not a common first name, it is the name of a gotra (i.e., male lineage) of Brahmins who still live along the Tamil-Andhra-Odisha coastline. Perhaps this is not a coincidence.[40]

The merchants of Kalinga, Tamilakam, Andhra, and Bengal took to the sea very early and well before the beginning of the Common Era, they were well acquainted with the Indian Ocean to criss-cross islands as far as Sumatra (Swarnadvipa), Bali and Java (Yavadvipa). No wonder, the entire East and Southeast Asian regions show deep Hindu/Buddhist connections. So much so that while the current Thailand royalty is referred to as King Rama, Korea is proud of its Ayodhya connection. Similarly, from Myanmar to Vietnam, Buddhism remains the dominant religion. Japan, too, has several Hindu temples, many of them belonging to Vedic gods such as Varun and Mitra for whom there's no shrine in Bharat itself.

The trade, both in the east and the west, was enormously advantageous to Bharat. For, the balance of trade was tilted too much in favour of Bharat, given that while 'consumers in the West have long hankered after Indian spices and luxuries but Indians were not particularly interested in western things; since books had to be balanced, they were balanced with gold and silver, and this meant a drain of precious metal from the West'.[41]

The Romans, thus, complained 2,000 years ago that their trade with Bharat was draining their empire of precious metals, with Pliny the Elder, in 77 AD, going to the extent of calling this country 'the sink of the world's precious metal'. He bitterly complained, 'Not a year passed in which India did not take 50 million sesterces away from Rome'.[42] Following Nero's death, the Roman emperor Vespasian passed a series of laws curbing the luxurious lifestyle of the upper classes, and the luxury items were stopped from being imported.

But the trade imbalance continued. So much so that Roman emperor Septimius Severus (193–211 AD) reduced the gold content in Roman coins, debasing the currency. Even the Eastern Roman Empire, called Byzantine Empire, founded in the fourth century AD, complained of their reserves of precious metals being 'leaked away to India'. The Portuguese bemoaned in the 16th century of losing their 'hard-won' silver from South America to Bharat. French physician Francois Bernier, too, as late as in the second half of the 17th century, on his visit during Mughal emperor Aurangzeb's time, wrote: 'It should not escape notice that gold and silver, after circulating in every other quarter of the globe, come at length to be absorbed in Hindostan'.[43]

After the Battle of Plassey in 1757, the world turned upside down for Bharat and its people. Within a hundred years, they were made dependent on the British for everything. This was the time for the drain of wealth from Bharat to the West.

V

There has been a constant, never-ending debate surrounding the Gupta period: Was it a golden period for Bharat? While one section of historians has no doubt in calling it a golden period, there are those, especially from the leftist ecosystem, who call it 'a vastly unequal society', where 'religion was used as an instrument for maintaining the *varna*-divided society'.[44] The reader is also told how 'the upper classes were happy and prosperous, and lived in comfort and ease, as can be judged from the contemporary art and literature', but this was 'hardly true for the lower orders'. The verdict is typically Marxist in nature: 'For the upper classes all periods in history have been golden; for the masses none. The true golden age of the people doesn't lie in the past, but in the future.'[45]

Both sets of arguments have problems. While there's no denying that the nationalist historians, during the British Raj, in order to instil a sense of pride among the people of this country, highlighted the Gupta period as the golden era, it did gloss over the 'varna inequality/varna discrimination' aspect, highlighted later by Marxist historians. But, then, our eminent distorians have overplayed the discrimination card too. For, which society, howsoever advanced and civilized it may be, doesn't have socio-economic inequality and discrimination? The statement—that the true golden age of the people doesn't lie in the past, but in the future—is more ideological than historical. For, it seems to imitate the grand communist wet dream of a classless society in future![46]

There's no denying that the Gupta period was a period of great affluence and prosperity.[47] Yet, to pick just this one out would be erroneous. The Guptas, no doubt, excelled, but so did the Pallavas and the Cholas. The Vijayanagara empire was at the zenith of socio-cultural-economic excellence. So were the Mauryans, Satavahanas, Karkotas, and Ahoms in their respective eras. To top it all are the civilizational exploits of the Indus–Saraswati civilization with its flourishing urban centres such as Rakhigarhi, Harappa, Mohenjodaro, Lothal, et al.

The most appropriate way of looking at this subject would be to stop analyzing Bharat's history in silos and, instead, see its civilizational journey as a consolidated effort from one dynasty to another. This explains why the greatness of the Guptas cannot be explained without the contribution of Mauryan and post-Mauryan rulers. The beauty of this great landmass lies in the fact that the end of a dynasty didn't mean the end of Bharat's civilizational journey.

Still, there was something about the Gupta period that made it stand out. It was the era that saw the fulsome flowering of the great Indic civilization, both physical and metaphysical, literary and artistic, spiritual (*dharma*) and sexual (*kama*). The sense of inquiry—both with a sense of the sacred as well as irreverence—was wholesome.

The manifestation of the holistic approach of life can be seen in what Rishi Vatsayana says in *Kama Sutra*.[48] According to him, *kama*, 'like food, is a means for the body's sustenance. It is also a fruit of *Dharma* and *Artha*. Its shortcoming should be taken into account, but will one not eat food because there are beggars who need it, or not sow seeds because there are beasts who may eat the crop?'[49]

Two verses from the *Kama Sutra* explain this further:

One who thus pursues
Artha, Kama and Dharma
enjoys untroubled happiness
in this world and the next.(39)

Civilised folk will act in ways
that give pleasure, but do no harm
to the end of material gain
nor cause worry about results
of their deeds in the world hereafter.
Their actions should be for achieving
all the three ends of human life,
or just two or even one,
but not to obstruct two of them
in pursuit of a single end.(40)[50]

4

The Age of Extremes

When Bharat Saw the Best and Worst of It

I

The post-Gupta phase, in popular parlance, is seen as a period of decline, when the 'existence of landed intermediaries, restrictions on the movement of artisans and peasants, and the decline of trade' strengthened under the 'rule of the Palas, Pratiharas and Rashtrakutas'.[1] The decline, we are told, had been all-encompassing: politically, Bharat was too decentralized to be strong; socially, it was too divided by caste equations; and, economically, trade was significantly down.

The post-Gupta reality was starkly different from what several of our eminent distorians have projected. Bharat, in this era, actually scaled new heights. The era can be divided into two parts—between 600 and 1000 AD, and between 1000 and 1200 AD. The first phase (600–1000 AD) saw the flowering of Bharat in every aspect of life—political, economic and cultural. In fact, in no other phase one saw the best of the Indic civilization coming up in all corners of the country, almost simultaneously. The north saw the rise of the great Karkotas of Kashmir, led by the incredible Lalitaditya Muktapida, who in some ways eclipsed the exploits of Samudra Gupta and his Western equivalent, Alexander. There was also the rise of the immensely underestimated Gurjara-Pratiharas in the north, who, as their very name suggests, were the real defenders of Bharat and one of the reasons why the Muslim invasion in the subcontinent was a failure at a time when they romped over most of the West and Central Asia and reached as far as the borders of France within a century of Prophet Mohammed's death in 632 AD. As for the south, the exploits of the great Pallavas were not just matched but, in many ways, outshined by the Cholas led by Rajaraja I and Rajendra I.

The second phase (between 1000 and 1200 AD) did see Bharat politically far more disintegrated and divided. This gave the Turks an opportunity to sneak into the heartland of Bharat. But as we will see in chapter 5, it was an intense and incessant battle for every inch of Bharat's territory. Historian Peter Jackson, in his book on the Delhi Sultanate, has no hesitation in highlighting 'the limits of Muslim successes'. He writes, 'Victory did not necessarily entail the displacement of Hindu rulers.'[2]

However, an era's excellence, or degeneration, can be gauged from the literature produced then, in both religious and secular spheres—and of course its ability to rewrite the rules of the sacred and the profane, to make divine and kingly figures look human and ordinary. Adi Shankaracharya (c. 788–820 AD) and his work epitomize the best in the realm of religion.

Born in the village of Kaladi in Kerala, Shankara was born after a lot of prayers. His father died when he was young, and it was his mother who raised him. Shankara's love for his mother has been well documented. For instance, as the legend goes, when she found it difficult to go to the Kaladi river daily to bathe, Shankara used his yogic powers to turn its course towards their house. There's another incident that shows his love for his mother even if it meant breaking the fundamental vow of being a *sannyasin*: to cut all familial ties.

At the time of accepting *sannyas*, he had promised to be by her side during her last moments. Not only did he keep his word, but also he performed her last rites for which he was ostracised by his community.

Shankara mastered the Vedas by the age of eight, and by 16, he had accomplished all he wished by way of education and spiritual learning. His mission from then on was two-fold: to consolidate the Advaita[3] tradition and to revitalize the Vedic practices.[4] With these objectives in mind, he travelled across the length and breadth of the country, debating with the best of minds in the opposite camps and spreading the ideals of Advaita. Such was the scale and intensity of his intellectual conquest that it was called 'Shankara Digvijaya'. He stole the intellectual thunder from Buddhism, though the latter continued to flourish in the country alongside Hinduism and receive liberal endowments from both Hindu and Buddhist rulers, as one can see from the contemporary descriptions of the Nalanda Mahavihara. It was the Muslim invasion that uprooted Buddhism from Bharat as it was easy for Turks, Arabs and Afghans, among other invading tribes, to target, loot and destroy a monastery-based order.

Shankara not just worked towards helping Hinduism regain pre-eminence in his own time, but ensured it retained its importance in the future as well. He, therefore, established monasteries (*mathas*) in all the four corners of the subcontinent: the Jyotirmatha near Badrinath in the north; the Kalikapitha in Dwaraka in the west; the Saradapitha in Sringeri in the south; and the Govardhanapitha in Puri in the east. A fifth *matha*, the Kamakotipitha in Kanchi, was also founded by him, according to its tradition. Shankara is also credited with organizing the itinerant monks into 10 orders (Dasanami Sampradaya). He also undertook the task of writing commentaries on the *Prasthanatrayi*: major *Upanishads*, *Bhagavad Gita*, and *Brahma Sutra*, besides unifying different theistic sects within the fold of Hinduism—Vaishnava, Shaiva, Shakta, among others.

What was, however, unique about Shankara was his ability to combine the impersonal Advaita philosophy with the personalised devotional philosophy. Tradition mentions two 'touching incidents' that moved Shankara to compose devotional hymns:

> One was when, as a student, he sought alms from a poor woman who offered the only gooseberry (*amla*) she had, with a heavy heart that she was unable to feed such a brilliant boy sumptuously, and who blessed him that the light of self-knowledge should shine as clearly as the fruit she placed on his palm. It is believed that, touched by her plight, Shankara composed the *Kanakadhara Stotra* in praise of the Divine Mother, and a shower of golden gooseberries filled the poor woman's courtyard. The other relates to his composing his famous hymn *Bhaja Govindam* at Kashi when he was stirred by pity on seeing an elderly scholar struggling with Sanskrit grammar. The futility of his effort at that age made him burst into song about directing his effort instead to devotion, along with self-inquiry, for attaining liberation.[5]

The story of Mandan Mishra's wife, who acted as an arbitrator when Shankara and Mishra engaged in a debate, is well-known. Author–diplomat Pavan K. Varma, in his book on Shankara, mentions another legend surrounding the monk, showcasing how knowledge during those days has trickled deep down the society and across genders. Varma writes,

> Local legend has it that when Shankara arrived in Srinagar, his entourage camped just outside the city. The teacher and his disciples were hungry and weary after their long travel, but had failed to light a fire to cook some food. A young Kashmiri girl then came to their help. Taking two pieces of

wood, she rubbed them while chanting a mantra, and the spark that emerged from the friction lighted the fire. The wood, the girl explained, is Brahman. The fire that sprang forth from it is Shakti, the power inherent in Brahman.

It is also believed that at the very outset of his advent into the Valley, Shankara entered into a *shastrartha* with a Kashmiri lady on the concept of shakti. The debate lasted for seventeen days, at the end of which Shankara conceded defeat. This apocryphal story signifies his acceptance of shakti worship, and his association with tantric interpretations of Advaita philosophy.[6]

If the religious arena was so argumentatively boisterous and exuberant, defining and redefining the notion of the sacred, the secular literature of the era showcased an unprecedented level of liberalism, wherein the limits of both the sacred and the profane got challenged and extended.

In *Bhallatashataka*, written by Bhallata, a ninth-century poet adorning the court of King Avantivarman of Kashmir (c. 855–883 AD), the poet mocked at gods and goddesses—he, for instance, described Goddess Lakshmi as 'a woman shamelessly eloping to her unworthy beau by paths black with impenetrable darkness', or even wrote about the sun god running about naked or wallowing in mud, much like a drunkard. When Bhallata was removed as court poet by King Shankaravarman, who succeeded Avantivarman, he seemed to take a jibe at him when he wrote that even if a dog, put up with a fake mane, took the place of the lion, it could not roar like the king of the jungle.[7]

Then there is *Mattavilasa Prahasana* ('The Farce of Drunken Sport'), a seventh-century play by Mahendravarman I, a prominent Pallava king, which deals with drunk, debased mendicants. The play begins with a discussion between two drunken mendicants—one Shaivite (Kapalin) and the other

Buddhist (Devsoma)—who, while describing the goddess of liquor as being as faultless as the city of Kanchi, compares the liquor shop to a sacrificial ground, the signpost of the shop signifies the sacrificial post, liquor is the soma juice, the drunkards are the priests, and the keeper of the liquor shop is the patron of the sacrifice! At one point, one of the monks is unhappy why Buddha did not prescribe women and liquor, but later wonders if these things have been blotted out of the scriptures. 'From where can I procure an uncorrupted text,' the monk asks.[8]

A society that humanises gods and ridicules kings cannot be status quoist. A society that debates, deliberates and engages with invoking the constraints of the sacred and the profane is innately liberal and deliberative. A society where a housewife judges the *shastrartha* of an intellectual of Adi Shankara's calibre is inherently progressive. And a society where a young girl expounds the fundamentals of Shakta philosophy through a mere lighting of firewood cannot be anything but vibrant and dynamic.

But not for our eminent distorians who are accustomed to looking at Bharat through their ideologically tinted glasses. Their projection, no doubt, is grimly coloured, acutely distorted and vastly prejudiced.

II

In a distorian's textbook, the post-Gupta period begins with Harshavardhana (c. 606–647 AD) of Thanesar and ends with the raid of Mahmud of Ghazni and Mohammed Ghori, with fleeting, often forced, references of the Gurjara-Pratiharas and Rashtrakutas, Pallavas and Cholas. No doubt, Harsha of Thanesar was an eminent ruler, but he definitely wasn't the greatest.

Be that as it may, Harsha's life and times need a relook—also, in a way because he was fortunate to have two biographers of repute, Bana and Hiuen Tsang: the first 'a rakish Brahmin' and the second a hard-core Buddhist.

Harsha was an accidental king. He wasn't the eldest of sons, but as fate would have it, his eldest brother died. Then, his sister's husband, who was a Maukhari king, died too, and that kingdom too came under his effective control.

Among his adversaries, Sashanka, king of Gauda, was the most prominent one. And he remained a challenge for Harsha for long. However, in later years, Harsha seemed to have strengthened his position, especially with the support of the king of Kamarupa, Bhashkaravarman. Chalukya king Pulakesin II was another prominent adversary of Harsha, and he is said to have defeated the king of Thanesar to stop his victory march from going to the south.

At the height of his prime, Harsha's army had overrun almost the whole of northern Bharat, from the snowy mountains of the north to the Narmada in the south, and from Ganjam in the east to Valabhi in the west.[9] His area of influence went beyond that. The king of Kamarupa, for instance, was more than just an ally, and the nature of the alliance becomes clear by an incident recorded by Hiuen Tsang, which shows how Bhaskaravarman dared not to detain the Chinese pilgrim at his capital against the wishes of Harsha. Even the kings of Kashmir and Sindh were seen to be afraid of antagonising Harsha.

Harsha wasn't just about kingly responsibilities. He was also a man with considerable literary talent, with three plays to his credit—while two of them were comedies, the third one was religious in nature.

How Harsha died is not known, but soon after he breathed his last in 647 AD, his empire collapsed. The throne of Thanesar itself was usurped by one of Harsha's ministers.[10]

At a time when Harsha was alive and kicking, a new dynasty emerged in Kashmir that was supposed to rewrite the political history of north Bharat. The *Rajatarangini*, an 11th-century work by Kalhana, outlining Kashmir's history since ancient times, provides detailed information on this dynasty, which saw themselves to be the descendants of the mythical snake-king (Naga) Karkota of the Mahabharata era.[11] However, in historical terms, Durlabhvardhana is said to be the founder of the Karkota dynasty in 625 AD. During his time, Hiuen Tsang visited Kashmir and was received with a warm reception by the king's maternal uncle in 631 AD. During his two-year stay in the valley, he wrote extensively about Kashmir, especially its Buddhist connections. Hiuen Tsang writes:

> They (Kashmiris) are light and frivolous, and of a weak, pusillanimous disposition. As the country is protected by a dragon, it has always assumed superiority among neighbouring people. The people are handsome in appearance, but they are given to cunning. They love learning and are well instructed. There are both heretics and believers among them.[12]

Hiuen Tsang tells us about the geographical stretch of Durlabhvardhana's kingdom. He says that five other states, viz., Takshashila (Rawalpindi district), Simhapura (Salt Range region), Urasa (Hazara or Abbottabad district), Pan-nu-tso (Poonch), and Rajapura (Rajouri) were subject to Kashmir. It would, thus, be safe to say that he ruled over not only Kashmir proper, but also a part of the western and northwestern Punjab.

Durlabhaka succeeded Durlabhvardhana around 661 AD and ruled for the next 50 years; his rule was largely peaceful but without any significant political development. His eldest son, Chandrapida, succeeded him in around 711 AD. Two years later, in 713 AD, given threats from Mohammed bin Qasim,

Chandrapida sent an envoy to the Chinese emperor asking for aid against the Arab invaders. Although Chandrapida did not receive any assistance from China, he was able to successfully defend his kingdom against Arab aggression.

King Chandrapida was well-known for his piety and justice. Kalhana records how, when the king decided to build a temple, it fell on the land that had the house of a tanner, who refused to give up his hut. When the matter was reported to the king, he considered his own officers to be at fault, not the tanner. He told them to stop the construction 'or have it erected elsewhere'. The tanner himself came to the king and said: 'Since my birth this hut has been to me like a mother, witness of good and evil days. I cannot bear to see it pulled down today.' Still he agreed to give up his hut 'if His Majesty would come to his dwelling and ask for it in accordance with propriety'. As soon as the king heard this, he went to the tanner's hut and bought it.[13]

Chandrapida's eight-and-a-half-year rule was followed by that of Tarapida, whose four years as king were full of cruelty and bloodshed. He was followed by his younger brother Lalitaditya Muktapida, who without doubt was the greatest king of the dynasty.

Lalitaditya, who ascended the throne about 724 AD and never lost a battle, in more ways than one, outdid the military exploits of Samudra Gupta and Alexander. He was aware of the Arab ambition to gain a foothold in Kashmir, and thus he made an alliance with the ruler of Kannauj, Yashovarman—and together they defeated the Arabs. One reason for Lalitaditya's victory was his reliance on cavalry and foot soldiers, and not on elephants, which was then a fetish for rulers in Bharat.

Tibetans were a rising imperial power in those times. Lalitaditya invited the Chinese emperor to join him in subduing them, but when the help was not forthcoming, he did that with the support of Yashovarman of Kannauj. Lalitaditya defeated not only the Tibetans,[14] but also other mountain tribes such as Dards and Kambojas. When Yashovarman tried to assert his influence, Lalitaditya took him head-on and defeated him to become the master of the north.

If Kalhana is to be believed, Lalitaditya's 'digvijaya' took him as far as Gauda (Bengal) and Kalinga (Orissa). That he could conquer Bengal is corroborated by a casual mention of an image of Buddha brought from Magadha! In the south, he successfully reached the bank of the Kaveri, then turning west he was said to have reached as far as Dwarka in the western Kathiawar Peninsula. He is also credited with defeating the Arabs. On this, R.C. Majumdar writes, 'The fact that the Arabs could not gain any lasting success in this direction supports the view that Lalitaditya thoroughly defeated them and freed the Punjab from their depredation.'[15]

Then, Lalitaditya did something that put him in the league, if not ahead, of Alexander: his far-north military campaign that took him deep into Xinjiang. At the time when Lalitaditya was preparing for this campaign, the Chinese empire was under a lot of pressure from the Tibetan troops. If this were not bad enough, they were attacked by Arabs, who could easily defeat the Chinese troops. This created a lot of chaos in the region, and it provided an opportunity to Lalitaditya to go into this unprecedented mission, more so after the T'ang ruler decided to withdraw his troops from western regions to curb internal dissension within China. In this backdrop, Lalitaditya decided to set out on what Kalhana called the Uttarapatha campaign.

German art historian Hermann Goetz writes in detail about this campaign:

> Lalitaditya successfully fought down the Tibetans, invaded the Tarim Basin, crossed the Taqlamaqan, seems to have

> conquered the kingdoms beyond, possibly Kucha and Turfan, and to have further advanced into the deserts. There his army was annihilated, and the great conqueror burned himself on a pyre with his ministers and generals, ca. A.D. 756/757. This Central-Asian war kept him away from his Indian dominions for years, but his prestige seems to have been strong enough to maintain the peace of his empire. The Kashmiris apparently tried to keep his death secret for some time, but when the news spread, everything broke up; and as Lalitaditya's sons quarrelled one with the other, the empire disintegrated within a few years.[16]

Kalhana writes about Lalitaditya's disappearance and death:

> Some say the king died because of the enormous snowfall in the Aryajak (or Aryanaka) country. Some even say he submitted himself to fire when faced with an imminent, inevitable danger to preserve his eternal prestige. Some others say, in the Uttarapatha that is beyond the human reach but easily reachable for the divine beings, that king went into the earth along with his army. Just like the story of his astonishing achievements is told, the various wondrous stories about his death are also narrated. When the sun sets, some say it drowned in the sea, some say it entered the fire and some say he (the sun) went to another country. Likewise, many marvellous stories are related to the death of the great men.[17]

Lalitaditya, who remained undefeated in his lifetime, was also a great administrator. He ran his empire with such efficiency that there was peace in Kashmir even after his death in 760 AD—till his demise could be kept secret. And he was a master builder. During his time, several new towns came up, and others were put up with fine buildings, monasteries, temples, and images of gods. The most famous of his works is the Martanda temple, whose ruins today are enough to suggest its past glory.

Lalitaditya's shoes were too large to be filled by his successors. The Karkota dynasty, however, could hobble for almost a century before collapsing in 855 AD. It was replaced by the House of Utpala. Avantivarman, the founder of this new dynasty, is famous for carrying out, under the supervision of Minister Suyya, his irrigation works. His son, Sankaravarmana, further strengthened the kingdom as he extended its boundaries. After him, Kashmir saw a series of not-so-competent rulers. There was also a dynastic change: the Loharas came to power in Kashmir in 1003 AD. King Harsha (1089–1101 AD), whose 'Turushka-like' behaviour we talked about in the introduction, belonged to this dynasty. Dynastic change, however, couldn't change the sagging fortune of Kashmir and it was reduced to the position of an insignificant power, to finally succumb to the Muslims in 1339 AD.

III

From the eighth century till the end of the tenth century, the politics of Bharat was dominated by the dynasty that controlled Kannauj. The city had become a symbol of imperial power. This battle saw three dynasties—Gurjara-Pratiharas, Rashtrakutas and Palas—taking on each other, and their military activities were primarily directed towards the conquest and retention of Kannauj.

Of the three, the Gurjara-Pratiharas were the most dominant force in central, western and northwestern Bharat, though in the initial part the Rashtrakutas had kept them on the leash. True to their name, the 'Pratiharas' (door-keepers) successfully defended Bharat against Muslim invasions as long as they were in power. Though their epigraphic records claim descent from Lakshmana, brother of Rama, of the solar race (Suryavanshi), who guarded the doors on the latter's command at an important occasion, historians mostly believe that they were a branch of the Gurjara race that began to play an important part in Bharat's history from the sixth century onwards. In the seventh century AD, they are mentioned in Bana's *Harshacharita*, Hiuen Tsang's writing and also in the Aihole inscription of Pulakesin II.[18]

The Gurjara-Pratiharas came into prominence in the second quarter of the eighth century AD by the successful resistance they offered under Nagabhata I to the Arabs. He is described in the Gwalior Inscription as 'having crushed the large armies of the powerful mlechchha king', who undoubtedly were the Arabs.[19]

About the time when Nagabhata I was firmly implanting his dynasty in the north, the Rashtrakutas were coming into their own in the Deccan and the south. The Rashtrakuta king Dantidurga, who reigned between c. 733 and 758 AD, is said to have defeated the Gurjara king and made him serve as a 'door-keeper' (Pratihara) when he performed the Hiranyagarbha ceremony in Ujjain. Such was the success of Dantidurga that he could even occupy the palace of the Gurjara-Pratihara king. However, the Rastrakutas couldn't hold it for long as they faced the Chalukya challenge down south.

Nagabhata I was succeeded by his brother's sons, Kakkuka and Devaraja, about whom not much is known. Devaraja was followed by Vatsaraja, who defeated Pala king Dharmapala to control Kannauj, but sustained defeat at the hands of the Rashtrakuta king Dhruva. Thus began the triangular struggle between the Gurjara-Pratiharas, the Rashtrakutas and the Palas for the control of Kannauj and supremacy in Bharat.

His son and successor Nagabhata II, however, retrieved the fortunes of his family. The Gwalior inscription of his grandson tells us that the rulers of Andhra, Saindhava, Vidarbha, and

Kalinga succumbed to him, that he defeated Chakrayudha and the lord of Vanga, and forcibly seized the hill-forts of the kings of Anartta, Malava, Kirata, Turushka, Vatsa, and Matsya.[20] Nagabhata's success, again, was fleeting, as the Rashtrakuta records show that he was defeated by Govinda III who overran his dominions and reached the Himalayas. If the success of Govinda III matched his father's in brilliance, it was equally ephemeral. He was called to the Deccan on account of internal troubles that had broken out during his long absence in the north, and for nearly half a century the Rashtrakutas ceased to play any dominant part in northern politics. This gave the Pratiharas and the Palas enough time to regain strength. The time was especially utilized by the Palas, under Dharmapala and his son, Devapala, to re-establish their supremacy.

The Pratiharas saw their glorious phase come during the rule of Bhoja I, the grandson of Nagabhata II, who ascended the throne in 836 AD. During his time, his state's boundaries stretched from the borders of Kashmir in the north to the Vindhyas in the south, and from Rajasthan–Gujarat in the west to as far as Paharpur in north Bengal in the east.

Bhoja I, in his 46-year reign, acted as the real bulwark against Muslims desperate to attack Bharat. Within a year of his accession, Imran ibn-Musa, the Arab governor of Sindh, tried to extend his hold over the adjoining territory. The Arabs were, however, driven out of Kutch between 833 and 842 AD. A few years later, most of Sindh was conquered by Bhoja. For, according to Masudi, the Indus ran right through one of the cities within the kingdom of Jurz (Gurjara).[21]

Sulaiman, an Arab traveller who visited in 851 AD, wrote about the king of Juzr, who is regarded as Bhoja. Sulaiman writes,

> This king maintains numerous forces and no other Indian prince has so fine a cavalry. He is unfriendly to the Arabs, still,

> he acknowledges that the king of the Arabs is the greatest of kings. Among the princes of India, there is no greater foe of the Muhammadan faith than he. His territories form a tongue of land. He has got riches, and his camels and horses are numerous. Exchanges are carried on in his states with silver (and gold) in dust, and there are said to be mines (of these metals) in the country. There is no country in India more safe from robbers.[22]

According to R.C. Majumdar, Bhoja I was 'one of the outstanding political figures of India in the ninth century, and ranks with Dhruva and Dharmapala as a great general and empire-builder'.[23]

Mahendrapala I, son of King Bhoja, maintained the prestige of the dynasty and even extended the empire eastward. Poet Rajashekhara adorned his court. It was a downward slide for the Pratiharas thereafter, and in 1018 AD, Pratihara king Rajyapala was defeated by Mahmud of Ghazni. Thus ended the empire that for three centuries stood as the bulwark of Bharat's defence against the aggression of the Muslims.

As for the Rashtrakutas, they were the second of the three pillars that dominated Bharat's political landscape between eighth and tenth century AD. Just as the Pratiharas saw Rama of Ayodhya as their ancestors, the Rashtrakutas claimed descent from Satyaki, a Yadava chief of the north and a close associate of Krishna. It's likely that the Rashtrakutas were 'Kannada-speaking military aristocrats settled at a strategic point in modern-day Maharashtra by the Chalukyas or some other powerful group to keep an eye on trade routes and various tribal peoples'.[24]

As we have seen in the chapter, the Rashtrakutas initially dominated the triangular fight with the Pratiharas and the Palas. It was only after the emergence of Bhoja that the Pratiharas got the upper hand in the fight, with the Palas occasionally dominating the proceedings. As we saw earlier in the chapter, the Rashtrakutas under Dantidurga (735–756 AD), Dhruva (780–793 AD) and Govinda III (793–814 AD) defeated the Pratiharas.

At the height of its power, the Rashtrakuta empire extended from South Gujarat, Malwa and Baghelkhand in the north to Tanjore in the south. Such was the success of the Rashtrakutas that all the great powers of their time, Pratiharas, Palas, Eastern Chalukyas, and Cholas, were subjugated by them at one time or another. In fact, Majumdar is categorical enough to say that 'no other ruling dynasty in the Deccan played such a dominant part in the history of India till the rise of the Marathas as an imperial power in the eighteenth century'.[25]

As in war, the Rashtrakutas also excelled in peace. The Kailasa temple in Ellora, built by Krishna I between 756 AD and 773 AD, is a case in study. Similarly, there was Amoghavarsha, who had no great military record to his credit but was a great litterateur with top books to his credit.

As fate would have it, just when the Pratiharas and Palas were weakening, the Rashtrakuta dynasty was overthrown by a feudatory of Krishna III, who claimed descent from the early Chalukyas of Vatapi.

The third axis of power struggle for the control of Kannauj was the Pala dynasty, which ruled over most of modern-day Bengal and Bihar. The Palas came into power at a time when there was complete chaos in Bengal, caused by a series of attacks from outside, starting with Yasovarman of Kannauj.

Buddhist monk Taranatha (1575–1634) explains the situation by using the term '*matysa nyaya*', an ancient philosophical theory referring to the idea that in times of chaos, the strong devours the weak. When people couldn't take anymore, they decided to elect a king, but on each occasion a demoness killed him soon after his selection. Finally, Gopala was elected, and he was given a club by Goddess Chandi to protect himself. As the story goes, Gopala killed the demoness with this club, and thus began the Pala dynasty.[26] In this backdrop, it can be safely said that unlike the Pratiharas and the Rashtrakutas, the Palas were commoners when they suddenly became rulers.

Be that as it may, Gopala established the Pala dynasty. It was, however, his son Dharmapala (780–815 AD) who made it a force to reckon with in north Bharat. Dharmapala extended the boundaries of the kingdom across the Gangetic Doab and at one time conquered Kannauj. He placed on the throne of Kannauj his protégé, Chakrayudha. While the Pratiharas desired Kanauj for their ambition to make it a base for military campaign in the Gangetic plains, the Palas seemed to have commercial interest in doing that: it might have secured them control over the vast river system, besides offering them access to Central Asian markets.[27]

Dharmapala's success in the Gangetic Doab was short-lived. Not only was his protégé expelled but also he was defeated by the Rashtrakutas and the Pratiharas. He was succeeded by Devapala, who continued to fight against the two traditional rivals. Though he couldn't achieve much success against them, Devapala could defeat the neighbouring kingdoms of Orissa and Assam. He is believed to have shifted his capital from Pataliputra to Monghyr. He died around 855 AD. The Palas remained in power for the next 240 years but could never regain the glory of the yore. In 1023 AD, when Rajendra Chola I raided the north via Orissa and Bengal, the latter was ruled by a Pala king.

The Palas were finally dislodged in 1097 AD by Vijayasena, who belonged to a family hailing from the Kanarese country in the Deccan. With this ended the dynasty that produced the last great Hindu emperor to rule from the historic city of Pataliputra. The Palas were also the generous patrons of the Nalanda Mahavihara, besides laying the foundation of the universities of Vikramshila and Uddandapura.

The Senas tried to bring back the good old days, but somehow the slide continued—till an Afghan plunder in Bakhtiyar Khilji knocked on the doors of Bihar and Bengal with his band of barbarians in 1200–01 AD. We have already seen in the introduction what he did with Nalanda Mahavihara, here we must look at the criminal negligence on the part of the then Sena ruler, Lakshmanasena, to not just ignore Khilji's murderous exploits in the region but also continue to indulge in luxuries. Such was administrative indifference that when Khilji reached the capital city, he found no armed troops guarding the gates. He marched with just 18 soldiers and reached the royal palace unopposed. They arrived during lunch time. As fate would have it, Lakshmanasena couldn't have his lunch and fled barefoot, as the 13th-century Muslim chronicler Minhaj Siraj writes gleefully in *Tabakat-i-Nasiri.*

Siraj adds:

> At this time Rae Lakhmaniah (Lakshmanasena) was seated at the head of his table, and dishes of gold and silver, full of victuals, were placed according to his accustomed routine, when a cry arose from the gateway of the Rae's palace and the interior of the city. By the time he became certain what was the state of affairs, Muhammad-i-Bakhtyar had dashed forwards through the gateway into the palace, and had put several persons to the sword. The Rae fled bare-footed by the back-part of his palace; and the whole of his treasures, his wives, and (other) females, his domestics and servants, his particular attendants, were taken, and the Musalmans captured a number of elephants, and such a vast amount of booty fell to their lot, as cannot be recorded.[28]

Bengal and Bihar were thus lost to Muslims. Unfortunately, while it took lakhs of Muslim soldiers to fight for centuries to make inroads into Bharat, it took just 18 Muslim soldiers to win Bengal—that too without a fight. Interestingly, Islam found its maximum converts during Bakhtiyar Khilji's rule.[29] There are several reasons for this, some of which have been deliberated upon by American historian Richard M. Eaton,[30] with a few obvious and deliberate distortions and misinterpretations, of course. But then, that is a debate for another day, another book.

IV

Economist-cum-historian Sanjeev Sanyal begins his 2016 book, *The Ocean of Churn*,[31] with an interesting turn of events in Pallava history. The year was 731 AD. Pallava king Parameswaravarman II had just died—suddenly, without a successor—in a battle with the arch-rival Chalukyas. It was a period of uncertainty, with a field day for conspiracy theorists. Amid all this, an assembly of leading scholars, chieftains and other prominent citizens of Kanchi decided to invite a Pallava prince from a collateral branch of the dynasty ruling a distant land across the seas in Southeast Asia.

Five generations earlier, a younger brother of the Pallava king Simhavishnu decided to go on a sea voyage. Reaching a distant kingdom, he married a local princess and became its ruler. His descendants were still ruling that land when the Kanchi branch of the Pallavas faced this problem. A delegation from Kanchi rushed to seek a prince from the distant land, which it could reach after 'a long and arduous journey crossing rivers, jungles, mountains and deep seas'. As fate would have it, the king of this distant land had four sons. The youngest prince, barely 12 years old then, took up the offer. This young prince, who was later known as Nandivarman II, not just survived the initial tumultuous years but ruled for 65 long years till 796 AD.

Scholars have long debated the origins of the Pallavas, with some claiming Vengi tribal roots in them while others have speculated on their Pahlava (Parthian) connections. Interestingly, all these theories had one thing in common: they all invoked the dynasty's connection with a Naga princess. As per one such tradition, which points at both the Pallavas' Naga connection as well as their foreign origin,

> a young prince fell in love with a Naga princess of the nether world, and, when he finally had to leave her, told her that if she set their child adrift with a young creeper or twig tied to its body he would recognise the child on finding it and bestow part of the kingdom on the child. This the princess did and the child was duly recognised and installed as the founder of the Pallava (literally meaning a young twig) dynasty.[32]

The Pallavas may or may not have a foreign origin, but what the story conveys without an iota of doubt is the deep and intense relationship Bharat had with East and Southeast Asia from ancient times.

One of the earliest mentions of a Pallava ruler was made when Samudra Gupta captured and then liberated Vishnugopa of Kanchi around the middle of the fourth century AD. The name Vishnugopa was referred to by several members of the Pallava dynasty, but the history of the dynasty becomes more definite from the time of Simhavishnu, who ruled in the second half of the sixth century AD. He was succeeded by Mahendravarman I (c. 600–630 AD), the author of *Mattavilasa Prahasana* ('The Farce of Drunken Sport'). His reign saw the beginning of the incessant struggle between the Pallavas and their northern arch-rivals—the Chalukyas of Vatapi—for the lordship of the south.

The struggle continued for several generations, with the pendulum swinging from one side to the other. Chalukya king Pulakesin II, who had defeated Harshavardhana, is said to have defeated Mahendravarman I. His Aihole inscription of 634 says that Pulakesin II 'caused the splendour of the lord of the Pallavas... to be obscured by the dust of his army and to vanish behind the walls of Kanchipura'.[33]

Narasimhavarman Mahamalla (630–668 AD), Mahendravarman's son and successor, retrieved the Pallavas' lost glory as he defeated Pulakesin and stormed his capital, Vatapi. Another striking achievement of Narasimhavarman was a successful naval expedition sent by him to Ceylon to reinstate a Sinhalese prince of his choice. Also, during his reign, Chinese traveller Hiuen Tsang visited Kanchi. Undoubtedly the greatest of the Pallavas, he also gave his name to the port of Mamallapuram, and some of the famous temples cut out of rock boulders (Rathas) that were constructed there during his reign.

After Narasimhavarman, his son, Mahendravarman II, ruled for two years from 668 to 670 AD; then came the latter's son Paramesvaravarman I (670–695 AD). Pulakesin II's son, Vikramaditya I, tried to take revenge as he attacked Kanchi, but the attack, after an initial success, was repulsed by Paramesvaravarman I. Paramesvaravarman was succeeded by his son, Narasimhavarman II Rajasimha (c. 695–c. 722), who enjoyed a peaceful reign. He built the Kailasanathar temple at Kanchi and the Shore temple at Mahabalipuram. His son and successor, Paramesvaravarman II, ruled between 722 and 730 AD. He was killed in a battle with the Chalukyas by Vikramaditya II.

It was his death that brought uncertainty in the Pallava kingdom, leading to the arrival of Nandivarman II in the picture. He ruled for almost six and a half decades, with mixed results. Though he stabilized the state, the slide in its overall fortune was obvious. He is believed to have built the Muktesvara temple and the Vaikunta Perumal temple in Kanchi, among others.

The Pallavas lost much of their importance under his successor, Dantivarman. By this time, there was a new rising power in southern politics, the Cholas, who defeated King Aparajita of Kanchi, to finally end the house of the Pallavas.

Though the Cholas were mentioned in Ashoka's edicts way back in the third century BC, along with the Pandyas and the Cheras, they joined the big league only after the decline of the Pallavas. The house of the imperial Cholas, as the later ones were called, was founded by Vijayalaya in the middle of the ninth century AD. However, the dynasty took off in 907 AD when Parantaka I came to power and ruled for almost half a century. He secured the southern frontier of the kingdom by campaigning against the Pandyas and capturing their capital, Madurai. In the later part of his rule, the Cholas suffered defeat at the hands of the Rashtrakutas.

After him, the Cholas saw a period of decline and uncertainty for the next three decades, till Rajaraja I became the king in 985 AD. He ruled till 1014 AD. He was succeeded by his son, Rajendra I, who ruled till 1044 AD. Together, this period, between 985 and 1044 AD, saw the Cholas scale new heights in the sphere of empire-building, administration, economic prosperity, and cultural affluence.[34]

Rajaraja began to expand his state early in his reign when he destroyed the Chera navy in Trivandrum. He next conquered Madurai and seized Amarabhujanga Pandya. The expedition to Ceylon resulted in the dislodgement of Mahendra V and the annexation of the northern part of the island. He also conquered the Maldives, 'the 12,000 ancient islands' of the Tanjore inscription. Rajaraja's empire thus included the whole of south Bharat up to the Tungabhadra, besides the Maldives, as well as a part of Ceylon. These victories were significant in the backdrop of flourishing south Bharat's maritime trade with the West. The Cholas, after these victories, became the main force in the south with which the Arabs were expected to deal with commercially.

Rajendra I continued his father's policy of territorial-cum-commercial expansion, comprehensively defeating the Chera and Ceylonese kings. But Rajendra is today known more for carrying out two daring, absolutely unprecedented, military campaigns in the history of Bharat: the first one took him northwards, leading him all the way to the Ganges as his troops marched through Bastar, Orissa and Bengal. From there, the holy Ganga water was carried back and poured into the Cholagangam, the large irrigation tank excavated near the new capital, Gangaikondacholapuram, near Chidambaram, built by Rajendra, who assumed the title 'Gangaikondachola'.

Even more ambitious was Rajendra's overseas campaign, involving both the army and navy against the kingdom of Srivijaya in Southeast Asia. The cause of the war seems to be commercial in nature. Romila Thapar explains:

> By the 10th century merchants in China and south Bharat had trading relationships. Ships passed through the seas held by the kingdom of Srivijaya (the southern Malay peninsula and Sumatra) which controlled the Malacca and Sunda Straits. The rulers of Srivijaya realised that it would be more lucrative for local traders if the China-India trade had to terminate in Srivijaya, with local middlemen taking the goods to their eventual destinations. But when Indian merchants in Srivijaya territory were threatened, this raised the wrath of the Chola, who may have had his own investment in this trade, and the result was an attack on Srivijaya.[35]

Interestingly, the Srivijaya campaign took place soon after the Cholas sent an embassy to the Chinese court. The first Chola embassy, sent by Rajaraja I, was received on 17 October 1015 AD.

The Chinese were highly impressed by the Chola delegation, so much so that the emperor ordered his officials to treat them with 'great regard' and invited them to participate in the emperor's birthday festivities in early 1016 AD. Anirudh Kanisetti writes,

> They departed soon after, bearing an 'imperial edict and rich gifts' and perhaps some trade concessions. That was not all they carried with them, for they had learned something very worrisome about the activities of Srivijaya, the maritime confederation that ruled the Straits of Malacca. The historian Tansen Sen argues that until the Chola embassy had arrived in the Song court, merchants from Srivijaya had been informing the Chinese that the Cholas—who were actually south India's undisputed superpower—were mere vassals of Srivijaya. This had secured preferential trade licences for them, as representatives of an ostensibly greater kingdom.[36]

Rajendra Chola wasn't going to take this Srivijayan duplicity lying down. In 1017 AD, he sent a small naval expedition, more like a warning message; but when things didn't change, a much larger fleet was sent in 1025 AD.

A Tamil *prashasti* gives a detailed narrative of the 1025 AD naval expedition:

> (Who) having dispatched many ships in the midst of the rolling sea and having caught Sangrama Vijayottunga Varman, the king of Kadaram, together with the elephants in his glorious army, (took) the large heap of treasures which (that king) had rightfully accumulated; (captured) with noise the (arch called) Vidyadharatorana at the 'war gate' of his extensive city; Sri Vijaya with the 'jewelled wicked gate' adorned with great splendour and the 'gate of large jewels'; Pannai with water in its bathing ghats; the ancient Malaiyur with the strong mountain for its rampart; Mayirudingam, surrounded by the deep sea (as) by a moat;

> Ilangashoka (i.e., Lankashoka) undaunted (in) fierce battles; Mapappalam having abundant (deep) water as defence; Mevilimbangam having fine walls as defence; Valaippanduru having Vilappanduru (?); Talaittakolam praised by great men (versed in) the sciences; Madamalingam, firm in great and fierce battles; Ilamuridesam, whose fierce strength rose in war; Manakkavaram in whose extensive flower gardens honey was collecting; and Kadaram, of fierce strength, which was protected by the deep sea.[37]

Historian K.A. Nilakanta Sastri tries to decode the places mentioned in the *prashasti*. According to him, Pannai is identified with Pani/Panei on Sumatra's east coast. Ancient Malaiyur is a principality 'at the southern end of the Malay Peninsula'. As for Mayirudingam, which had the deep sea for its moat, this place is quite obviously the same as Ji-lo-ting mentioned by Chau Ju-kua among the dependencies of Srivijaya. Ilangaashokam, identified as Ling-ya-sseu-kia, was to the south of the state of Kedah in the Malay Peninsula. Mapappalam could be a place in the Tailang region of lower Myanmar. Talaittakkolam, most probably the same place as Takkola of the *Milinda-Panha* and Takkola of Ptolemy, is in the modern Takuapa district south of the isthmus of Kra. Madamalingam (Temiling or Tembeling) is at the mouth of the Kwantan river in Pahang on the east coast of the Malay Peninsula. Ilamuridesam is quite obviously the country in the northern part of the island of Sumatra, known to Arab geographers under the name Lamuri, called Lambri by Marco Polo. Manakkavaram, clearly, applies to the Nicobars, while Kadaram is a place mentioned under the name of Kataha in Sanskrit literature and epigraphy, and of Kadaram or Kidaram in the *Kalingattuparani* (a 12th-century Tamil poem).[38]

It's thus obvious that the 1025 AD expedition led to a widespread Cholan conquest in the Malay Peninsula. The attack was so swift and sudden, showcasing the deft planning that would have gone behind such a distant overseas operation, that it gave no opportunity to the Srivijayans to organize themselves and respond, resulting in a complete rout.

The Cholas continued to rule with some authority for the next two-and-a-half centuries, but what Rajaraja I and Rajendra I could achieve was not to be repeated again—not by their descendants, not even by other rulers of Bharatavarsha.

Still when the history of Bharat was written post-independence, the Cholas were reduced to being a regional power by our eminent distorians. They just couldn't comprehend, deliberately or otherwise, that a dynasty so far away from Delhi could be anything but not that.

5

Of Invaders and Infidels

From Delhi's Puffed-up Sultans to Vijayanagar's Forgotten Kings

I

When one reads Bharat's dominant colonial-leftist history from 500 to 1200 AD, one gets the feeling that one is aboard a time machine, randomly jumping from one era to another—from the Guptas and Harshavardhana to the Pallavas and Cholas, with significant dynasties such the Karkotas and Gurjara-Pratiharas being reduced to footnotes. The same pattern is repeated while recording the raids, lootings and massacres of Muslim invaders. It begins with Mohammed bin Qasim's Sind attack in 712 AD. Then, the focus shifts to the raids of Mahmud of Ghazni in the early 11th century, climaxing with the destruction of the Somnath temple in 1025 AD. And, finally, the invasion of Mohammed Ghori in 1191 and again a year later. The idea, one suspects, is to suggest, without saying in as many words, that, first, there was nothing worthwhile in Bharat in those years (quite a well-curated myth, as we see in the previous chapter), and, two, Hindus capitulated meekly to Islamic attacks—it was as if they came, they saw and they conquered!

Sadly, this distorted nature of historiography still persists and, worse, retains primacy in the mainstream intellectual ecosystem of the country. In fact, over the decades since Independence, it has managed to get a sense of venerability in a milieu where writing matter-of-factly about an Islamist tyrant spontaneously becomes an act of Islamophobia. So, Mahmud of Ghazni's obsession to become a 'ghazi' or a 'but-shikan' (idol-breaker) is projected by some of our eminent distorians in economic terms.

In fact, there has been a powerful clique of historians among the left that still swears by this theory, first propounded by Mohammad Habib, father of Irfan Habib. According to Mohammad Habib, commerce, and not religion, played a major role in Mahmud of Ghazni's act of vandalism.[1] This despite the fact that he had 'vowed that every year he would undertake a holy war against the Hind'.[2] (He is believed to have attacked Bharat 17 times between 1000 and 1027 AD.) This despite the fact that Abu Nasr al-Utbi, Mahmud's secretary, wrote how in 1011 AD the 'blood of the infidels flowed so copiously (at Thanesar) that the stream was discoloured, notwithstanding its purity, and people were unable to drink it'.[3] This despite the fact that in Mathura in 1018 AD, 'nearly 50,000 men were killed' and how 'all the temples should be burnt with naptha and fire, and levelled with ground'.[4] This despite the fact that in Shrawa, the 'Muslims paid no regard to the booty till they had satiated themselves with the slaughter of the infidels and worshippers of sun and fire'.[5] This, despite the fact that the Somnath temple was destroyed even when the attending Brahmins pleaded with them to take away all its wealth and leave the *murti*[6] alone—Mahmud chose to become *but-shikan* (idol-breaker) rather than *but-parast* (idol-seller), and when he found resistance, he took to killing them all.[7] In fact, he ordered two pieces of the *murti* 'to be broken off and sent to Ghazni, so that one might be thrown at the threshold of the public mosque, and the other at the court door of his own palace… Two more fragments were reserved to be sent to Mecca and Medina.'[8]

While Habib and his followers indirectly blame Hindus for parking so much wealth at temples, thus luring the 'secular' sultan to target them, there are other historians who blame Hindus directly. Romila Thapar, for instance, tries to connect Somanth with an early Arabic goddess, Manat, saying Somnath might be a bastardization of the Arabic 'su-manat'. Manat was one of the goddesses Prophet Mohammed once said could be worshipped, but then retracted, claiming that the assertion was influenced by Satan. These lines came to be known as the 'Satanic Verses' and were subsequently withdrawn. Thapar also quotes a tradition to say that the image of Manat was 'secreted away to Kathiawad for safekeeping in a land where idol worship was considered normal'.[9]

So, when Mahmud attacked Somnath, he wasn't actually desecrating a Hindu temple, we are now being told; the sultan of Ghazni was actually targeting a place that had provided sanctuary to a pre-Islamic Arabian goddess!

Ironically, one of the meekest defences came from Jawaharlal Nehru, Bharat's first prime minister, who said that Mahmud was a soldier who 'came to India to conquer and loot, as soldiers unfortunately do, and he would have done so to whatever religion he might have belonged'.[10]

Coming to the issue of Hindus capitulating meekly to Muslim invaders, one needs to relook at historical facts, used selectively, if not dubiously, by our eminent distorians. The truth is that it took a full 500 years of intense struggle before a Muslim sultan could ascend to a throne in Delhi. In fact, as R.C. Majumdar writes, 'Ultimately, after three centuries of unremitting efforts, we find the Arab dominion in India confined to two petty states of Mansurah and Multan.'[11]

In sharp contrast, by the time Mohammed bin Qasim attacked Sind in 712 AD, the forces of Islam had overrun the vast swathe of landmass comprising today's West Asia, which included the Byzantine provinces of Egypt, Palestine and Syria, the great Sassanid empire of Persia, and a large part of Central Asia, including Inner Mongolia, Bukhara and Samarkand.

As historian Ram Gopal Misra writes,

> Astonishing as these victories of Islam were, equally amazing was the ease and rapidity with which people of different creeds and races were assimilated within the Islamic fold. Syrians, Persians, Berbers, Turks and others—all were rapidly Islamised and their language and culture Arabised.[12]

Bharat not only withstood the Muslim attacks for more than five centuries, but it also survived, though with deep wounds, the 'Islamic conquest', which, according to American historian Will Durant, was 'probably the bloodiest story in history'.[13]

Muslim attacks on Bharat didn't begin in 712 AD, as it is generally believed. The reality is that in 637 AD, within five years of Prophet Mohammed's death, the armies of Islam had begun raiding Al-Hind, as Bharat was referred to in the Arab world then. Yet, repeated attempts only got them humiliation and defeats. So much so that the first four caliphs of Islam died without hearing a single victory in Sind, let alone in Al-Hind.

In 636 AD, Umar ibn al-Khattab, the second caliph, appointed Uthman ibn Abi al-As al-Thaqafi as governor of Bahrain and Oman. A year later, Uthman sent Arab contingents first to Thane on the Maharashtra coast, followed by two more raids—to Baruz (modern-day Bharuch) in Gujarat and Debal (a port near today's Karachi). The three naval raids failed to gain any success for the Arabs. The Arab historians record a Muslim victory in Debal, but according to *Chachnama*, Muslims were defeated and their leader was killed.[14] The defeat enraged the caliph, who wrote an angry letter to Uthman, swearing by God that 'if our men had been killed, I would have slain an equal number from your tribe'.[15]

Uthman ibn Affan, the third caliph, wanted to send a land army to Makran, in today's Balochistan region—a part of the then kingdom of Sind—but was advised against doing that by the governor of Iraq, quoting what one of his informers had told him about Makran: 'Its water is dark; its fruit is bitter and poisonous; its land is stony and its earth is selfish. A small army will soon be annihilated there, and a large army will soon die of hunger.'[16]

Caliph Uthman decided not to send any military expedition to Makran!

In 659 AD, he was succeeded by Ali ibn Abi Talib, who sanctioned the next attack to Al-Hind under Haras ibn Mara-al-Abidi. After initial success in 662 AD, Haras was encouraged to attack Kikan, a small state in the hilly region surrounding the Bolan Pass and is referred to by Hiuen Tsang as 'a kingdom whose people led pastoral lives amid the great mountains and valleys in separate clans, without any ruling chief'.[17] In this battle, fought at the Bolan Pass, a small contingent of local Jats defeated a much bigger and superior Arab army.

On this massive victory, which unfortunately doesn't find space even in the footnotes of most history textbooks, R.C. Majumdar writes:

> The Bolan Pass was protected by the brave Jats of Kikan or Kikanan… If there had been a history of India written without prejudices and predilections, the heroic deeds of these brave people, who stemmed the tide of Islam for two centuries, would certainly have received the recognition they so richly deserve.[18]

Despite defeat, the Arabs continued to attack Kikan. During the next 20 years, no less than six expeditions against this frontier post of Sind were recorded, but to no avail. The only solace for them during this time was the conquest of Makran. This was followed by two decades of relative peace, which was broken in 708 AD when a ship from Ceylon, carrying some Muslim women to the Arab world, was captured by pirates near the port of Debal. Al-Hajjaj ibn Yusuf, the Umayyad governor of Baghdad, wrote to Dahar, king of Sind, to set the women free, but the latter excused himself, saying he had no control over those pirates.

The caliph was at first unwilling to sanction the risky expedition, but ultimately gave in to the persuasion of Al-Hajjaj, who appointed his nephew and son-in-law, Mohammed bin Qasim, as the commander of the ambitious expedition with 6,000 men from caliph's well-equipped army joining him from Syria. Fortunately for him, Dahar, though he fought the Arab army bravely, was complacent, hoping that the Arabs would be defeated again. Even after the Arabs took over the fortified town of Debal, he wrote to Qasim with an air of arrogance, reminding him how Debal, 'which you have taken, is an insignificant town where only traders and artisans reside'.[19]

Dahar's confidence was short-lived as Qasim next moved to occupy his capital, Brahmanabad, which he did, thanks to the former's overconfidence and his army's lack of preparedness. Two more factors sealed his fate, and incidentally, these two factors continued to repeat themselves in other historic defeats for Hindu rulers: one, about 500 Arabs fighting under Dahar's army banner deserted the Hindu camp just before the war as they were reluctant to fight their co-religionists[20]—this was repeated during the time of the Vijayanagar empire when it faced a do-or-die battle against the combined onslaught of neighbouring Muslim states. The second factor was even more common: a burning arrow fired by an Arab rear guard hit Dahar's white elephant, which made it run helter-skelter, causing chaos and confusion in the army. Anyway, a king on an elephant was a sitting duck for enemy archers. And this sealed the fate of several Hindu rulers from Hemu to Rana Sanga in battles that decided the destiny of this country.

Sind had finally fallen into the Arab hand in 712 AD.

Though we are often reminded of Qasim's successes in Sind, what is quietly sidestepped is the fact that these successes were peripheral and short-lived. By the middle of the eighth century, the Arabs started facing major military reverses. Not only had the Pratiharas, led by King Nagabhata, but also Chalukya ruler Avnijnashraya Pulikeshi defeated them comprehensively. The Gurjara King Jayabhata IV of Nandipuri also claims to have defeated the Arabs. But a bigger defeat awaited them in the north where Karkota ruler Lalitaditya Muktapida and King Yashovarman of Kannauj joined hands to give the Arabs a crushing defeat.

Such was the situation that, according to the Arab chronicles, 'a place of refuge to which the Muslims might flee was not to be found', and so the governor of Sind built a city on the far side of the lake, on which later the city of Mansurah stood, as a place of refuge for them.[21]

By the 10th century, Arab travellers to the subcontinent would mention only two small Arab principalities in Bharat—Multan and Mansurah. Interestingly, Multan could survive, especially the assault of the unrelenting Pratiharas who were hell-bent on getting back the sacred Hindu city of Moolsthan (Multan) and its famous *murti* of the sun god, through indulging in a 'non-Islamic' act.

The 10th-century Arab traveller Abu Ishaq al-Istakhri writes, 'When the Indians make war upon (Multan) and endeavour to seize the idol, the (Mussalmans) bring it out, pretending that they will break it and burn it. Upon this the infidels will retire.'[22]

Historian Ram Gopal Mishra sums up the Arab condition well. He writes:

> Thus after three centuries of unremitting effort, we find the Arab dominion in India limited to two petty states of Multan and Mansurah. And here too, they could exist only after renouncing their iconoclastic zeal and utilising the idols for their own political ends. It is a very strange sight to see them seeking shelter behind the very 'budds' they came here to destroy.[23]

There has been constant criticism of the ruling class in Bharat for being oblivious to threats arising from the outside. They never stitch a united front, we are told. In fact, at the time when Mahmud of Ghazni was busy vandalizing Hindu temples in Mathura, Ujjain and Somnath, the south of Bharat was being ruled by one of its greatest rulers, Rajendra Chola I, who rewrote the history of this country by successfully crossing the Indian Ocean and invading Srivijaya in Southeast Asia.

Yes, Rajendra Chola seemed unperturbed by the happenings in Bharat's northwest. But then it's an unfair criticism given the length and breadth of the country. Even in modern times, in the aftermath of Emergency (1975–77), north and south Bharat gave contrasting responses to Mrs Indira Gandhi's political excesses. But to say there was complete indifference towards foreign threats, would be a lie.

Lalitaditya and Yashovarman were rivals, but they collaborated to stop the march of Islam in the subcontinent. Likewise, in Central Bharat and Deccan, one would see a confederacy of several kings, such as Nagabhata of the Pratihara dynasty, Bappa Rawal of Mewar, Vikramaditya II of the Chalukya dynasty, et al., coming together to take on the Muslim invaders. Even the common Hindus were seen contributing in their own way to the war against the Arabs. Firishta, for instance, mentions how Hindu women 'sold their jewels and melted down their gold ornaments (which they sent from distant parts), to furnish resources for the war' against Muslim invaders.[24]

Even when Mahmud of Ghazni began attacking Bharat from 1000 AD onwards, one saw attempts being made to come up with a sort of alliance to take him down. In 1008 AD, for instance, when Mahmud led an army against Anandapala, the Hindu Shahi ruler,[25] in response, led a well-equipped and well-armed army. According to Firishta, many rajas of Hindustan despatched, on the appeal of Anandapala, big contingents to the ruler's aid. They had done this before as well, on a similar occasion, about 30 years earlier, during the reign of Anandapala's father, Jayapala. The Khokars or the Gakkhars of Punjab also joined the Shahis in full strength.[26]

The third big endeavour to breach Bharat's citadel came from Mohammed Ghori, who was eager to replicate Mahmud's exploits. But by the time he first decided to attack Gujarat in 1178 AD, almost 550 years had passed of successive attempts by Islamic armies to establish a firm foothold in Bharat.

Ghori's Gujarat battle brought forth another hero in Bharat's long history—Naiki Devi, queen of King Ajayapala of Gujarat's Chalukya dynasty, who died early. Naiki Devi was ruling on her son's behalf when Ghori invaded her kingdom. She was up to the challenge; she not only prepared the army for the invasion but also opened diplomatic channels seeking support from neighbouring kingdoms, including the famous Prithviraj Chauhan. However, the coalition couldn't come up, as 'none of these provinces, including that of Chauhan, seemed to share the foresight of Naiki Devi in forging a united alliance against the recurring menace'.[27] She made it up by coming up with a better war strategy wherein she lured Ghori to fight from a battleground that was more suitable for Naiki Devi's troops. The invading troops were badly routed.

Such was the demoralizing impact of the defeat that Ghori didn't dare to attack the heart of Bharat for the next 13 years—he did raid peripheral areas such as Peshawar, Sialkot and Lahore in between. And when he attacked the heartland, as in the Battle of Tarain in 1191, he again met with a crushing defeat by Prithviraj Chauhan.

Sir Jadunath Sarkar writes about the first battle of Tarain, thus:

> The rout of the Turki army was complete, but such a victory did not yield its full fruits as the Rajputs were incapable of making a relentless pursuit, and their ponies were outpaced by the Khurasani horses of the Muslim army. Prithviraj merely followed up his victory by laying siege to Bhatinda, which held out for 13 months and at last capitulated.[28]

Next year, he was back again in Tarain—this time with more soldiers and better luck. As for the Hindu army, this time it 'was much smaller than in the first battle. Prithviraj had delayed in mobilising his force; many of his former allies were too lazy or indifferent to fight again for him, and his domestic enemy, the Raja of Kannauj, held off in unpatriotic pride.'[29]

Prithviraj lost the battle and his life. And the heartland of Bharat was finally breached, leading to the foundation of the first Muslim dynasty with its capital in Delhi.

On the Muslim conquest of Bharat, K.M. Munshi once said, 'The conquest of India is the conquest of culture by those who lacked it'.[30] There is no doubt that faster horses and smarter military strategies helped the Muslim invaders shock and awe

Hindu troops. But Hindus didn't lose the war because they were not brave enough. They lost because they didn't really know their new enemy well. These invaders were unlike the invaders of the past: the Hindu ethics of war were vastly different from the Islamic, if there were one among the latter. While Hindus obsessively tried to fight battles as per the established dharma of war, for their latest adversaries the end mattered the most.

Ghori did exactly that in Tarain. When the two armies were face to face, he made the Hindus believe that war could still be avoided by peace talks. The ruse worked. The Rajputs got complacent. And Ghori did what he was best at—deception. He made the plan to launch the attack the next morning. The Hindu soldiers woke up to find their enemies right in front of them, all prepared to launch an assault. In contrast, Prithviraj and his men had not even answered nature's call or even taken a bath, forget about breakfast. The Muslim soldiers, thus, seized the tactical initiative, forcing Hindus 'to fight on the ground and in the manner of Turks' own choosing'. And worse, 'Hindus had to fight on empty stomach'.[31]

And then Ghori's army played a tactical game which would remind one of a group of hyenas taking on a solitary lion by teasing it one after another, thus exhausting the latter's energy. The Turks did something similar.

Sarkar writes:

> They (Turkish archers) were ordered to advance turn by turn and keep the Rajputs in play by shooting at them from a distance, but when the Indians advanced to engage them they were to feign and retreat beyond a horse's course, so as not to be entangled in combat… These Parthian tactics bewildered and baffled the Hindus. They spent all their energy and time in the futile game of chasing and trying to catch up the elusive Central Asian horsemen before them. In this fashion the battle, or rather the series of skirmishes,

> raged from 9 o'clock in the morning till 3 o'clock in the afternoon, at the end of which the Hindus were utterly dispirited by the futility of their exertions and exhausted from hunger and thirst.[32]

Ghori had kept a corps of 12,000 steel-clad special warriors on superb horses as 'strength in reserve'. When he unleashed them at tired and exhausted Rajput, the game was over for Prithviraj Chauhan and his men. Thus, the Muslims found their first footholds in the heart of Bharat and the Sultanate of Delhi came into existence.

II

It took almost 500 years for a Muslim ruler to get a foothold in Delhi and, as Sandeep Balakrishna writes, 'From 1206 to 1526, it (Delhi Sultanate) comprised a total of five dynasties, with only one powerful sultan emerging from each dynasty… Each such dynasty inevitably became extinct within a few years of the death of its most powerful sultan.'[33]

Before we look deeply into the Delhi Sultanate, we need to make it clear that the occupation of Delhi was not an earth-shattering event in the history of Bharat. Yes, it was a setback that a Muslim dynasty found a foothold in the heart of the country, but we seem to be projecting the future glory of Delhi into the past to assume that the Turkish invaders occupied the capital of Bharat. At that time, Kannauj, Ujjain, Varanasi, Devagiri, Madurai, etc., were bigger, much significant cities. In fact, looked dispassionately, the Muslim conquest of cities like Multan, Peshawar and Lahore[34] was an equally momentous development, given that they were strategically more important urban centres than Delhi.

Be that as it may, the fact of the matter is that the first dynasty of the Delhi Sultanate—called the Slave (Mamluk) dynasty—began to formally rule from 1206 AD. The first sultan was Qutub-ud-din Aibak, who was originally Ghori's slave but rose in hierarchy through sheer talent, hard work and good luck. Aibak had two stints, first as Ghori's general and then as a full-fledged sultan of Delhi. Under Ghori, he had a stupendous record: while Ghori conquered Punjab, Sind, Delhi, and the Doab up to Kanauj, Aibak extended the conquest to Ajmer and Ranthambore in Rajasthan, Gwalior, Kalinjar, Mahoba, and Khajuraho in Bundelkhand, and Katehar and Badaun beyond the Ganges. But by the time Ghori was assassinated by the Khokhars in 1206 AD, when Aibak formally assumed power as Delhi's sultan, Kalinjar had been re-conquered by the Chandellas, Ranthambore had renounced Delhi's suzerainty, Gwalior had been re-occupied by the Pratiharas, and the Gaharwar and Katehar Rajputs were in rebellion. Aibak failed to re-conquer these areas before he died in 1210 AD in a freak accident while playing polo in Lahore.

Aibak's successor, Iltutmish, again a slave, succeeded in regaining control over Ranthambore and Gwalior, and in tightening Delhi's noose around Ajmer, but he also suffered defeats at the hands of the Chandellas of Bundelkhand, the Paramars of Malwa, the Chauhans of Bundi, and the Guhilots of Nagda. His control over the Doab remained slippery and grip over Ajmer had slackened towards the end of his life. Iltutmish died in 1236 AD.

He was succeeded by a series of incompetent rulers, though his immediate successor, Razia Begum, gained eminence for being the first female Muslim ruler of the subcontinent, and also the only female Muslim ruler of Delhi.

The Delhi Sultanate's slide was prevented by Balban, who wielded effective power through the dreaded 'Forty' (a powerful class of Turkish nobility) from 1246 AD onwards, though he formally sat on the throne as sultan in 1266 AD. Himself being a prominent member of the Forty, he knew very well the threat this clique of nobility posed, and he worked incessantly to cut this group to size. It took him a full decade, and by 1276 AD, the Forty had ceased to exist.

Meanwhile, Balban continued to respond to rising Hindu resistance. He sent a strong army to crush the neighbouring Mewatis. If Firishta is to be believed, more than a lakh Mewatis were killed.[35] Balban also ordered his army to clear the entire forest region in the circumference of 100 miles. He then built four forts in the area and garrisoned them with Afghan troops. Elsewhere in the Sultanate too, Balban was ruthless in crushing the Hindu resistance. In Katehar, for instance, according to Ziauddin Barani, he personally led a contingent of soldiers and ordered them to 'burn down Katehar and destroy it, to slay every man, and to spare none but women and children… The blood of the rioters ran in streams, heaps of the stain were to be seen near every village and jungle, and the stench of the dead reached as far as Ganga'.[36] He was equally assertive in putting down a rebellion in Bengal. However, by the time of his death in 1289 AD, the Sultanate had again lost most of the gains he had made.

R.C. Majumdar sums up the Delhi Sultanate situation in the 13th century in the following words:

> India south of the Vindhyas was under Hindu rule in the 13th century. Even in north India during the same century, there were powerful kingdoms not yet subjected to Muslim rule, or still fighting for their independence... Even in that part of India which acknowledged the Muslim rule, there was continual defiance and heroic resistance by large or small bands of Hindus in many quarters, so that successive Muslim rulers had to send well-equipped military expeditions, again and again, against the same region... As a matter of fact, the Muslim authority in northern India, throughout the 13th century, was tantamount to a military occupation of a large number of important centres without

> any effective occupation, far less a systematic administration of the country at large.[37]

Within a year, the Slave dynasty was uprooted from Delhi. Ironically, it was Balban, the 'purest' of the Turks, who heralded the extinction of his own dynasty through the systematic purge of the dreaded 'Forty'. In order to decimate them, he patronized non-Turkish generals and nobles, led by the Khiljis. And it was a Khilji—Jalaluddin Khalji—who put an end to the Slave dynasty in 1290 AD.

Jalaluddin's stint as the sultan of Delhi was largely uneventful. He failed to reconquer any land that had been lost during the last years of Balban. But he did bring in some sort of order and normalcy in the administration. By the time he ascended to the throne of Delhi, he was 70 and had begun spending most of his time in prayers and preparing for his death. This was also aided and abetted by his guilt of betraying Balban by becoming the sultan.[38] This sense of pacifism created uneasiness among his nobles. When one of his loyalists who warned him against being so merciful and prone to giving leniency to those indulging in rebellion, the ageing sultan said:

> I know better than you what Sultans in the past have done to rebels. But I am an old Mussalman now and I am not habituated to shedding the blood of the Mussalmans… A short life remains before me now… I would rather renounce this throne for I cannot endure the wrath of Allah.[39]

Firishta shows the popular mood of the nobility as he writes, 'Clemency is a virtue which descends from Khuda, but the degenerate nobles of that age didn't deserve it'.[40]

It was only a matter of time before someone displaced Jalauddin. His nephew, Alauddin, did so in 1296 AD.

Alauddin Khilji was by far the most successful of Sultanate rulers. His army conquered Gujarat in 1298 AD. After initial setbacks, he defeated Ranthambore in 1301 AD, followed by the conquest of Chittor in 1303 AD. It was, however, his southern exploits that became more popular. His own as well as Malik Kafur's expeditions against Devagiri (Maharashtra), Warangal (Andhra Pradesh), Dvarasamudra (Karnataka), and Madurai (Tamil Nadu), though primarily raids in nature, opened the south to Muslim invaders for the first time. Again, with his death in 1316 AD, the Khalji dynasty collapsed and within four years, the Sultanate squandered much of the territorial gains it had made in the past decade and a half.

Alauddin was 'the first sovereign of the Turkish line to have taken a keen interest in fiscal and revenue reforms'.[41] These so-called reforms were aimed at allowing cultivators, who were overwhelmingly Hindu, 'only a bare subsistence'.[42] Historian K.S. Lal writes,

> Alauddin's measures were truly oppressive. The very idea of leaving the bare minimum to the peasantry, which formed the bulk of the population, was to impoverish the countrymen. In years to come Ghiyasuddin Tughlag also more or less followed the same policy. His instructions to the revenue officers were that 'there should be left only so much to the Hindus that neither on the one hand should they become intoxicated on account of their wealth, nor on the other hand should they become so destitute as to leave their lands and cultivation in despair'.[43]

Next came the Tughlaq dynasty. Established by Ghiyasuddin Tughlaq, the dynasty saw a few successes, such as in Bengal, but it was under the regime of his successor, Mohammad bin Tughlaq, that the Delhi Sultanate not just consolidated its hold over north Bharat but also exposed in a big way the chink in the armour of southern kings. He consolidated his hold over Devagiri, conquered the small kingdom of Kampili on the Tungabhadra, and forced Dvarasamudra to pay tribute to the imperial authority of Delhi. Madurai also came to be included in his empire. He transferred his capital to Devagiri in order to keep a close watch on Hindu resurrection in the south, and for establishing another centre of Islamic power in Bharat. However, his capital experiment failed, and he had to shift his capital back to Delhi.

Interestingly, at the very start of his reign Mohammed bin Tughlaq had been defeated by Maharana Hammir of Mewar, taken prisoner, and released only after he ceded all claims to Ajmer, Ranthambore and Nagaur, besides a payment of 50 lakhs of rupees as indemnity. Again, as was customary with all Sultanate rulers, his empire south of the Vindhyas was lost to Delhi in his own lifetime, and Delhi's hold over large areas even in the north disappeared soon after his death in 1351 AD. In fact, his failed capital-shifting endeavour—from Delhi to Daulatabad—was aimed at finding a balance between the north and south of his empire. Sadly for him, even the best of his plans lacked the finesse to make it a success on the ground.

Firuz Shah Tughlaq succeeded him. Though Firuz's reign was very long, it saw a slow but steady decline. It was during his time that the mighty Vijayanagar empire had come to control the region south of Krishna. And in Rajasthan, Rajput princes, led by Mewar's king, regained most of their lost territories.

The next two Sultanate dynasties—the Sayyids and the Lodis—were hardly imperial dynasties. They could barely hold on to power. In fact, when Babur defeated Ibrahim Lodi in the First Battle of Panipat in 1526 AD, Mewar under Rana Sanga was the strongest power in north Bharat. As for the biggest power in the country, it, without an iota of doubt, had to be the Vijayanagar empire that attained its zenith under Krishnadevaraya (1505–1530 AD).

In his evaluation of the 14th and the 15th centuries, R.C. Majumdar writes:

> The Khalji empire rose and fell during the brief period of twenty years (1300–1320 AD). The empire of Muhammed bin Tughlaq... broke up within a decade of his accession (1325 AD), and before another decade was over, the Turkish empire passed away for ever... Thus barring two very short-lived empires under the Khaljis and Muhammad bin Tughlaq...there was no Turkish empire in India.[44]

III

Ramdhari Singh Dinkar, a well-known Hindi litterateur, writes in his milestone book, *Sanskriti Ke Char Adhyay*, how the Hindu–Muslim relationship before the arrival of Turks, led by Mahmud of Ghazni and Mohammed Ghori, was cordial and amicable. It was the plunder and destruction of the Turks that pushed the two communities away from each other, he says. While lamenting this turn of events, Dinkar writes, 'Mahmud of Ghazni and Mohammed Ghori neither belonged to the Arabic or Iranian race, nor were they the true representatives of Islam... They lacked the tolerance of Arabic and Iranian cultures.'[45]

Dinkar seemed to be pursuing the ideological line taken by communist leader M.N. Roy, who in his essay, 'Historic Role of Islam', bemoaned the fact that 'Islam came to India after it had played out its progressive role, and its leadership had been wrested from the learned and cultured Arabs'. According to him, Mohammed bin Qasim conquered Sindh with the active assistance of the Jats and other agricultural communities oppressed by the Brahmin rulers. Having conquered the country, he followed the policy of the early Arab conquerors.

> He employed the Brahmans in pacifying the country by taking them into confidence. He allowed them to repair their temples and to follow their own religion as before, placed the

> collection of revenue in their hands, and employed them in continuing the traditional system of local administration.[46]

When one revisits the tumultuous era and goes through the contemporary or near-contemporary writings, a different picture of the 'cultured Arabs' emerges. This Qasim is starkly different from what Dinkar and Roy wanted us to believe.

As reported in *Chachnama*, soon after his victory at Raor, Qasim received a letter from the 'cultured' Hajjaj, who wrote thus:

> The great God says in the *Quran*: 'O true believers, when you encounter the unbelievers, strike off their heads.' The above command of the Great God is a great command and must be respected and followed. You should not be so fond of showing mercy, as to nullify the virtue of the act. Henceforth grant pardon to no one of the enemy and spare none of them, or else all will consider you a weak-minded man.[47]

R.C. Majumdar writes in detail about Qasim's Debal victory. He states:

> After his men had scaled the walls of the fort of Debal, the besieged Indians opened the gates and asked for mercy. Muhammad replied that he had no orders to spare anyone in the town, and so, no quarter was given, and for three days the inhabitants were ruthlessly slaughtered. The local temple was defiled and '700 beautiful females, who had sought for shelter there, were all captured'. The same tragedy was enacted after the capture of Raor; Muhammad massacred 6,000 fighting men who were found in the fort, and their followers and dependents, as well as their women and children, were taken prisoners. Sixty thousand slaves, including 30 young ladies of royal blood, were sent to Hajiaj together with the head of Dahar. We can now well understand why the capture

> of a fort by the Muslim forces was followed by the terrible *jauhar* ceremony (in which the females threw themselves in fire kindled by themselves), the earliest recorded instance of which is found in the *Chachnama*.[48]

The *Chachnama* also talks about *jizia* being imposed on Hindus. It writes,

> He who received the honour of Islam and became a convert was exempt from slavery as well as tribute and was not injured. Those, however, who did not accept the true faith were compelled to pay the fixed tribute (*jizia*). These latter were divided by him into three classes. The first and highest class had to pay 48 dirams of silver in weight per head. The second, or the middle class, had to pay 24 dirams in weight, and the third, or the lowest class, had to pay 12 dirams in weight only. He then dismissed them with the following words: 'I let you go this day. Those among you who become Mussalmans and come within the fold of Islam shall have their tribute remitted, but those who are still inclined to be of their own faith, must put up with injuries (*gazand*) and tribute (*jizia*) to retain the religion of their fathers and grandfathers.'[49]

Five hundred years later, when the Turk rulers of Delhi were killing Hindus at will and destroying temples, they were only pursuing the violent path of their 'cultured' Arabic predecessors. The process, the procedure, and the modus operandi all seem to be the same. One needs to look at historian A.L. Srivastava's description of Balban's massacre at Katehar in the late 13th century, and how similar it appears to Qasim's exploits in Sind. Srivastava writes:

> There he ordered his men to attack the villages, to set fire to the houses and to slay the entire adult male population. Innocent women and children were dragged into slavery.

> By these barbarous methods he struck terror into the hearts of the people and depopulated the entire region. In every village and jungle heaps of human corpses were left rotting. The remnants of the people, lurking here and there, were thoroughly cowed down. We are told by the historian, Barani, that the Kateharias never after raised their heads and the entire region became safe for the traveller, the peasant and the government officer.[50]

Almost a century later, Firuz Shah Tughlaq would first sack the temples in Orissa, including the famous Jagannath temple, and then go to Nagarkot (Kangra) to destroy the shrine of Jvalamukhi. Firishta writes quite gleefully how the God-fearing sultan 'broke the idols of Jvalamukhi, mixed their fragments with the flesh of cows and hung them in nosebags round the necks of Brahmins. He sent the principal idol as trophy to Medina.'[51]

From Debal to Katehar to Jvalamukhi, and from Qasim to Balban to Firuz Shah, there's a common ideology/belief system that makes Islam's foot soldiers act zombie-like. This was what V.S. Naipaul was pointing at when he called Islam 'the most uncompromising kind of imperialism', where the 'converted peoples have to strip themselves of their past; of the converted peoples nothing is required but the purest faith (if such a thing can be arrived at), Islam, submission'.[52] The attitude of the latter-day Turkish sultans of Delhi, thus, was in continuance of—and in consonance with—what the Arabs had done in Sind a few centuries ago, and not in any way contrary to their actions and worldview. The 'cultured Arabs' were as brutal and barbaric as the 'uncouth Turks'!

IV

The Muslim invasions in south Bharat—first by Alauddin Khilji and Malik Kafur, and then by Mohammed bin

Tughlaq—upended the politico-social condition south of the Vindhyas.[53] Politically, there was a vacuum: the old kingdoms were weakened beyond repair, and the one that was behind all this mayhem was too distant to effectively replace them.[54] Mohammed bin Tughlaq's decision to transfer his capital from Delhi to Daulatabad was aimed at creating a geographical balance, but the endeavour failed miserably.

When Tughlaq returned to Delhi, he appointed Malik Muhammad as the governor of Kampili. His letter to the Delhi sultan is quite revealing. Malik Muhammad told sultan—as recorded by Portuguese traveller Fernao Nuniz—that 'the land was risen against him', 'everyone was lord to what he pleased and no one was on his side'; the people came to 'besiege him in the fortress, allowing no provisions to go to him, nor paying him the taxes that had been forced on them'.[55]

This politico-social ferment in Bharat south of the Vindhyas was just right for two young Hindu princes, Harihara and Bukka, to lay the foundation of the Vijayanagar kingdom.[56] The two brothers were believed to be once feudatories of either the Hoysala or the Kakatiya king. In around 1327, they seemed to have been captured by Muslim troops and taken to Delhi. There, the two were converted to Islam before being told to go to the south as feudatories of Mohammed bin Tughlaq. It was their encounter with sage Vidyaranya[57] of the famous Sringeri *math* that made them reconvert to Hinduism, besides inspiring them to lay the foundation of 'the great Hindu kingdom of the south'.[58]

From the very beginning, Vijayanagar was engaged with Bahmani rulers in incessant battles. At issue between the two was a fertile tract of land between the Krishna and Tungabhadra rivers known as the Raichur Doab. To command this territory, the Bahmanis, like the Rashtrakutas many centuries earlier, moved their capital from Daulatabad to Gulbarga and finally Bidar. At another level, the battle was also religious, given that Vijayanagar 'was committed from the start to the preservation of a Hinduism that had already been violated, and culturally and artistically it preserved and repeated'.[59]

It was this hatred for the *other* that explains why when thoroughly defeated in 1565, Vijayanagar was completely erased from the map of the earth. As V.S. Naipaul writes:

> It was conquered, and totally destroyed, by an alliance of Moslem principalities in 1565. The city was then one of the greatest in the world, its walls twenty-four miles around—foreign visitors have left accounts of its organisation and magnificence—and the work of destruction took five months; some people say a year.[60]

After 1565 AD, nothing was left to remind of the splendour of Vijayanagar, which so many visiting foreigners talked about. Iranian traveller Abdur Razzak believed the 'city of Vijayanagar simply has no equal in the world'. 'It is such that the pupil of the eye has never seen a place like it, and the ear of intelligence has never been informed that there existed anything to equal it in the whole world', he said. Writing about Vijayanagar, he said how he passed through seven concentric rings of fortifications, each having its own citadel, with the innermost ring containing the palace and the audience hall of the king.[61]

Portuguese traveller Domingo Paes, too, was at a loss of words to see the opulence at Vijayanagar. He wrote,

> I cannot possibly describe it all, nor should I be believed if I tried to do so… For I went along with my head so often turned from one side to the other that I was almost falling over backwards off my horse with my senses lost… Truly, it

seemed as if, that what I saw was a vision, and that I was in a dream.[62]

Despite being more populous and prosperous, militarily, in the first 100 years, the Bahmanis had an upper hand over Vijayanagar. However, these Bahmani victories remained largely inconclusive. The Muslim troops could never reach the Vijayanagar capital. But then, as is often the case, power, success and riches often blunt the force of ideology. And this happened when the empire was at its apex, just over 100 years after its foundation.

During the reign of Devaraya II (1425–46 AD), a decision was taken by the king that first led to great success but ended up being the cause of its decline. It would bother Devaraya II to see his more populous and prosperous empire being constantly beaten up by the Bahmanis. It would irk him, and he summoned his advisers to come up with answers. At this meeting, the king was told that the strength of the Bahmanis came from their horses and mounted archers. In the end, it was decided not just to import more horses and improve the archery training of the Hindu soldiers, but also open the doors of the Vijayanagar army for Muslim soldiers.

Muslims were thereafter eligible for service in the Vijayanagar army. They were allowed to freely practice their religion, and a Quran was placed before the Hindu king's throne so that they 'might perform the ceremony of obeisance in his presence, without sinning against their laws'.[63]

This did give Vijayanagar instant strength. At the end of Devaraya II's reign, the empire was the strongest in south Bharat, if not in the whole of the country. The empire's golden era, however, came half a century later when not just the armies of Krishnadeva Raya (1509–1530 AD) had turned into an invincible war machine but also Vijayanagar had become the most prosperous empire in Bharat—economically, culturally and intellectually.

Writing about the Vijayanagar of Krishnadeva Raya's time, Paes wrote:

> The people in the city are countless in number, so much so that I do not wish to write it down for fear that it should be thought fabulous... What I saw... seemed as large as Rome, and very beautiful to the sight; there are many groves of trees within it... many orchards and gardens with fine trees... many conduits of water which flow in the midst of it, and in places there are lakes... This is the best provided city in the world.[64]

But after the death of Krishnadeva Raya, Vijayanagar saw a period of decline. Its rulers became too arrogant, taking the infallibility of Vijayanagar for granted. Also, by then, Vijayanagar's ideological positioning was dangerously diluted. The empire that fundamentally saw itself as a bulwark against the expansion of Muslim influence in the south lost its ideological moorings in over two centuries of its rule—not a surprising development given the fact that power corrupts, but absolute power corrupts absolutely.[65]

Rama Raya, the king who fought the disastrous 1565 war, was an apt example as to where things went wrong for Vijayanagar. By that time the Bahmani empire had long disintegrated into five independent kingdoms: Ahmadnagar, Bijapur, Berar, Golconda, and Bidar. This gave Rama Raya a newfound confidence to toy with each of them, putting one against another. With this, he not only succeeded in falling out with all his neighbours, but also managed to unite them in hatred and envy of the rich and powerful Vijayanagar empire. The Muslim rulers could see clearly that their division gave the advantage to Rama Raya.

They all came together to challenge Vijayanagar at the Battle of Talikota in 1565 AD. Rama Raya's army seized the first advantage and nearly won the battle, but at this momentous occasion two of his Muslim commanders, each in charge of 70,000 to 80,000 soldiers, switched to the Muslim side. This turned the tide in favour of the Muslim confederacy.

K.A. Nilakanta Sastri blames Rama Raya for his tragic fate. He writes:

> Firishta says that Rama Raya destroyed many of the ancient nobility and raised his own family to the highest rank, a point which is confirmed by the evidence of other writers and of the inscriptions. Rama Raya also began to admit large numbers of Muslims into the army, a practice that had, indeed, been started in a small way by Devaraya II. No important offices at that time had been entrusted to them, but Rama Raya departed from this prudent policy employing Muslims in places which gave them an intimate knowledge of the internal affairs of the state.[66]

Tragically, for the later Vijayanagar rulers, while they might have diluted the ideological moorings of the empire, for the enemy, it remains an object of utter derision and hate. While the Hindu empire might have compromised on its Hindu identity, for its enemy it remained the Hindu bulwark against the forces of Islam. Such a state had to be decimated, with no space for redemption. Sewell writes:

> The victorious Mussulmans had halted on the field of battle for rest and refreshment, but now they had reached the capital, and from that time forward for a space of five months Vijayanagar knew no rest. The enemy had come to destroy, and they carried out their object relentlessly. They slaughtered the people without mercy, broke down the temples and palaces; and wreaked such savage vengeance on

> the abode of the kings, that, with the exception of a few great stone-built temples and walls, nothing now remains but a heap of ruins to mark the spot where once the stately buildings stood. They demolished the statues, and even succeeded in breaking the limbs of the huge Narasimha monolith. Nothing seemed to escape them… With fire and sword, with crowbars and axes, they carried on day after day their work of destruction. Never perhaps in the history of the world has such havoc been wrought, and wrought so suddenly, on so splendid a city; teeming with a wealthy and industrious population in the full plenitude of prosperity one day, and on the next seized, pillaged, and reduced to ruins, amid scenes of savage massacre and horrors beggaring description.[67]

Vijayanagar's destruction wasn't an ordinary event, but then it wasn't an ordinary empire either.

6

The M Factor

Evaluating the Contributions of the So-called Mughals and Marathas

> The Great Mughal is a foreigner in Hindustan. To maintain himself in such a country he is under the necessity of keeping up numerous armies, even in the time of peace.
>
> —Francois Bernier, a 17th-century French traveller

I

In September 2020, Uttar Pradesh chief minister Yogi Adityanath put the cat among the left-'liberal' pigeons when he asked, 'How can our heroes be the Mughals?' The statement ruffled many feathers, as they saw this comment as an assault on the country's liberal, secular ethos.

Among many, the response of an 'eminent' journalist, who could easily claim the status of royalty if the Lutyens' zone were to ever become a princely state, is worth exploring. The journalist Karan Thapar wrote in an article,

> I want to ask him (Adityanath) a few questions myself. What gives a chief minister the right to question who our heroes are? He may have the authority to govern us but not to determine our values and shape our ideals. It's arrogance

> on his part to presume to tell us who to look up to and which rulers of our past to consider great.[1]

At a cursory glance, it seems to be a valid assertion, though with moralistic overtones. Sadly, the truth is that the 'eminent' journalist commits the same mistake he accuses the Uttar Pradesh chief minister of indulging in. For, as one goes through the article, one finds him assuming the role of a guardian angel—not an unlikely posture from someone hailing from the family of presiding deities of the pretentiously moralistic Nehruvian order—and exhorts us how 'the greatest of our rulers is the Mughal emperor Akbar or, to use his full name, Abu'l Fath Jalalud-din Muhammad Akbar'.

He then claims pompously: 'I know many consider the Mauryan emperor Ashoka, who ruled 18 centuries earlier, Akbar's equal or, possibly, heroically superior but I disagree. Akbar was not responsible for 100,000 deaths at Kalinga.'[2]

In chapter 2, we have already examined the great Nehruvian project of amplifying Ashoka's greatness. Interestingly, the same ecosystem—of which the 'eminent' journalist has been an elite member—is mostly preoccupied with the task of making the Mughals in general, and Akbar in particular, great. Then comes the well-oiled sleight of hand, perfected by our eminent distorians: first, project the greatness of Ashoka, saying there was no one like him in the Indic scheme of things; and then, compare him with Akbar to say that the former was good but with the Kalinga blemish. The result: if there ever was a great ruler in Bharat, it was Akbar! What's, however, not realized is that for every Kalinga, there was Chittor (1568 AD), where Akbar, after conquering its almost impregnable fort, ordered the massacre of 30,000 non-combatant civilians, including old and infirm men, women and children.[3]

Abul Fazl writes in his *Akbarnama*:

> There were 8,000 fighting Rajputs collected in the fortress, but there were more than 40,000 peasants who took part in watching and serving... From early dawn till midday the bodies of those ill-starred men were consumed by the majesty of the great warrior. Nearly 30,000 men were killed. The reason of so many being killed was that on the former occasion... when Sultan Alauddin (Khilji) took the fort after six months and seven days, the peasantry were not put to death as they had not engaged in fighting. But on this occasion they had shown great zeal and activity. Their excuses after the emergence of victory were of no avail, and orders were given for a general massacre.[4]

At the very outset, it must be clarified that the usage of the term 'Mughals' for Babur and sons is erroneous. Author Aabhas K. Maldahiyar is quite categorical on the issue as he writes:

> While penning the *Baburnama*, Babur ensured a clear distinction between him being a Timurid prince establishing a Timurid Gurkaniyan Sulṭ̤anate and not the Moghul, which has been a popular claim of late. One may argue that Babur may have not used the term 'Moghul' at all and hence the different term. But that too is not the reality. Babur has used the term 'Moghul, Mughal, Mugal' more than 400 times in the *Baburnama*, drawing a clear distinction.[5]

To this John Zubrzycki adds:

> In the 15th century, the term 'Mongol' carried the connotations of barbarism. As Babur would say, 'Were the Mongols a race of angels, it would still be a vile nation.'[6]

Coming back to Adityanath's words, all he said was, 'How can our heroes be Mughals?' He didn't single out Akbar. But the 'eminent' journalist turned the so-called Mughals (Timurids) into Akbar, as if the two were one and the same.

Can the Timurids as a whole be our heroes?

The Timurid empire in Bharat was established by Babur after the Battle of Panipat in 1526 AD. Interestingly, Babur has largely been introduced to schoolchildren as a naturalist, a poet and a doting father who prayed to Allah to take his life but spare his ill son's. He, for Jawaharlal Nehru, was 'an attractive person, a typical Renaissance prince, bold and adventurous, fond of art and literature and good living'.[7] But then the lurid details he provides of his repeated massacres of 'kafirs', especially his propensity to raise towers of Hindu heads cut off during and after every battle, leave very little doubt about Babur's fondness for infidel blood. Babur would also take the title of 'Ghazi' after his victory in the battle of Khanwa against Rana Sanga in 1527 AD.[8] Babur explained this nature of his with the following quatrain:

> For the sake of Islam I became a wanderer;
> I battled infidels and Hindus.
> I determined to become a martyr.
> Thank God I became a holy warrior.[9]

Salman Rushdie, in his introduction to Wheeler M. Thackston's translation of *The Baburnama*, written by Babur himself, too, highlights this two-facedness of the Timurid king. He writes:

> Who, then, was Babur—scholar or barbarian, nature-loving poet or terror-inspiring warlord? The answer is to be found in the *Baburnama* and it's an uncomfortable one: He was both... Both Baburs are real, and perhaps the strangest thing about the *Baburnama* is that they do not seem to be at odds with each other.[10]

Rushdie brings out Babur's dual personality during his conquest of Chanderi in 1528. He writes:

> First comes the blood-thirsty description of the killing of many 'infidels' and the apparent mass suicide of two or three hundred more. ('They killed each other almost to the last by having one man hold a sword while the others willingly bent their necks… A tower of infidels' skulls was erected on the hill on the northwest side of Chanderi.') Then just three sentences later, we get this: 'Chanderi is a superb place. All around the area are many flowing streams… The lake… is renowned throughout Hindustan for its good, sweet water. It is truly a nice little lake.[11]

Babur lost his father in a freak accident in 1494 AD, when he was just 11. Then onwards it was a phase of political wilderness for him as he, while trying to conquer Samarkand, lost his little kingdom of Ferghana to his half-brothers. When he could not achieve much in the next ten years, he shifted his gaze to Kabul, whose ruler had just passed away, leaving behind an infant son. Once in Kabul, the road to Delhi wasn't far away, especially given the sorry state of affairs it was under the Lodis. After initial hesitations, in 1526, he reached Panipat with 12,000 cavalry, which, according to Sir Jadunath Sarkar, 'must have been the number of his choice Turkish horsemen or first-class troops'.[12] Lt Col Wolseley Haig estimates Babur's forces in Panipat at 25,000 men.[13] Babur won the battle against Ibrahim Lodi and thus founded the famous Timurid (Mughal) dynasty in Delhi–Agra, which was further consolidated a year later when he defeated Rana Sanga, believed to be the most powerful ruler of north Bharat, in the battle of Khanwa.

Babur came to Bharat out of desperation and not love. He, thus, found it to be 'a place of little charm', with 'no beauty in its people, no graceful social intercourse, no poetic talent or understanding, no etiquette, nobility or manliness'. Even the arts and crafts have 'no harmony or symmetry'.[14]

No wonder, when he died in Agra in 1530 AD, Babur was buried there, but soon after his body was taken to Kabul and reburied in a tomb there, the place where it was felt he belonged.[15]

Babur's son, Humayun, largely led the life of a vagabond. North Bharat during his time was dominated by Sher Shah Suri, an Afghan ruler from Bihar who defeated the Timurids in 1540 AD to send them into exile. It was the accidental death of Sher Shah Suri, who was an administrator par excellence, in 1545 AD that gave Humayun another opening. But by the time Humayun could capture Delhi back in the mid-1550s, it was too late for him to leave any credible mark behind. A year later, in 1556 AD, he died after he slipped on the stairs in his library.

Akbar's was an era of religious tolerance and universal peace (*Sulh-i-Kul*). But his religious tolerance couldn't successfully transcend a generation as his successor, Jahangir, infamously ordered the killing of the fifth Sikh guru, Arjan Dev, in the very first year of his reign. Jahangir's contempt for Hindus comes out clearly in his *Tuzuk-i-Jahangiri*:

> In Gobindwal, which is on the river Blyah (Beas), there was a Hindu named Arjun, in the garments of sainthood and sanctity, so much so that he had captured many of the simple-hearted of the Hindus, and even of the ignorant and foolish followers of Islam, by his ways and manners, and they had loudly sounded the drum of his holiness. They called him Guru, and from all sides stupid people crowded to worship and manifest complete faith in him. For three or four generations (of spiritual successors) they had kept this shop warm. Many times it occurred to me to put a stop to this vain affair or to bring him into the assembly of the people of Islam.

> At last when Khusrau passed along this road this insignificant fellow proposed to wait upon him. Khusrau happened to halt at the place where he was, and he came out and did homage to him. He behaved to Khusrau in certain special ways, and made on his forehead a finger-mark in saffron, which the Indians (Hinduwan) call 'qashqa', and is considered propitious. When this came to my ears and I clearly understood his folly, I ordered them to produce him and handed over his houses, dwelling places, and children to Murtaza Khan, and having confiscated his property commanded that he should be put to death.[16]

Sir Jadunath Sarkar also recalls an episode where Jahangir claimed to have cut the Akshay Bat of Allahabad 'down to its roots and hammered a redhot iron cauldron on to its stump. He flattered himself that he had killed it. But lo! In a year the tree began to grow again and pushed the heavy obstruction to its growth aside'.[17]

As for Aurangzeb, Jahangir's grandson, his intolerance towards Hindus was legendary, as he, among many others, got the ninth Sikh guru, Tegh Bahadur, brutally tortured and killed. In the very first year of his reign in 1658 AD, in a charter granted to a priest of Varanasi, he avowed that 'his religion *forbade* him to allow the building of new temples, but did not enjoin the destruction of old ones'.[18] As his hold over his administration strengthened, his Islamist tenacity increased. On 9 April 1669, for instance, he issued a general order 'to demolish all schools and temples of the infidels and put down their religious teaching and practices'.[19] Some of the holiest Hindu shrines such as the temple of Somnath, the Viswanath temple of Varanasi and the Keshav Rai temple of Mathura became the victims of his Islamist fury. A decade later, 'Akbarian liberalism' saw a total rollback as Aurangzeb, through imperial orders on 2 April 1679, re-imposed the *jizya* to 'spread Islam and put down the practice of infidelity'. Hindus protested vehemently but to no avail. [20]

Various other anti-Hindu measures were also adopted during Aurangzeb's reign. As per an edict in April 1665, the customs duty on the commodities brought in for sale was fixed at 2.5 per cent for Muslim merchants and 5 per cent for the Hindu merchants. Two years later, in May 1667, this duty in the case of Muslim traders was abolished, but Hindu merchants were forced to pay at the old rate of 5 per cent. In 1671 an order was passed for the dismissal of all Hindu head clerks and accountants and replacing them with Muslims, but due to fewer qualified Muslims, half of these posts were allowed to be held by Hindus. In 1668 all Hindu religious fairs were prohibited, and in March 1695 another order was passed forbidding the Hindus, except the Rajputs, to ride in palanquins, on elephants, and on good horses; they were also forbidden from carrying arms.

Such was Hindu disquiet and anger against such measures that even Maharaj Jaswant Singh, a loyal Rajput general serving Aurangzeb and fighting some of the most arduous battles for the Timurid empire, couldn't stop himself from writing a letter just before his death in 1678 AD: 'God is the God of all mankind, not just the God of Muhammadans alone. To vilify the religion or customs of other men is to set at naught the pleasure of the Almighty.'[21]

In sharp contrast, Shah Jahan, son of Jahangir and Aurangzeb's father, had the image of a humane, love-stricken Mughal, thanks to his association with the Taj Mahal. But this is a historical hoax based on such dubious records that even a colonial historian like V.A. Smith could see through. He writes,

> Jahangir had raised no objection to the erection of new temples, which is opposed to strict Muhammadan law.

> Shahjahan now resolved to put a stop to the practice, and gave orders that 'at Benares, and throughout all his dominions in every place, all temples that had been begun should be cast down. It was now reported from the province of Allahabad that seventy-six temples had been destroyed in the district of Benares'. No record of the destruction in other parts of the empire has been preserved, but it must have been considerable.[22]

If Hindu persecution resumed under Jahangir, it gained momentum under his son, Shah Jahan. This is what his biographer, Abdul Hamid Lahori, had to say about Shah Jahan in *Badshahnama:*

> It had been brought to the notice of His Majesty (Shah Jahan) that during the late reign many idol temples had been begun, but remained unfinished at Benares, the great stronghold of infidelism. The infidels were now desirous of completing them. His Majesty, the defender of the faith, gave orders that at Benares, and throughout all his dominions in every place, all temples that had been begun should be cast down. It was now reported from the province of Allahabad that 76 temples had been destroyed.[23]

Today as our eminent distorians romanticize the Timurids, especially the reign of Shah Jahan, often calling it the 'golden era', one must realize how famines were the order of the day then. There was no food for the masses as Shah Jahan was busy collecting taxes for building the tomb for Mumtaz. Here, it needs to be emphasized that while the traditional Hindu rate of taxation was one-sixth of the farm produce, something which the Vijayanagar rulers too followed, most of the contemporary Muslim rulers, including the Timurids, sought as taxes more than half of what the peasants would produce.

Abdul Hamid Lahori adds,

> The inhabitants… were reduced to the direst extremity. Life was offered for a loaf, but none would buy; rank was to be sold for a cake, but none cared for it; the ever-bounteous hand was now stretched out to beg for food; and the feet which had always trodden the way of contentment walked about only in search of sustenance. For a long time dog's flesh was sold for goat's flesh, and the pounded bones of the dead were mixed with flour and sold… Destitution at length reached such a pitch that men began to devour each other, and the flesh of a son was preferred to his love. The number of deaths caused obstructions in the roads, and every man whose dire sufferings did not terminate in death and who retained the power to move wandered off to the towns and villages of other countries. Those lands which had been famous for their fertility and plenty now retained no trace of productiveness.[24]

As for Akbar, he began his rule at the age of 13 under the stewardship of Bairam Khan. He was incredibly lucky that in the Second Battle of Panipat in 1556 AD, a stray arrow hit the eye of Hemu, who was leading the army against the Timurids, thus scaling the balance of the war in favour of Akbar. Coming to Akbar's liberal outlook, there is no doubt his reign saw, for the first time since the establishment of the Muslim rule in Bharat, the state officially relinquishing its anti-Hindu stand—the most obvious sign of which was the abolition of the pilgrimage and *jizya* taxes in 1563 and 1564 AD, respectively, imposed on Hindus for visiting their pilgrimage centres and also remaining Hindus in an Islamic state. In the early 1560s, he also gave the Timurid dynasty a long-term stability by going in for matrimonial alliances with Rajput kingdoms of Rajasthan. It all began with Akbar marrying a Rajput princess from Amber in January 1562. Over the years, his association with the Rajput kingdoms increased.

As historian A.L. Srivastava writes, Akbar's Rajput policy 'was not the outcome of thoughtless sentiment or a mere chivalrous regard for their valour, generosity and patriotism', but the result of 'a deliberate policy, and was based on the principles of enlightened self-interest, recognition of merit, justice and fair play'.[25] Akbar could see unflinching loyalty and unwavering support that Rajput warriors like Man Singh gave to the Timurid emperor, which stood in sharp contrast to the questionable allegiance of Muslim generals.

One can gauge Akbar's understanding of the Rajput psyche and also his respect for the new relationship from the following conversation: Soon after the marriage of the daughter of Raja Bhagwan Das to Jahangir, it is said that when Bhagwan Das was seeing off his daughter, he told Akbar, '*Mhari re beti thare mahion ki cheri, ham bandh ghulam re*' (My daughter is the maid of your palace, and we are your slaves). To which Akbar promptly replied, '*Thari re beti mhare mahlon ki rani, tum sahib sardar re*' (Your daughter is the queen of our palace, and you are [our] great lord).[26]

In the reign of Akbar, there were no less than 38 Rajput princesses married in the royal family—12 to Akbar, 17 to Prince Salim (Jahangir), six to Daniyal, two to Murad, and one to Prince Khusrau (Shah Jahan).[27] There was bound to be a reaction to the presence of a large number of 'free-willed' Hindu women in the Timurid harem, given the fact that the Muslim ruling classes were conscious of their ethno-political superiority. If James Tod were to be believed, even Akbar became aware of the fact 'that his policy of strengthening his throne by Rajput alliances was not without hazard, these alliances introducing a direct influence in the state'.[28] No wonder, one sees a lesser number of marriages with Rajputs in the future with seven in Jahangir's time, five in Shah Jahan's, and nine in Aurangzeb's time.

The Rajput relationship remained the bedrock of Timurid rule in Bharat. But once Aurangzeb tampered with it, thanks to his untamed Islamist zeal, it hit the foundation of the empire, which collapsed like a pack of cards. Aurangzeb died in 1707 AD, and within 50 years the Timurid empire found itself confined to the area from 'Delhi to Palam'!

II

Towards the end of his life in 1707 AD, when Aurangzeb, then 88 years old, looked back at his life, all he could see was failure. From his deathbed in the Deccan, where he was stuck for the last 26 years of his life in his desperate attempt to quell the Maratha challenge and where he ultimately died in Ahmednagar, Aurangzeb wrote in a letter to one of his sons, Azam Shah:

> I came alone and I go as a stranger. The instant which has passed in power has left only sorrow behind it. I have not been the guardian and protector of the Empire. Life, so valuable, has been squandered in vain. God was in my heart but I could not see him. Life is transient. The past is gone and there is no hope for the future.[29]

During his 49-year-old reign, Aurangzeb took the Timurid empire to its maximum spread—from Afghanistan in the west to Bangladesh in the east and from Kashmir in the north to Tamil Nadu in the south. He was unstoppable in the first three decades of his reign. But the last two decades saw Aurangzeb squandering most of the gains he had made. He failed to be 'the guardian and protector of the empire'. Worse, after the rebellion of his son, Mohammed Akbar, he seemed worried about karma catching up with him. For what he had done to his father Shah Jahan and brothers, especially Dara Shikoh,[30] at the time of his accession, he was now worried about it being repeated during the last days of his life, if not immediately after his death. He, therefore, in his will, advised his three sons to divide the empire among themselves. But a genie once out of the bottle cannot be put inside so easily. Aurangzeb's sons too fought the war for succession.

At its prime, the empire had become too large to be ruled by one man, especially with Aurangzeb antagonizing almost everyone—from his allies to potential friends. As Jadunath Sarkar writes, Aurangzeb, 'like the boa constrictor, had swallowed more than he could swallow'.[31] The Rajputs were anyway unhappy by his overt anti-Hindu policies in general, but Aurangzeb's pernicious attempt to take over the Marwar kingdom after the death of Jaswant Singh, who had valiantly fought for the Timurid empire in Afghanistan, infuriated them the most.[32]

It was, however, the Maratha challenge that did the maximum damage to the Timurid reputation. Napoleon Bonaparte used to say, 'It was the Spanish ulcer which ruined me.' The Deccan ulcer seemed to have ruined Aurangzeb.[33]

The Marathas, with their guerrilla warfare tactics, incessantly raided Mughal territory. The Maratha troops were light, fast and had the advantage of knowing the land too intimately to their advantage. Ghost-like, they were present wherever Aurangzeb's army moved in the Deccan. As Sarkar writes,

> They seemed to be ubiquitous and elusive like the wind. The movable columns frequently sent out from the imperial headquarters to 'chastise the robbers', only marched and countermarched, without being able to crush the enemy. When the Mughal forces had gone back, the scattered Marathas, like water parted by the oar, closed again and resumed their attack as before. There was an exultant and menacing Maratha army always hanging five or six km behind the emperor's camp wherever it marched or halted.[34]

The never-ending war with the Marathas took a heavy toll on the Timurid state and army. Sarkar adds,

> The wastage of the Deccan war, which raged intensely for nearly 20 years, was one hundred thousand soldiers and followers and three times that number of horses, elephants, camels and oxen on the Mughal side every year. In the imperial camp pestilence was always present and the daily mortality was heavy. The economic exhaustion of the Deccan was complete: the fields were left devoid of trees and bare of crops, their places being taken by the bones of men and beasts. The country was so entirely desolated and depopulated that neither fire nor light could be found in the course of a three or four days' journey? (Manucci)[35]

Aurangzeb could have easily avoided the Maratha disaster. He just needed to take a cue from his great-grandfather, Akbar, on how to deal with a difficult adversary. Beyond a point, Akbar would never make it a prestige issue. Even with Maharana Pratap, as the next segment of the chapter would show, he was desperate to win him over, first through diplomacy and then with arms, but when he realized the high cost of it all after almost a decade of incessant warfare, he chose to ignore him for good. Aurangzeb could do neither: he was neither tolerant nor generous; worse, he never stopped taking setbacks personally. The result was that he got stuck with an enemy—Marathas in this case—for 26 years, and only his death could free him from that.

Shivaji belonged to the Bhonsle clan of the Marathas, claiming its origin from King Porus (who fought Alexander) and the ranas of Udaipur.[36] (Interestingly, Shivaji's battle strategies resembled in so many ways Maharana Pratap's fight against Akbar's troops, as we shall see in the next segment of the chapter.) A look at the geography of the core Maratha land (or for that matter, the rugged region of Mewar) would explain why it produced such an incredible leader in Shivaji (Maharana Pratap in Mewar's case), and a class of people who refused to give in even in the face of insurmountable adversities.

Sarkar writes,

> The Maratha people's inborn love of independence and isolation was greatly helped by nature, which provided them with many ready-made and easily defensible forts close at hand, where they could quickly flee for refuge and whence they could offer a tenacious resistance. Unlike the Gangetic plain, this country could not be conquered and annexed by one cavalry dash or even one year's campaigning. Here the natives had the chance of making a long struggle against superior numbers and, it may be, of recovering their own when the invader was worn out.[37]

In fact, as early as in the 7th century AD, a Chinese traveller found the Marathas to be 'proud-spirited and warlike, grateful for favours, and revengeful for wrongs, self-sacrificing towards suppliants in distress and sanguinary to death with any who treated them insultingly'.[38]

Those born in the Maratha land, thus, were traditionally tough people. In fact, Jadunath Sarkar goes to the extent of calling it a society where 'nature enforces a Spartan simplicity'. There can, thus, be 'no luxury, no learned leisure (except among the priests), no aesthetic development, no polished manners even'.[39] Sarkar elaborates,

> The Marathas, when they rose to political power, did not impress the subject population favourably. To the over-polished decadents of the Mughal capitals, the warriors from the South appeared as a race of upstarts, insolent in prosperity, and lacking in grace, refinement and even good manners. They had no taste for the fine arts, no elegance of address, no aptitude for the amenities of social life. Even their horsemanship was awkward and graceless, though

> eminently practical. The period of Maratha ascendency has not left India richer by a single grand building, or beautiful picture, or finely written manuscript. Even the palaces of the Peshwas are low, mean-looking, flimsy structures, with small rooms and narrow staircases—relieved from utter insignificance only by their richly carved wooden facade.[40]

One may or may not agree with Sir Jadunath's assessment, but what is undeniable is the fact that Aurangzeb chose the worst possible adversary in Marathas in general, and Shivaji in particular. Had he known a little more about Shivaji and his people, he would have been more accommodating and forthcoming than what he was when Shivaji visited the court of Aurangzeb in Agra with his son Sambhaji after being forced to ink the Treaty of Purandhar by Raja Jai Singh on 12 June 1665 AD. As per the treaty, Shivaji agreed to cede 23 out of 35 forts to Aurangzeb, retaining only 12 for himself, besides acknowledging the suzerainty of the Timurid emperor and promising to serve him loyally in the Deccan.

Aurangzeb's 50th birthday on 12 May 1666, as per the lunar calendar, coincided with the day Shivaji was scheduled to arrive at the Timurid court. Ram Singh, Raja Jai Singh's son, and Fidai Khan were ordered to welcome and escort Shivaji to Agra. Due to a series of miscommunications and missteps, the arrival of Shivaji to Aurangzeb's court was delayed, and when he could finally meet the emperor, he found that his reception at the Timurid court was not what Raja Jai Singh had promised: Shivaji was made to stand 'before the emperor among Mughal noblemen, especially below the despised lackey Jaswant Singh, steeped in abject servitude'.[41]

He was raging with anger as Ram Singh approached him. Shivaji said, 'You have seen, your father has seen, your Emperor has seen what a man I am, and yet you have deliberately kept me standing! I cast off your *mansab*. If you wanted me to stand, you should have done it with proper thought.' Then he turned his back to the emperor and immediately began to walk away. Ram Singh tried to pacify him, but Shivaji refused to listen. 'The day of my death has arrived! Either you kill me or I shall kill myself! Cut off my head and take it there if you like; but I am not going into the emperor's presence again,' Shivaji said. Noticing the escalating situation, Aurangzeb asked Ram Singh to take Shivaji to his residence and conciliate him.

One oft-asked question is why Aurangzeb didn't try to use this excuse to get rid of Shivaji. There may be two reasons: One, Raja Jai Singh had personally pledged about Shivaji's security in Agra; the words of a senior member of Aurangzeb's court couldn't have been overturned so directly. The other, equally credible, reason could be Aurangzeb's duplicity to use Shivaji's presence in Agra, which was more like a house arrest, to gain access to the remaining twelve Maratha forts as well.

Sir Jadunath Sarkar believes that Shivaji's audience with Aurangzeb went wrong because of a series of missteps, the first of which, according to him, was Shivaji's late arrival at Agra. He writes: 'Shivaji could enter Agra only about noon on the 12th (May), and he had therefore to be rushed immediately to the fort for his audience, without being taught the court etiquette beforehand. This was the real seed of all the trouble that followed.'[42]

This seems to be too simplistic an assessment for someone as smart and shrewd as Shivaji. To expect that he had no idea about Timurid court etiquette would be naïve. The assessment of biographer Gajanan Bhaskar Mehendale seems closer to the truth. Quoting Mountstuart Elphinstone who criticizes Aurangzeb in his book, *The History of India, Vol. II*, for not suppressing his narrow religious views in his court, thus squandering 'an opportunity... of turning a formidable enemy into zealous servant', Mehendale wonders 'if a robe of honour and a place in the front rank of Mughal nobility would have induced Shivaji to give up his aim and become a Mughal *mansabdar*, a "zealous servant" of Aurangzeb!' Mehendale writes, 'Elphinstone certainly knew his Aurangzeb, but he had not understood the character of Shivaji.'[43]

If one looks at the agreement between Raja Jai Singh and Shivaji, it becomes apparent that the latter never accepted a *mansab* for himself but for his son, Sambhaji; he would, thus, have been spared from attending the Agra court. As Khafi Khan writes, 'Raja Jai Singh had flattered Shivaji with promises; but as the Raja knew the Emperor to have a strong feeling against Shivaji, he artfully refrained from making known the promises he had held out.'[44]

No wonder, when he reached the Agra court, Shivaji thought he was treated as a *mansab*, and that too below Jaswant Singh; he flared up. For Shivaji, the Purandhar treaty might have been a temporary arrangement provided him some respite to strengthen his hold in the region. Shivaji would have, at the time of his choosing, thrown off the Timurid yoke.

Soon, Shivaji with his son made a daring escape from Agra. Disguised as travelling mendicants and by taking a long circuitous route, he reached his capital Rajgad. His presence enthused the Marathas, and they regrouped as never before. Shivaji used this time to not just strengthen his hold in the region but also initiated several significant administrative and military reforms, including the system by which the army was raised and paid. Various sources give an account of his cavalry that ranged from 40,000 to 1,00,000 men.

The Maratha army travelled light, with three horses assigned for two riders. But his true genius, Jadunath Sarkar writes, 'as a born statesman' lies in 'his creation of a Navy and Naval bases'.[45] Beginning with 20 ships in 1659, the Maratha Navy had over 80 ships in the 1680s.[46] (In the next chapter, we will discuss the contribution of Kanhoji Angre in making the Maratha Navy a fearsome battle machine, incessantly defeating the British and Portuguese navies for over five decades.) Shivaji also took good care of his forts, which without a doubt were his strongest defence. Writes author Uday S. Kulkarni,

> By the end of his (Shivaji's) life he had 240 forts and it was said that if each fort fought for a year, it would take the Mughals many centuries to take this kingdom. Remarkably, in his entire reign no fort was lost to treason by his men.[47]

The Maratha journey towards *swarajya* took off in June 1674 when Shivaji declared himself an independent king with the title 'Chhatrapati', though he couldn't live long, and died at the age of 50 in March 1680. Soon after his death, Aurangzeb camped in the Deccan, and as fate would have it, he remained stuck in the south for 26 years till his death in 1707 AD. Kulkarni writes,

> By about 1705 the Marathas had won the Deccan simply by not losing. As in many guerrilla wars, the Mughal defeat was not the loss of any particular fort or town, but the loss of the will to keep chasing an enemy that struck and disappeared into the hills, or merged with the local population.[48]

Manucci, too, had observed something similar in 1704 AD:

> These (Maratha) leaders and their troops move in these days with much confidence, because they have cowed the Mughal commanders and inspired them with fear. At the present time they possess artillery, musketry, bows and arrows, with elephants and camels for all their baggage and tents... In short, they are equipped and move about just like the armies of the Mughuls... Only a few years ago they did not march in this fashion.[49]

Our eminent distorians would like us to believe that the British took over Bharat from the Timurids, but the fact is long before the English could establish themselves as political masters in this country, the Marathas were already the *numero uno* power, thanks to leaders like Baji Rao I (1720–40), the greatest of the Peshwa who remained undefeated despite fighting more than 40 wars across the country. No wonder, when Afghan ruler Ahmed Shah Abdali[50] invaded Bharat in 1761, he wasn't challenged by a Timurid ruler in Delhi, but the Marathas whose 'Hindu Pad-Padshahi' at one time stretched from the Afghan border in the west to Orissa coastline, and from Punjab in the north to Tamil Nadu down south. And it took the British three Anglo-Maratha wars, the last one being fought between 1817 and 1819, to finally take over the country's reigns.

III

If Shivaji had a role model to look up to before challenging Aurangzeb, it would without a doubt be Maharana Pratap. In every possible way, Pratap first came up with a manual to deal with the imperial Timurids: hit and run, never engage in a pitched battle, and never be bothered about 'running away' from the battlefield in order to keep the larger war going. As R.C. Majumdar writes,

> The Maharana loses battles, but never gives up the principle for which he stands—independence, and he regains for posterity the soul of India The great Shivaji will be proud to claim him as his ancestor, and the revolutionary movement in Bengal in the twentieth century will draw inspiration from his untiring fight against foreign domination.[51]

Pratap became the king of Mewar in 1572 AD, at a time when the Rajputanas were witnessing a major transformation in their relationship with the Timurids. A number of prominent Rajput families went into matrimonial alliances with Akbar and his family. The Sisodia dynasty of Mewar not just refused to have any matrimonial relationship with the Timurids but also vowed to keep its independence intact. The Maharana's decision to keep the banner of fight alive even when Chittor had seen a massacre of epic proportions in 1568 AD, just four years before his accession to the Mewari throne was creditworthy.

Also, the illustrious history of Mewar must have stopped Uday Singh II and his son, Maharana Pratap, from going in for any alliance with the Timurids. The Sisodias saw themselves as the descendants of King Rama of Ayodhya, calling themselves 'Suryavanshis'. The clan had once been known as Guhila, named after one of their ancestors, Guhaditya, who had grown up in a cave among the Bhils in the mid-sixth century AD. As per Mewar's traditions, Guha ruled around 568 AD.

The next high (or low) point in Mewar's history came in 1303 AD, when Rawal Ratan Singh and his men perished resisting Alauddin Khilji's forces in Chittor for eight months. All the womenfolk, led by Padmavati, Ratan Singh's beautiful wife, committed *jauhar* (self-immolation) to safeguard their honour.

In around 1326 AD, Prince Hammir, hailing from the immediate collateral branch of the Guhilas that had its seat of power at Sisoda, took over Chittor and revived the fortune of Mewar. Hammir, in fact, took on Mohammed bin Tughlaq, whose armies were completely routed by the Mewar troops, and even the sultan was taken prisoner for three months and could be released on a bond of Rs 5 lakh and a promise to never interfere with Mewar's politics. The ruling clan thereafter preferred to be called Sosodias and the king called themselves rana or maharana, and not Rawal, as was the case earlier.

Mewar reached its zenith of power under Maharana Kumbha who ruled between 1433 and 1468. During his time Mewar remained undefeated even when the powerful sultans of Malwa and Gujarat joined hands to launch a simultaneous attack. Maharana Kumbha was also a master builder: out of the 84 fortresses for the defence of Mewar, 32 were built by Kumbha alone, including the famous Kumbhalgarh Fort, which has under its name the Guinness World record for being the longest fort wall in the world.[52]

Be that as it may, the fact remains that Pratap had an illustrious legacy to abide by when he came to the throne. And given the strength and preparedness of the Mewari army in the battle of Haldighati in 1576 AD, it's but obvious that Pratap, in the first four years of his reign, used every moment to prepare for the fight against the Timurids: he raised a strong army, besides getting the support of Afghans like Hakim Sur Pathan and the neighbouring Bhils, who fought alongside Maharana Pratap in Haldighati. It was especially the support of the Bhils that let the Maharana wage the much-effective guerrilla warfare against the Timurids after the battle of Haldighati.

The battle of Haldighati was fought on 21 June 1576. The first flush of Rajput attack, led by the Maharana, broke through the Timurid army, and the rout could only be stopped by the timely rumour that Emperor Akbar himself was fast approaching the battlefield. After inflicting massive strikes, the Maharana left the battle on the advice of his generals to keep the war running in the future.

The battle was so closely fought that at one point some Muslim commanders, in the panic of the moment, shot their arrows indiscriminately on the Rajputs, whether they belonged to the imperial ranks or formed a part of the Maharana's army. At this moment, Badayuni curiously asked a commander how the imperial Rajputs and the Maharana's men were being differentiated. The officer was brutally frank in his reply and declared: 'Let them experience the whiz of arrows be what may; for, to whichever side they may belong, their being killed will be a gain to Islam!'[53]

One can gauge the level of Mewar's planning (including the Maharana leaving the Haldighati battle) and preparedness from the fact that after the battle, Man Singh, the general of Akbar's army, could find no trace of Pratap, his family or his nobles. Actually when Man Singh reached Gogunda, the Maharana's temporary capital, the day after the battle, the town was deserted.

Such was the terror of Maharana's army that the Timurid troops barricaded the streets in Gogunda and dug a trench and a wall of such a height that horsemen could not leap over it. But their plight was not done yet. The Maharana cut all supplies to Gogunda, and soon the Timurid *amirs* (nobles) 'were reduced to killing their horses for meat, the only other food available being mangoes and wild fruits that grew with Gogunda—and not enough of those either'.[54] Even this did not last long. There were skirmishes and the Mughal losses therein compelled Man Singh to forbid even this means of rationing his armies.[55]

It wouldn't have happened without meticulous planning and preparation. After all, from the Haldighati battlefield the Maharana had rushed to Gogunda, collected his family, found an inaccessible hideout, and then organized his men and begun to harass Akbar's army. As professors Lloyd I. Rudolph and Susanne H. Rudolph write in the introduction to Kesri Singh's milestone book, *Maharana Pratap: The Hero of Haldighati*,

> Pratap... did not flee the battlefield in a manner inconsistent with the Rajput ethic. His withdrawal was strategic as well as tactical, both deliberate and planned. Rana Pratap...

> did not 'lose' the battle, as partisans of Akbar or Raja Man Singh want to claim. But neither did he win. As Kesri Singh so felicitously puts it in his Haldighati essay: 'The field no doubt remained with Man. But for the emperor's army no victory was ever more like defeat; for Mewar, no retreat more glorious.'[56]

No wonder Akbar was not happy with the results of Haldighati. He was vexed with Man Singh for 'having abandoned the pursuit of the Rana, and so allowing him to remain alive'.[57] Man Singh, Asaf Khan and Qazi Khan were called back, with the first two even excluded for some time from the court.

Akbar continued to send expeditions to Mewar to subdue the Maharana, but each time, the Rajput forces after making strategic retreats, would make a comeback. Even almost a decade later, in 1585, Akbar sent an expedition under Raja Jagannath, who attempted to surprise the Maharana. However, the latter got timely information, and when Jagannath reached his residence, he found it empty. Interestingly, Abul Fazl remarks: 'From foresight they (the raiding Timurid troops) did not judge it proper to return by the same way, and so proceeded towards Gujarat.' This indicates that the mountain passes and roads were under Maharana's control so as to strike terror in the Timurid army.

The Maharana's sense of generosity and fair play too won over the Timurids. On one occasion, Prince Amar Singh, Maharana's son, attacked a Mughal camp and captured the wife and children of Abdul Rahim Khan-i-Khana, who was then the governor of Ajmer. When the Maharana learnt about this, he admonished Amar Singh and told him to immediately release them with respect. Indebted, the Khan-i-Khana would later write in praise of the Maharana:

All is unstable in this world
Land and wealth will disappear
But the virtue of the great name lives forever
Patta (Pratap) abandoned wealth and land
But never bowed the head
Alone of all the princes of Hind
He preserved the honour of his race.[58]

The Maharana died in a freak accident during a hunting expedition in 1597 AD. Such was his aura that even a poet in Akbar's court, Dursa Adha, couldn't stop himself from writing an obituary praising Pratap:

You did not let your horses be branded by the imperial seal,
Your turban remained unbowed before all.
Songs of your valour were sung far and near…
Pratap-si(ngh), on hearing of your passing
The Shah (Emperor Akbar) has bitten his tongue
And let out his breath slowly,
While tears are welling up in his eyes.
Behold, your victory O Guhilot Rana.
Indeed, you have won (the ultimate round).[59]

Rajasthani records say Akbar generously rewarded the poet for the composition. This was the Maharana's ultimate victory.

IV

If Shivaji was inspired by Maharana Pratap, the former, in turn, influenced a military general in faraway Assam. The Ahom general closely followed the exploits of the Maratha warrior in the Deccan and used his tactics to stop the march of Aurangzeb's army in the northeast. Interestingly, the similarity didn't stop here: while Raja Jai Singh was sent by Aurangzeb to defeat Shivaji, the former's son, Ram Singh, led the Timurid army to Assam. In fact, a powerful group in

Aurangzeb's court had even accused the father–son duo of helping Shivaji escape the Agra Fort prison in 1666.[60]

The Ahom general in question was Lachit Barphukan, about whom author S.K. Bhuyan writes:

> Lachit was a contemporary of Shivaji Maharaja, and like the latter stemmed the advance of Mogul imperialism in his land. In fact, the Assamese hero's great antagonist was a person most intimately associated with the turning point in the career of the Maharatta empire-builder, and his presence in Assam at the head of a formidable army was the outcome of the part he had played in that connection. Besides, we have evidence to prove that Shivaji's successes at one time had supplied an additional incentive to the Assamese to organise an effective opposition to Mogul aggressions in Eastern India.[61]

In a letter to the king of Cooch Behar on 7 February 1666, the then Ahom king Chakradhwaj Singha wrote:

> You have sent the verbal message informing me that war had commenced between Shewa (Shivaji) and the Moguls, and that Shewa having defeated the Moguls has pushed them back to a distance of twenty days' march; that Daud Khan has fallen, and Dilel (Dilir) Khan is wounded, and that the Badshah has come from Delhi to Agra. It cannot be predicted as to who becomes vanquished and who becomes victorious. You have further informed me that you are engaged in putting your forts and dikes in order; and you have asked us to strengthen our fortifications and to train our soldiers… Because the Moguls have humiliated us once, does it follow that we should make no attempt to throw off this position of subordination to them? They have discomfited us once, and we have dealt them severe blows on repeated occasions, and of this fact you are fully conversant.[62]

The result was the decisive Ahom victory against Aurangzeb's army at the Battle of Saraighat in 1671 AD. Such was the shattering blow to the Timurid troops in Assam that it never attempted another military adventure in the northeast. This victory 'stopped the Muslim flood from penetrating' into the other northeastern states and also 'into Burma and beyond in a wave of aggressive warfare and conquest... Otherwise the history of Burma and Indo-China might have been different.'[63]

Still the battle of Saraighat, in which the Timurids were decisively defeated in Assam under the leadership of the Ahom general Lachit Barphukan, remained a largely unknown and un-talked-about saga in Bharat's history.

The Ahoms were among the longest-running dynasties in the country, being in power for almost 600 years. It all began in 1228 AD when a group of Shan or Tai warriors, led by Sukapha, left their home in Myanmar and travelled to upper Assam. Here they established the powerful Ahom empire, which continued to rule till it was annexed by the British in 1826 AD.

Assam was attacked several times, without much success, by the Delhi Sultanate. Its successor, the Timurid dynasty, too kept its ambition alive to conquer Assam. The first such invasion took place in 1615 AD when Jahangir was the ruler and it ended in a disaster for the Timurids. After a brief respite, the hostilities resumed during Shah Jahan's time. The independence of eastern Assam remained intact through the Ahom rule, but western Assam kept changing its rulers from Ahoms to Kochs and even Timurids. In December 1636, Shah Jahan's troops crossed the traditional eastern boundary for the Timurids (Manaha river) to occupy Kamrup. According to the Treaty of Asurar Ali, between the Ahoms and the Timurids in 1639 AD, the whole of western Assam, beginning with Guwahati, passed into Shah Jahan's hands.

However, when the Timurid dynasty faced a succession war among Shah Jahan's sons, led by Aurangzeb, this gave the Ahoms an opportunity to regain the lost western portion.

When Aurangzeb became the emperor, he assigned Mir Jumla to invade Assam in 1662 AD. Jumla found the Ahoms badly divided and imposed a humiliating treaty in January 1663, following their defeat: the Ahoms were again forced to cede western Assam to the Timurids. They also promised a war indemnity of Rs 3 lakh and 90 elephants, and an annual tribute of 20 elephants. What further added to their disgrace was the only daughter of the Ahom king Jayadhwaja Singha was forcibly picked for Aurangzeb's harem.[64]

All this while Jayadhwaja Singha was hiding at Chorai-Khorong in Namrup in the foothills of the Naga Hills. This wasn't the first time an Ahom king took refuge in or near Naga Hills—and this was not supposed to be the last one either. Almost a century later, an Ahom prince, Godapani, too, went into hiding in the Naga Hills to escape being hunted by a rival claimant to the throne. He even married a Naga girl of the Konyak tribe. Later, Godapani ascended to Ahom throne in 1681 AD with a new name of Godadhar Singha. The Nagas would also recruit themselves in large numbers in the Ahom army.

The close relationship between the Ahoms and the rest of Bharat (as we see in the case of the Ahoms eagerly following the exploits of Shivaji) as well as the Ahoms and the Nagas busts the myth of the northeast's, especially the Nagas', splendid isolation. Reading the Naga folktales and folklores reveals a sense of civilizational oneness. It was actually a British colonial mischief to, first, bracket these people out of the Hindu fold by calling them 'animists', and then to further divide them between the valley and the hills. Unfortunately, Bharat's political leadership post-Independence blindly followed this divisive policy of splendid isolation of the northeast.

Prof. B.B. Kumar, in the *Tribal Societies of India*, quotes the Census of 1921, as saying: 'Animism as a religion should be entirely abandoned, and all those hitherto classed as Animists should be grouped with Hindus'.[65] Even sociologist Herbert Risley found 'no sharp distinction' between Hinduism and animism.[66]

Their folklores, too, share a similar story: of one people, with an overarching civilizational unity. Prof. Kumar, in another book, *Folklores and Folklore Motifs*, invokes several local legends that hint at common cultural, civilizational continuity. As per a Naga story,

> (a) God known as Jillmasa had connection with a cloud, and as a result of that god, tiger and three others namely Asapu, Tuthoh, and Kepi were born. Asapu and Tuthoh went to the valleys of Brahmaputra and Manipur, respectively. Kepi stayed there. The three became the ancestors of Mayangs (Indians), Meitheis (Manipuris), and Huas (Nagas), respectively.[67]

Kumar also recounts an Angami (Naga) story that says that the Nagas and the plainsmen were,

> the descendants of two brothers and their followers, who used Chombu and Chemu trees to lighten their paths. The former gave light for several days, but not the latter. Thus, most people who followed the brother using Chombu tree for blazing the path went to the plains. The ancestor of the Nagas was the second brother.[68]

According to another Angami legend, Nagas and Teprima (Indians) are the descendants of Ukepenopfu and her wise husband, who had a long moustache and beard reaching down to his feet. 'He imparted all his knowledge and wisdom to the younger son, who became the ancestor of Teprimas. The elder one (i.e., the ancestor of the Nagas) was frightened to see him and ran away and thus remained poor in knowledge and wisdom.'[69]

Coming back to King Jayadhwaja Singha, he came out of hiding and started regrouping the Ahoms for retaliation once the Timurid troops left. He also reached out to the rajas of neighbouring Cooch Behar, Jaintia, and Chachar to build a grand alliance against the Timurids. Sadly, he could not seek revenge and passed away in November 1663. Since he had no offspring of his own, he was succeeded by his uncle's son, Chakradhwaj Singha, who invoked a meeting of his advisers and generals in 1665 AD to expedite the process of expelling the Timurids from western Assam. But his prime minister, Atan Buragohain, stepped in with a request not to hurry without adequate preparations.

> His Majesty (Chakradhwaj) has only voiced the sentiments of his ministers when he declares that we should fall upon the Moguls this very moment if possible. But we must provide the army with sufficient quantity of food provisions and war materials, and must hold in stock sufficient reserve to enable us to replenish the stores of the expeditionary army as soon as they become empty. This task of supplying reinforcements will become a matter of frequent occurrence.[70]

The king enquired publicly in the court about the quantity of war materials deposited in the royal arsenal. He was told that there were plenty of provisions in the store. But when the king was alone, he was informed about the sorry state of affairs: 'We do not possess even a single box of gun-powder. As regards shots and pellets we have not got in store even four boxes, nor do we possess even a stack of arrows.'[71]

The Ahoms used the next two years in preparing for the big war, not just replenishing the arms and weapons needed for the army, but also strengthening the navy (another similarity with the Marathas) given the vast riverfronts that surrounded the kingdom. Also, the army organization was reset, making it a lean, efficient war machine.

The Ahom army was ready to strike by the summer of 1667. On 20 August, it sailed downstream the Brahmaputra river in two divisions under the command of Lachit Barphukan, who was accompanied by Atan Buragohain. After offering prayers at the holy Kamakhya temple, they began their offensive against the Timurids. Within two months, the Timurid forces were completely routed and pushed out of Guwahati and west Assam. The Ahoms, however, knew the bigger Timurid offensive was round the corner.

And it did come sooner than later. Raja Ram Singh, son of Raja Jai Singh, was given the task of leading the Timurid army. It was more like a punishment posting for him, given his alleged role in the escape of Shivaji from the Agra jail.[72] In fact, Aurangzeb had placed several Muslim generals with Ram Singh, with the orders to keep a close watch on the Rajput general and do the needful, if ever the latter thought of switching sides in the war against the Ahoms.

Ram Singh was well aware of Aurangzeb's subterfuge. But then saying no to the emperor was equally dangerous. On his family's advice, he consulted guru Tegh Bahadur. 'It is certain death to command the invading army', he told the ninth Sikh guru, 'but it would be equally fatal to me to disobey the emperor's orders.' To this, the guru advised him to take the Assam assignment, and also decided to accompany the Rajput general.[73]

Taking a cue from the Maratha style of guerrilla warfare, the Ahoms under Lachit used the Assamese topography to their advantage to launch a hit-and-run battle strategy. Lachit knew very well that the Ahoms stood no chance in a pitched battle, but at night amidst the uncertainties of a jungle and on the Brahmaputra waters, they had a definite edge.

The Ahom's guerrilla strategy annoyed the Timurid forces so much that Ram Singh sent an emissary to Lachit, saying: 'Do you know what our commander-in-chief calls such dirty tactics? He calls them "thieves' affairs". Only thieves steal into a house at night to commit mischief.' To this, Lachit replied, 'Ah, that is our way of fighting… You see only tigers fight at night.'[74]

After a series of battles, which saw fortunes shifting sides, the two sides finally met at Saraighat in March 1671. As fate would have it, the Ahoms had it tough initially, with Lachit falling severely ill. But as is often the case with great leaders, Lachit, when he saw things not going his way, chose to fight in that condition. This galvanize his followers, and the Ahoms dealt a mortal blow to Aurangzeb's hegemonistic ambitions. The Timurids faced a complete rout and their forces had to retreat from Guwahati and western Assam.

Lachit summed up to his soldiers the reasons that would ultimately push the war in the Ahoms' favour:

> We have an advantage over Raja Ram Singh. The Mughal commander is fighting under compulsion. We can note by the nature of his war tactics that his heart is not in this campaign. You and I, on the other hand, are fighting for king and country, as are our officers and men. Our passion will give us ultimate victory.[75]

Ram Singh, too, was quite impressed by the Ahom attitude, courage and strategy. He said: 'Glory to the king! Glory to the counsellors! Glory to the commanders! Glory to the country! One single individual leads all the forces! Even I, Ram Singh, being personally on the spot, have not been able to find any loophole and opportunity!'[76]

7

White Mischief

The Predatory Nature of British Rule in Bharat

I

Nassim Nicholas Taleb begins his book, *The Black Swan*,[1] with the story of 'an unassailable belief' in the 'Old World' that 'all swans were white'. The belief was 'confirmed by empirical evidence'. But then the sighting of the first black swan in Australia after the continent's discovery in 1606 AD reversed the conventional understanding, showcasing 'a severe limitation to our learning from observations or experience and the fragility of our knowledge'. Taleb writes, 'One single observation can invalidate a general statement derived from millennia of confirmatory sightings of millions of white swans. All you need is one single (and, I am told, quite ugly) black bird.'[2]

What does the black swan phenomenon suggest? It tells us that once in a while an outlier event takes place that would be beyond the 'realm of regular expectations'. Such a highly improbable event, however, would have an extreme impact, though once the incident is over, the human mind would come up with explanations suggesting it wasn't random after all!

Very few people would have believed in 1913 that the world was so close to a world war. When the Berlin Wall fell in 1989, it came as a surprise; so was the collapse of the erstwhile Soviet Union in 1991. No one would have predicted the United States going into a war in Afghanistan a day before the terrorist attacks on the Twin Towers in 2001. But howsoever surprising these events might have been, they all ended up with immense consequences and impacts.

The rise of British rule in Bharat was one such black swan event. No one saw it coming, but when it happened, there were countless theories explaining the same. As we discussed in the previous chapter, the 18th-century Bharat belonged to the Marathas, and unlike what our eminent distorians would want us to believe, the British took the country from the Marathas, and not the Timurids. And this rivalry began not with the First Anglo-Maratha War in 1775 AD, but from the early 1700s itself.

The initial battles were largely fought on the waters of the Arabian Sea. And the man who kept the British, along with the Portuguese and the Siddis of Janjira, high and dry in the narrow, but strategically significant coastal strip of Konkan, was Maratha general Kanhoji Angre, who took forward Shivaji Maharaj's vision of a strong navy being the foundation of a strong state. As historian Jon Wilson writes:

> The first British victory in its 50-year sea war against the Marathas occurred in 1755 but by then Kanhoji Angre had died, and his sons had fallen out of favour with the Peshwa, the chief administrator of the Maratha regime. The Company only defeated the Angres because, by then, they fought as allies of the Maratha regime.[3]

If in the initial years of the 18th century, 'any of the foreign powers along the coast of Konkan had been asked to nominate a common enemy ... [t]heir answer would have been the same: Kanhoji Angrey!'[4] Such was the Kanhoji phobia that the British 'dug a ditch around the town in Bombay as a protection against him, and then they erected a wall behind the ditch'.[5] They even joined hands with their bitterest rivals, the Portuguese, but the Maratha strongman managed to push them back.

Not much is known about Kanhoji's initial life. Clement Downing, a contemporary English sailor who disparagingly called him 'Angria the Pirate', traced Kanhoji's ancestry to an 'Arabian Cofferey (Arab's kafir), one that renounced the Mahometan Faith'.[6] One finds several such claims of dubious origins, especially from his adversaries, but according to his family lore, Kanhoji was a Maratha Kshatriya with the original surname of 'Sankpal'. It was only after his ancestors settled in the village of Angarwadi near Poona that the surname of Angre (or Angria) was adopted by them.

Kanhoji is believed to have been born around 1669 AD, and was eight years old when his father kept him under the guidance of a Brahmin guru in a village in today's Ratnagiri district. As per a Konkani folktale, Kanhoji once fell asleep while herding his guru's cows. When he didn't return home on time, the guru went looking for him and saw a five-headed cobra guarding the boy's head from the scorching midday sun. This convinced the guru that kingship was in store for Kanhoji, and he started giving him education befitting his destiny. Later, the guru asked Kanhoji what he would give him if the prophecy came true. 'Anything you ask', the young boy said. 'All I ask for is the field I now cultivate for the landlord; the field and the orchard surrounding it'. Kanhoji promised and, if the folktale is to be believed, he did fulfil his promise later.[7]

Whatever be the veracity of the story, there's no denying that the guru gave the boy a good education. Kanhoji didn't just become one of the best maritime commanders of his era, but also was equally adept in the art of diplomacy (as one saw when he successfully put a wedge between the British and the Portuguese when the two rivals joined hands to fight the Maratha general) and fluent in Sanskrit scriptures.

During his growing years, Kanhoji is said to have developed a friendship with Balaji Vishwanath, who later rose to the position of Peshwa. This friendship was tested later when the two found each other on different sides of the Shivaji family: while Vishwanath supported Shahu Maharaj, who had spent most of his childhood in Aurangzeb's prison and was released only after his death in 1707 AD, Kanhoji continued to side with Tarabai, the wife of Rajaram, who became the king after Shahu was locked up in the Timurid prison. It took Vishwanath a personal visit to Kanhoji and also a lot of persuasion to make him switch loyalties in favour of Shahu.

Kanhoji's father, Tukoji, had served under Shahaji, the father of Shivaji Maharaj. Later, Tukoji worked under Shivaji too, who made him a commander in his fleet. His father's presence must have introduced Kanhoji very early in his life to the Maratha navy, where he rose to become an illustrious general.

Kanhoji's tussle with the British began as early as in 1702 AD, when he seized a private trading merchant ship that had six Englishmen on board. Next year, in retaliation, the British detained in Bombay a ship from Aden, loaded with cargo, even when it had Kanhoji's *dastak* for passage. The Maratha strongman didn't react immediately. Instead he waited for over a year, after which, in November 1704, he sailed with seven armed boats and camped at the mouth of the Pane river near Bombay. His troops stayed put there for a week, without firing a single shot. As his objective was to just choke Bombay and thus hurt the Company's maritime activity, the message was loud and clear: Don't mess with Kanhoji.

As we see, the battle of supremacy between the Marathas and the British began on the seas and it continued for most of the 18th century—and till the mid-1750s, Kanhoji's forces had an upper hand over the British and also the Portuguese. Interestingly, the Portuguese and British forces were, on their own, superior to the Maratha navy. What, then, explains the success of Kanhoji's troops against the much superior British and Portuguese navies? It was sheer understanding of one's strength and weaknesses—and, of course, Kanhoji's adroitness in utilizing the available resources to his advantage. The Marathas, for instance, since the days of Shivaji, had built forts at strategic locations on hills as well as coastal areas. These were strong, well-provisioned forts that complemented the lean and mean naval forces they had.

Author Uday S. Kulkarni writes about the Marathas' naval strategies:

> The Maratha strategy of capturing an enemy ship was to fire and destroy the masts of the ships by keeping astern of these ships. Once the European ships became immobile in water, they were boarded and taken charge of. By staying astern of the European ships, they were not vulnerable to being fired at a broadside.[8]

The *Ajnapatra* tells us more about the Maratha naval war.[9] It writes:

> Navy is an independent limb of the state; just as a king's fame for success on land is in proportion to the strength of his cavalry, so the mastery of the sea is in the hands of him who possesses the navy. Therefore a navy should necessarily be built.[10]

The Maratha royal edict has a few pieces of advice on how to fight naval battles too. It writes,

> The ships (Ghurabs) should be neither too large, nor too small. Make separate commands of groups of ships with a commander for each. If the navy and the hostile ships meet each other and begin fighting all should strive to join in the fight. The enemy should be put on the leeside… Owing to the force of the wind if the enemy does not fall on the leeside and we fall on the leeside and our ship is not able to move with the help of the wind, then, whatever may be our strength, without coming into contact with the enemy and gradually cutting off our contact from the enemy, our fleet should be brought under the protection of a sea-fort. The safety of ships and sailors should never be risked.[11]

Kanhoji died in 1729 AD. He was succeeded by Sekhoji, who continued to keep his ties with the Peshwas, then under Bajirao I, intact. Sekhoji died early in 1734 AD, but his sons—Sambhaji Angre, Manaji Angre and Tulaji Angre—decided to cut their ties with the Peshwas. Sambhaji, in fact, rendered no assistance to the Peshwas even when the whole Maratha country was engaged in an intense battle with the Portuguese during 1737–39 AD.[12]

It was this division between the Peshwas and the Angres that led to the first naval defeat for the latter against the English in 1755–56 AD. In this battle of Vijaydurg, Tulaji was defeated by the British with the support of the Peshwa. Tulaji's armada was burnt and he was made a prisoner for life. It is truly tragic to see the family of Kanhoji being exterminated by the British with the help of the Peshwa.

This internal divide gave the British an opening. Sixty-three years later, the Marathas under the Peshwas too lost the country to the British after the Third Anglo-Maratha War (1818–19).

II

In December 2022, when *Al Jazeera* came up with an article stating that British colonialism killed more than 100 million people in Bharat between 1880 and 1920 AD, it created a sense of outrage and disbelief.[13] One thought the article would create a serious debate and discussion in the country on not just those 40 years but also how one of the oldest civilizations met with a series of cataclysmic and existential assaults in the past 1,300 years.

But then the story died down.

Given this nature of mass amnesia, it is a matter of sheer good luck that Hindus didn't go the Persian, Greek or Roman way. Maybe they were just too many to be killed or converted. Maybe they were too decentralized and 'scattered in all directions like the atoms of dust', to use Alberuni's words,[14] to be stormed and destroyed at once—and yet there was an innate sense of unity pervading the utter chaos that Hinduism would appear from the outside. Maybe our intellectual and martial classes didn't let down the civilization the way it has been projected to us. And, maybe the so-called lower castes didn't join the invaders the way our eminent distorians would make us believe. In fact, as Prof. K.S. Lal explains, the so-called lower castes, instead of meekly surrendering to Muslim invaders—some distorians go to the extent of saying that they welcomed the Arabs when they first invaded Bharat—actually fought the invaders with vigour and strength when the class of 'traditional Hindu warriors, mostly Rajputs, stood exhausted by the time of the Mughal invasion, having fought the earlier invaders at every step for well-nigh eight centuries'.[15]

Taking into account all the available details, Prof. Lal comes to the conclusion that about 60 to 80 million Hindus died between 1000 and 1500 AD.[16] Now add to them the exploits of Babur, who after one of his victories got 'a tower of infidels' skulls' being 'erected on the hill on the northwest side of Chanderi'—and this wasn't an exception during his four-year rule in Bharat. Things hardly improved for Hindus thereafter. Even during Akbar's largely nonpartisan rule, the Chittor massacre of 30,000 Rajput civilians, including women and children, took place soon after the Timurid victory.

But then we forgot—or were made to forget by our eminent distorians—those battles. However, they remained deeply etched in our popular imagination, and in our folktales and folklores. Interestingly, the mainstream historiography is deeply divided on the horrors of Islamic and European atrocities in Bharat. While a section of historians would whitewash the Islamic barbarism but write in detail about European cruelties, there are scholars who love painting a largely rosy picture of the Raj.[17]

If one takes *Al Jazeera*'s 100 million casualties in 40 years to be true—there's no reason to disbelieve this—it would not be an exaggeration to say that more than 200 million people died or were killed under British rule. And this would be a highly conservative number for the 190 years of British rule between 1757 and 1947 AD.

The British colonial history in Bharat began on a rapacious note in 1757 when the East India Company under Robert Clive defeated Siraj-ud-Daullah, the ruler of Bengal, in the Battle of Plassey. Such was the level of loot[18] and corruption that on his return to England, Clive took home £2,34,000 (over £23 million in today's time), and transferred to the Company's treasury no less than £2.5 million (£262.5 million today) seized from Siraj-ud-Daullah's coffers.[19] Worse, the Company officials resorted to the worst-possible predatory measures in collecting exorbitant taxes from farmers. This came at a time when Bengal was facing a terrible famine after missing two consecutive monsoons.

Combined with British loot and 'shaking of the pagoda tree', Bengal, during the famine of 1770, saw the death of an estimated 10 million people, which was a third of the total population of the region. W.W. Hunter, a civil servant who in 1871 became the first director general of statistics, writes in *Famine Aspects of Bengal Districts*, 'Five in every 16 were officially admitted to have perished.'[20]

American philosopher and historian John Fiske, in his 1876 book, brings out the horror of 1770:

> Throughout the entire course of recorded European history, from the remote times of which the Homeric poems preserve the dim tradition down to the present moment, there has occurred no calamity at once so sudden and of such appalling magnitude as the famine which in the spring and summer of 1770 nearly exterminated the ancient civilisation of Bengal… The Black Death of the 14th century was, perhaps, the most fearful visitation which has ever afflicted the Western world. But in the concentrated misery which it occasioned the Bengal famine surpassed it, even as the Himalayas dwarf by comparison the highest peaks of Switzerland.
>
> All through the stifling summer of 1770 the people went on dying. The husbandmen sold their cattle; they sold their implements of agriculture; they devoured their seed-grain; they sold their sons and daughters, till at length no buyer of children could be found; they ate the leaves of trees and the grass of the field; and in June, 1770, the Resident at the Durbar affirmed that the living were feeding on the dead…
>
> The extent of the depopulation is to our Western imaginations almost incredible. During those six months of horror, more than ten millions of people had perished! It was as if the entire population of our three or four largest States—man, woman, and child—were to be utterly swept away between now and next August, leaving the region between the Hudson and Lake Michigan as quiet and deathlike as the buried streets of Pompeii…

> This unparalleled calamity struck down impartially the rich and the poor. The old, aristocratic families of Lower Bengal were irretrievably ruined. The Rajah of Burdwan, whose possessions were so vast that, travel as far as he would, he always slept under a roof of his own and within his own jurisdiction, died in such indigence that his son had to melt down the family plate and beg a loan from the government in order to discharge his father's funeral expenses... The wealthy natives who were appointed to assess and collect the internal revenue, being unable to raise the sums required by the government, were in many cases imprisoned, or their estates were confiscated and re-let in order to discharge the debt...
>
> For fifteen years the depopulation went on increasing... From lack of cultivators, one-third of the surface of Bengal fell out of tillage and became waste land... In 1789, Lord Cornwallis, after three years' vigilant inquiry, pronounced one-third of the company's territories in Bengal to be a jungle, inhabited only by wild beasts.[21]

Even the East India Company's own officials reported about the misery on the ground. One Mr Alexander, the supervisor of Bihar, wrote about the 'extremity of immediate distress' and that 'each day lost in deliberation adds to the calamity'.[22] Mohammed Ala Khan, the foujdar (judge) of Purnea, in today's north Bihar, wrote to Calcutta, saying, 'hardly a day passes without 30 or 40 people dying'.[23] An aumil (collector of revenue) of Jessor wrote about people eating tree leaves and selling their sons and daughters. Most shockingly, the resident of the durbar (of Murshidabad) reported that 'in several parts the living have fed on the dead'.[24]

At a time when people were dying in hordes in Bengal, the Company officials not just did nothing to provide them respite but, worst, 'the revenue assessment was increased by 10 per cent during the height of the famine and there were several accusations of British collusion in the inevitable hoarding and profiteering'.[25] The British indifference could be gauged from the fact that 'only £9,000 was expended on relief by government'.[26]

Warren Hastings, who became the governor general of Bengal, in 1772 AD, too, did nothing but exploit the poor. Widely regarded as someone who studied and admired Bharatiya culture, and under whom several Orientalists, including Sir William Jones, found liberal patronage, Hastings[27] lived a two-faced life: while he admired and studied Bharat's ancient past—unlike Clive, he not only spoke good Bengali and Urdu but also fluent court and literary Persian—he did pretty little to improve the situation of famine-hit Bengal.

Hastings, at a time when Bengal lost so many people, wrote to the Court of Directors on 3 November 1772 with a sense of contentment about raising revenue taxes in the province. He wrote: 'Notwithstanding the loss of at least one-third of the inhabitants of the province, and the consequent decrease of the cultivation, the net collection of the year 1771 exceeded even those of 1768'.[28]

Hastings also mentioned how revenue taxes were 'violently kept up' by the Company, but never once did he show any repentance for the dead and the dying! In 1770–71 AD, in the midst of the Bengal famine, a staggering £1,086,255 was transferred to England, equivalent to nearly £120 million in today's times.[29] Ironically, British author Philip Mason finds the same Hastings to be the next best thing to have happened to Bharat after Akbar. He writes, 'Since Akbar no one of his stature had walked the Indian state'.[30]

Author Sumanta Banerjee explains this Dr Jekyll and Mr Hyde personality of Hastings thus:

> He... represented the complex combination of sensitive literary and artistic tastes with ruthless administrative

> policies. His forte combined specialisation in oriental classical literature with an expertise in the most savage criminal methods to promote the East India Company's interests, as well as his own career, displaying in both capacities an equally intense passion… Hastings seemed to have smoothly moved in and out from his role as a connoisseur of oriental classics to that of a rapacious felon of the highest order.[31]

In fact, if British control of Bharat started with a famine in Bengal in 1770, as fate would have it, it ended with a famine—again in Bengal—in 1943.[32] Ironically, even the last famine, whose man-made nature can be understood from the fact that a series of decisions by Winston Churchill, the then British prime minister, 'directly and inevitably led to the deaths of some three million Indians', as Madhusree Mukerjee writes in *Churchill's Secret War*. 'The streets of eastern Indian cities were lined with corpses, yet instead of sending emergency food shipments, Churchill used the wheat and ships and his disposal to build stockpiles for feeding post-War Britain and Europe,' she adds.[33]

If this was the situation in Bengal, which was the richest province during the Timurid era, aptly described by Aurangzeb as 'the paradise of nations',[34] one can gauge the situation of other provinces as the Company extended its territorial wings across the country. Famines spread from Bengal to across the country as the Company Raj spread itself territorially. Author Cornelius Walford calculated that in the 120 years of British rule there had been 31 famines in Bharat, compared with only 17 recorded famines in the entire previous two millennia.[35]

Apart from the wanton, rapacious loot that allowed Company officials like Clive to become one of the wealthiest men at the age of 33, institutionally too, the East India Company acted like a predatory organization caring to just extort more and more revenue taxes even when people were in no position to pay them. Bishop Heber wrote in 1826 that 'the peasantry in the Company's provinces are, on the whole, worse off, poorer, and more dispirited than the subjects of the Native princes... No Native prince demands the rent we do'.[36]

In the past, too, there were attempts to heavily tax the masses, especially in the mediaeval times, but they never had the wherewithal to collect the rentals. The British zealously ensured the taxes were collected even when people were in no position to pay them. Such was the predatory nature of the British Raj that even technological innovations such as the railways were largely used to exploit the country's natural resources, draining them out for the unquenchable appetite of British factories. Bharat was first de-agriculturized and then de-industrialized. Its only usage was to become the raw material supplier for British industries in the West, obviously at throwaway prices.

The fate of the textile industry in Bharat is a case in study. Handloom fabrics from the subcontinent were in demand in the West from Roman times and as late as the mid-18th century, the country's textiles were being exported across the world, including Europe. Bharat had a one-fourth share of the global trade in textiles in the 18th century. But post-Plassey, this was destroyed. So much so that Lord William Bentinck, the governor general of Bengal between 1828 and 1834, observed that 'the bones of the cotton weavers were bleaching the plains of India'.[37]

Shashi Tharoor rips apart the apologists of the Raj who say that Bharat's textile industry would, in any case, have not survived the Industrial Revolution. Questioning this line of thinking that says that 'if they hadn't collapsed to British power, the weavers would have been replaced within fifty years by Indian textile mills using modern machinery'.

Tharoor says, 'It is plausible that, in due course, handlooms would have found it difficult to compete with mass-produced machine-made textiles, but they would surely have been able to hold on to a niche market, as they do to this day in India.'[38]

Bharat's fall was dramatic. In the beginning of the 18th century, the country generated almost a quarter of the world economy—24.4 per cent to be precise. A century later, in 1820, it went down to 16 per cent, to fall again to 12.1 per cent 50 years later. In 1913 AD, Bharat's share of the world GDP was 7.5 per cent, which by the time the British departed shrunk further to 4.2 per cent.[39]

Famines, however, weren't the only killing machines. The country saw hundreds of rebellions, climaxing with the Revolt of 1857, against the British, most of which were crushed with an iron fist. The kind of upheaval British rule created in Bharat led to widespread discontent and rebellions. From the Rangpur peasant uprising of 1783 AD in Bengal to the Bareilly rising of 1816 AD, and from the Cole outbreak of 1831–32 to the Santhal insurrection of 1855–57, the country had seen hundreds of popular rebellions. The 1857 rebellion, in that way, was the apogee of native protests against the Raj.

The Revolt of 1857 was the outcome of the changing socio-economic conditions, but the leading factor was political, which had its origin in Lord Dalhousie's policy of annexation of native princely states, such as Oudh, Maratha, Jhansi and even Delhi.

In this phase of anger and uncertainty, the issue of greased cartridges came up. Many sepoys believed that the cartridges that were being used with the new rifle were greased with pig and cow fat, angering both Muslims and Hindus. The issue first blew up when Mangal Pandey, a sepoy in the 34th Bengal Native Infantry regiment of the East India

Company, refused to use the greased cartridge and attacked British officers on 29 March 1857. This was followed by a mutiny of sepoys in Meerut, about 60 km northeast of Delhi, on 19 May 1857. Soon these sepoys reached Delhi, freeing it from British control and announcing Bahadur Shah Zafar as the leader of the rebellion. Others such as Rani Lakshmibai, Nana Saheb, Tatya Tope, Begum Hazrat Mahal and Kunwar Singh joined the rebellion from their respective places.

There have been efforts to colour the Revolt of 1857 as per one's prejudice: while the British merely confined it to being a sepoy rebellion, the nationalists led by Veer Savarkar called it the 'First War of Independence'. A closer look at the event, however, suggests something in between, where the rebellion was guided as much by the love of the land, tradition, culture, and religion, as it was driven by one's personal grievances and ambitions.

In fact, the religious aspect was often too overwhelming to ignore. William Dalrymple writes:

> By the time Padre Jennings was cut down, one of his two star converts had also been killed. Dr Chaman Lal had been attending to his patients at his hospital in Daryaganj when the sawars first charged through the Rajghat Gate. Hearing the uproar, he had gone out of the hospital to investigate, whereupon he was pointed out by the people in the street. Immediately, 'one soldier pinned him down, sat on his chest, and asked what religion he was. When Dr Lal replied that he was a Christian, the sawar shot him dead at point blank range with his pistol. The cavalry then ransacked and burned the clinic'... British men and women who had converted to Islam were invariably spared, yet all Indian converts to Christianity—Hindu or Muslim—were sought out and hunted down. While Chaman Lal was one of the very first victims, as were

> Jennings and his two missionary assistants—both cut down as they ran to escape along the Chandni Chowk—an Anglo-Indian Christian named Mrs Aldwell managed to save herself because she knew the *kalima*, the Islamic profession of faith, and told her captors that she was a Muslim. The soldiers replied that if they were to kill a Muslim 'they would (themselves) be as bad as infidels; but that they were determined on killing all the Christians'.[40]

In his study of the Revolt of 1857, R.C. Majumdar hardly finds any nationalistic fervour and patriotic incentive to set free the country from the foreign yoke. He writes:

> The Muslims in Hyderabed were excited by the events of North India and developed strong anti-British feeling, but they were more hostile to the Marathas and would have gladly fought under the British against Holkar and Sindhia, The Sikhs hated the Mughuls, and joined the British in order to prevent the restoration of Mughul rule under Bahadur Shah. It is on record that high British officials in the Panjab were able to persuade the Sikhs to cast in their lot with them by describing in vivid language the injuries and insults they had suffered in the past in the hands of the Mughul Emperors. Having impressed this point on their mind, they held out before them the grand opportunity they now had of taking full vengeance. There can be hardly any doubt that the Sikhs were largely influenced by such considerations in wholeheartedly offering their services to the British Government. There are good grounds to believe that the same spirit alienated the Rajputs and the Marathas, as they, too, for historical reasons, did not favour the restoration of the Muslim rule. It is to be noted that none of the Rajputs and Maratha Chiefs responded to the invitation of Bahadur Shah, and all the propaganda in Maharashtra was carried on in the name of Nana. These

> considerations, as well as the fact that by far the greater part of India was free from any overt act of hostility against the British Government, divest the outbreak of 1857 of a 'national' character.[41]

Majumdar also puts forward the examples of Sanyasi (1770s), Wahhabi (1837–65), Santhal (1855–56), and Pindari rebellions and says that these uprisings carried similar characteristics to those of 1857. Thus the latter was in no way different from what had already been witnessed in different parts of the country. Majumdar's assessment was thus quite scathing: the 'First War of Independence' was neither the first nor a war of independence.[42]

The conduct of its supreme leader, Bahadur Shah Zafar, too exposes the nature of the rebellion. While there are apologists who sanitize his role during the Revolt of 1857,[43] his conduct from the very beginning was dubious, to say the least.

When the sepoys from Meerut took over Delhi, Zafar was like 'the king on the chessboard after the checkmate', as nobleman Abdul Latif put it:[44] if he joined the rebels, he would invite the British fury, and if he didn't, the rebel won't take it gracefully. He, therefore, played it safe: while Zafar agreed to lead the rebels, he also kept a line of communications open with the British. Majumdar writes, 'Not only had Bahadur Shah no confidence in the sepoys or sympathy for their cause, but even after he had joined them he maintained his loyalty to the British.'[45] He also sent out letters to various British military officers, for example, to the lieutenant governor of Agra, treacherously revealing the location and other details of the sepoys in Delhi.[46]

The British reconquest post-rebellion was marked by wanton, indiscriminate violence. There seems to be a consensus for vengeance in British society. Such was the polarized milieu that even Charles Dickens, who warmed our hearts with *Oliver Twist*-like tales, had this to say on the Great Mutiny: 'I wish I were commander-in-chief in India… I should proclaim to them that I considered my holding that appointment by the leave of God, to mean that I should do my utmost to exterminate the race.'[47] Thomas Macaulay too noticed the British nation's 'one terrible cry for revenge' but was, he felt, 'half ashamed only half ashamed, for the craving for vengeance which I feel'. Macaulay wrote, 'I could be very cruel just now if I had power'.[48]

Post-rebellion, Delhi was one of the most brutal sites of revenge. At least 200 suspected rebels were hanged from gallows in the centre of the city without trial. Bahadur Shah Zafar was promised no harm if he gave himself up. But then, after being captured, he was found guilty of treason and exiled to Burma for the rest of his life. His two sons were summarily shot. Worst of all, the entire city was ransacked and looted at the Company's behest. Only those who could provide evidence of loyalty to the British escaped the state-sponsored terror. Jon Wilson quotes an observer from nearby Mhow saying, 'No one ever thought that the capture of Delhi by Englishmen would be attended with more cruelty to the general population, than that by a Nadir.'[49] Afghan ruler Nadir Shah had attacked and plundered Delhi in 1739 AD. After the Revolt of 1857, Delhi became a very different city, as the city's 300-year history as the cultural capital of the Timurids came to an abrupt end.[50]

The looting of Lucknow was second only to the sacking of Delhi. So much so that the city, like Delhi, 'never regained its former glory, not even when it was made the capital of the North-Western Provinces, redubbed the United Provinces in 1902'.[51]

Other cities faced no less British wrath. Jon Wilson writes about the fate of Allahabad and Kanpur, for example:

> The 47-year old Scottish Brigadier General James Neill was author of some of the earliest, most brutal violence at Allahabad and Kanpur. Early in the war he hanged six supporters of Maulvi Ahmadullah on thin evidence, nervously writing about carrying out 'a duty I never contemplated having to perform'... on his march upcountry Neill killed indiscriminately, gunning down bystanders on the banks of the Ganges from his steamship and burning entire villages. Like other British soldiers, Neill justified cruelty with cruelty, believing that barbarity could only be stopped by reciprocal acts. As time passed Neill would deliberately offend Indian religious sensibilities. At the site of the Bibighur massacre he forced the men accused of rebellion to clean the blood of Europeans with their tongues before hanging them.[52]

Author Amaresh Misra has tried to come up with a toll number of the 'untold holocaust'. According to him, almost 10 million people had died over 10 years since 1857.[53]

In this backdrop, the estimated toll—that more than 200 million people had died or were killed during British rule—doesn't seem to be an exaggeration. We, as a nation, have neither holistically examined the predatory nature of British rule nor sought an apology, far less any accountability, for the omissions and commissions during that time. It was an era of wanton violence, which killed over 200 million people, and institutionalized loot that led to the drain of at least $45 trillion from Bharat to Britain between 1765 and 1938 AD.[54]

III

V.S. Naipaul, in *India: A Million Mutinies*,[55] tells us the story of Irish reporter William Howard Russell, who was in

Lucknow when the British laid the siege of the city after the Revolt of 1857. The invading British army largely comprised Scottish Highlanders and Sikhs. Russell was surprised to see the Sikh sepoys, who, less than ten years ago, were engaged in an intense war that led to the decimation of the Sikh empire in 1849 AD, fighting with purpose and intent for the East India Company against their own countrymen.

The rage with which the Sikh soldiers fought against the Oudh army even left Russell, otherwise a tough man who had seen and covered several battles, shocked. When it became obvious to the British generals that the defenders won't be going down without a fight, they asked their soldiers to step back and let artillery do the talking. Those who survived the shelling were then ruthlessly bayoneted by the Sikhs. In no time everyone but one person was killed.

What happened thereafter was particularly awful. Russell writes:

> one of their member was dragged out to the sandy plain outside the house, he was pulled by the legs to a convenient place, where he was held down, pricked in the face and body by the bayonets..., whilst others collected fuel for a small pyre, and when all was ready—the man was roasted alive!... The horror of this infernal cruelty was aggravated by an attempt of the miserable wretch to escape when half-burned to death. By a sudden effort he leaped away, and with the flesh hanging from his bones, ran for a few yards... he was caught, brought back, put on the fire again, and held there by bayonets till his remains were consumed.[56]

According to Naipaul, at the heart of the 'Sikh fierceness' lay the desire 'to get even with the Pandies' who had about a decade back helped the British defeat the Sikhs in Punjab. Also at play was the innate tendency among Sikhs to settle accounts with Muslims, having internalized the sufferings of their gurus who had to face heinous barbarity at the hands of the Timurid rulers.[57]

Maybe the Sikhs should have read Maharaja Ranjit Singh's life and times to know that the decline of his empire was a foregone conclusion. As the story goes, Maharaja Ranjit Singh was with an English cartographer who was showing him a map of Hindustan. 'What does the red colour stand for?', asked the maharaja. 'Your Majesty,' replied the Englishman, 'red indicates the extent of British possessions in the country.' The maharaja, then, looked at the map closely to find that the whole of Bharat except the Punjab was painted red. Pausing for a while, he remarked: '*Ek roz sab lal ho jaiga*' (One day it will all be red).[58]

Ranjit Singh knew at the height of his power that threats for Punjab would come from the British. If anyone, it was he who had the strength and the wherewithal to stop the British charge, but the maharaja dithered, even when the English made no secret of their design to take over Punjab. In fact, in 1809, they extended their frontiers from the banks of the Jumna to the Sutlej, taking all the Sikh chiefs of Malwa under their protection. The only time the maharaja refused to be bulldozed by the Company was when he shot down the proposal to have a British resident in Lahore.

It was, therefore, a matter of time, especially after the death of Ranjit Singh in 1839 AD, before Punjab merged with the British Raj. The maharaja was succeeded by weak rulers, and the troubles were further compounded by divided loyalties of the Sikh nobility, with several of them eager to play by the English rules. The two Anglo-Sikh wars saw the defeat of the Sikh empire on both occasions, though there were occasions when the British were on the verge of humiliating defeats. In 1849, the Sikh empire was finally merged with the British.

Noted author Khushwant Singh was aghast to see the Punjabis, within eight years of the annexation of the Sikh empire by the British, helping their erstwhile conquerors to defeat their Hindustani counterparts in the Great Mutiny of 1857.

> A new generation of Punjabis who disowned their past was born. Instead of having nostalgic regret over the passing of the last independent kingdom of India many, were proud to be the foremost in loyalty to the British Crown; instead of boasting of their forefathers' achievements in hurling back foreign invaders, they were pleased to be known as 'The Sword Arm of the British Empire'. Thus was the sponge of oblivion passed over the slate of history.[59]

General Sir John J.H. Gordon explains this with a touch of colonial superiority when he writes: 'As they fought for their Gurus and for their Maharaja, so they have fought for Britain. Loyalty is in their blood.'[60]

Looked at dispassionately, there are reasons for Punjab embracing the Raj so tightly. The most obvious being the very nature of Sikhism, having internalized the sufferings of its gurus who had to face insurmountable barbarity at the hands of Muslims.[61] So much so, to use Naipaul's words, it 'created in the believer the feeling of injustice and persecution, and perhaps even the wish to be persecuted'.[62]

This internalization of the sufferings made the Punjabis opt for a regime that had liquidated the Timurid and other Muslim dynasties. Also, the British used the Machiavellian divide-and-rule ploy to officially give the Sikhs a special status, thus providing them preferential treatment in services such as the army and the police, and also separate electorates. Under the British, they became the martial race of Bharat. This created a powerful bogey not just in favour of the British but also against Hinduism, with whom they historically shared '*roti-beti ka rishta*' (breaking bread together and giving daughters in marriage).

As Khushwant Singh writes,

> Sikhism is an offshoot of Hinduism. Punjabi Hindus regard Sikhs as one of them and till recently brought up one of their own sons as a Sikh, intermarried with Sikh families, worshipped in Sikh *gurdwaras* and recited the Gurbani which they could understand in preference to *slokas* from the Vedas, Upanishads or the Gita which they could not.[63]

Rebutting a new breed of Sikh scholars who bend backwards to prove Sikhism has little or nothing to do with Hindu practices, or balance it by bracketing Hinduism with Islam (as author Amandeep Sandhu has done with his 2019 book, *Punjab: Journeys Through fault Lines,*[64] where he says that Guru Gobind Singh 'raised an army to defend the society from the unjust oppressors, both Hindu and Mughal'), Khushwant Singh writes:

> All they need to be told is that of the 15,028 names of God that appear in the *Adi Granth*, Hari occurs over 8,000 times, Ram 2,533 times, followed by Prabhu, Gopal Govind, Parbrahm and other Hindu nomenclatures for the Divine. The purely Sikh coinage 'Wahe Guru' appears only 16 times.[65]

He also reminds how the *Adi Granth*, though an eclectic work with compositions of Hindu and Muslim saints, 'echoes the Vedanta through most of its 6,000 hymns'.[66]

Historically, Sikhs and Hindus lived together, dined together and even fought wars together. Guru Tegh Bahadur, the ninth Sikh guru, was a shining example. He died fighting against Aurangzeb's fanaticism for the cause of the Pandits of Kashmir. It so happened that in June 1675, a group of Kashmiri Pandits met the guru at Makhowal (Anandpur) and complained about being persecuted by Aurangzeb's men for their forced conversion into Islam. After much deliberation, the guru asked them to go back and tell their perpetrators that they were the disciples of Guru Tegh Bahadur, and that if the guru could be persuaded to convert, then they all would follow the suit. Aurangzeb immediately sent orders for the arrest of Guru Tegh Bahadur, who was soon brought in chains to Delhi along with five disciples: they were given the choice between Islam and death. The guru chose the latter and was tortured to death on 11 November 1675. His death was accompanied by the slaughter of his disciples: Bhai Mati Dass, Gurditta, Uda, Chima, and Dayala. In order to strike terror in the hearts of the Sikhs, Mati Dass was bound, in his standing position, between two pillars and cut into two with a saw like a log of wood.[67]

On his father's martyrdom, Guru Gobind Singh, the 10th Sikh guru, wrote:

> To protect their right to wear their caste-marks and sacred threads,
> Did he, in the dark age, perform the supreme sacrifice.
> To help the saintly he went to the utmost limit,
> He gave his head but never cried in pain.
> He suffered martyrdom for the sake of his faith.
> He lost his head but revealed not his secret.[68]

Guru Tegh Bahadur's execution created widespread anger both in Punjab and outside, as his supreme sacrifice was regarded by Hindus as a sacrifice to protect their faith. This changed the nature of Sikhism completely from being a pacifist, non-violent religion to one that calls for taking up arms to fight injustice.

It was, however, Guru Hargobind, the sixth guru and the father of Guru Tegh Bahadur, who actually began the transformation of Sikhism, seeing the fate of his father Guru Arjan Dev, the fifth Sikh guru, at the hand of Jahangir. The young Hargobind took the seat of his father with two swords girded round his waist—one symbolizing spiritual power, and the other temporal. 'My rosary shall be the sword-belt and on my turban I shall wear the emblem of royalty,' he said. It was Guru Hargobind who told his followers that he would welcome offerings of arms and horses instead of money. As a result, he had at his service 'eight hundred horses in his stables, three hundred troopers on horseback, and sixty men with firearms'.[69]

Guru Gobind Singh took the militarization of Sikhs to an altogether different level. He fought Aurangzeb till the end of his life and then passed the baton to Banda Bahadur. Khushwant Singh writes about the first meeting between the guru and Banda Bahadur, who was then a Hindu ascetic: 'The Guru caught the fanatic gleam in the hermit's eye and felt that in the spare frame of the ascetic smouldered the Promethean fire which could be fanned into a flame.'[70] He armed Banda Bahadur with five arrows from his quiver and gave him his own standard and battle drum. After Guru Gobind Singh's assassination in 1708 AD, Banda Bahadur shifted his base to Punjab and in a couple of years created a state for himself and the Sikhs. He retained his independent identity till his death in 1716 AD when he was cornered by the Timurid forces in the fort of Gurdas Nangal.

The Gurdas Nangal fort confinement continued for eight months. Such was the reputation of Banda Bahadur and his followers that it 'was feared that the garrison might, by a sortie en masse and by sacrificing themselves, secure the escape of their leader'.[71] The Timurids were also overwhelmed by the belief that Banda Bahadur, through supernatural powers, could turn into a dog or a cat to escape the fort. 'Thus every dog or cat they saw from their entrenchments was at once a target for stones or arrows.'[72]

As the confinement continued, the provisions within the fort began to run out. Soon, differences arose between Banda Bahadur and his right-hand man, Binod Singh, who with a small band slipped out of the fort under the cover of darkness, cut his way through the Timurid forces and escaped to the hills. Banda held on doggedly, but the situation deteriorated. There was no food left to eat. His men ate their horses, mules and even the forbidden oxen. Then dysentery broke out in epidemic form. The fort finally fell on 17 December 1715, after Timurid general Abdus Samad Khan offered to secure an imperial pardon if they submitted. He went back on his word soon after the gates of the fort were opened, ordering an immediate execution of over two hundred of the prisoners and filled 'that extensive plain with blood as if it had been a dish'.[73]

Banda Bahadur lived a braveheart's life and died as such too. Mirza Muhammad Harisi, an eyewitness to the procession in Lahore where Banda Bahadur and his men were presented *tamasha*-like, writes in *Ibrat Namah*:

> There was hardly anyone in the city who had not come out to see the tamasha or to enjoy the show of the extirpation of the accused ones. Such a crowd in the bazaars and lanes had been rarely seen. And the Mussalmans could not contain themselves for joy. But those unfortunate Sikhs, who had been reduced to this last extremity, were quite happy… with their fate; not the slightest sign of dejection or humility was to be seen on their faces. In fact, most of them, as they passed along on their camels, seemed happy and cheerful, joyfully singing the sacred hymns of their Scripture. And, if any one from amongst those in the lanes and bazaars called out to them that their own excesses had reduced them to that condition, they quickly retorted saying that it had been so willed by the Almighty and that their capture and misfortune was in accordance with His Will. And if anyone said: Now you will be killed, they shouted: 'Kill us, when were we afraid

> of death? Had we been afraid of it, how could we have fought so many battles with you? It was merely through starvation and want of food that we fell into your hands, otherwise you know already what deeds we are capable of.'[74]

If this were not terrible enough, Banda Bahadur's four-year-old son was cut into pieces in front of his eyes, and then his 'quivering liver' was pulled out and pushed inside the father's mouth, who stood stoically, waiting for his turn to die. So were his men who, as Ghulam Hussain Khan, the author of the *Siyar-ul-Mutakherin*, writes, '[N]ot only behaved firmly during the execution, but they would dispute and wrangle with each other for priority in execution.'[75]

The supreme sacrifice of Banda Bahadur and his men stirred the emotions of the people in Punjab. It impacted the Punjabis the same way the killing of Sambhaji angered and united the Marathas. In a way, the challenges faced by the Sikhs were way more daunting than those of Marathas. For, unlike someone like Shivaji or even Maharana Pratap, Banda Bahadur didn't have topographical advantages that could have provided him strategic retreat in times of distress.

The Banda Bahadur saga was another example of close Hindu–Sikh ties when a Hindu ascetic instantly became a member of the Sikh community at the call of Guru Gobind Singh. He lived and died for the Sikh cause.

The Hindu–Sikh divide, thus, is a colonial construct that was further accentuated by the vote-bank politics of the post-Independence era. Even during the time of Maharaja Ranjit Singh, whose kingdom was the last to be absorbed into the British Raj soon after his death, there was a strong civilizational–cultural unity between Hinduism and Sikhism. No wonder the Sikh maharaja, when it came to determining the future of the Kohinoor diamond, decided to donate it to Puri's Jagannath temple, rather than bequeathing it to one of his sons. Also, it was he who got the Kashi Vishwanath temple's crown covered with gold.

Sir Gokul Singh Narang summed up the Sikh phenomenon well when he wrote:

> The sword which carried the Khalsa's way to glory was undoubtedly forged by Gobind (Singh), but the steel had been provided by Nanak, who had obtained it, as it were, by smelting the Hindu ore and burning out the dross of indifference and superstition of the masses and the hypocrisy and phariseeism of the priests.[76]

IV

If the Marathas were the toughest of adversaries that the East India Company faced in the 18th century, it was Tipu Sultan of Mysore whom it detested the most. Post-independence, he has also been among the most controversial and least understood personalities in the country. The state of Karnataka, and with it the rest of Bharat, is deeply divided with one section hailing him as a freedom fighter and feting him with the annual Tipu Sultan Jayanti, promising to also build a 100-ft statue of Tipu Sultan;[77] while the other side looks at him as a self-confessed Islamist ruler who worked ceaselessly to either convert or kill non-Muslims during his reign.

For a generation grown up with Sanjay Khan's portrayal of Tipu Sultan based on Bhagwan S. Gidwani's hagiographical work—*The Sword of Tipu Sultan*[78]—it seems hard not to see the Mysore ruler as a repository of all things good. The makeover was clear and absolute. So much so that author Charles Allen, during his travels around Bangalore, found it difficult to distinguish between the real and the perceived sultan of Mysore. He writes,

> During my travels in the Bangalore region I was frequently surprised to hear local people speaking warmly of Tipu. I

> could understand why local Muslims admired him, even to the point of veneration as a saint and martyr. But what I found mystifying was that Tipu Sahib should be seen by wider sections of the general community as a patriot who fought and died in a vain attempt to halt British imperialism in India.[79]

The reasons can be found in the dubious role played by our eminent distorians post-Independence: they systematically extricated episodes of Islamist violence from the pages of history. Economic reasons were invented to explain, and even justify, Islamic invasion and violence. As for Tipu Sultan, he had an added advantage: of being an uncompromising adversary of the British, which helped our distorians give him a 'freedom fighter' makeover.

Celebrated Kannada author S.L. Bhyrappa, in his foreword to Vikram Sampath's book *Tipu Sultan: The Saga of Mysore's Interregnum (1760-1799)*, adds another dimension to this makeover saga. He writes:

> During the freedom struggle, *laavani* singers, who were skilled in oral renditions but often lacked formal education, used to sing with an instrument called *damadi*, exaggerating Tipu Sultan. Some Muslim merchants encouraged these singers by giving them money. Tipu's reputation grew largely due to his opposition to British rule. He was painted as a patriot and dramas were performed to praise him. The audience believed this false narrative as true history. Marxists, politicians concerned with vote banks, Muslim artists, drama writers and directors, filmmakers portrayed him as a national leader in post-Independence India. True history lost its life. I have often written and lectured that authors of historical novels have the moral responsibility to present historical facts without distortions.[80]

The real Tipu Sultan was a rabid Islamist who hated non-Muslims, especially Hindus. And he abhorred Kannada culture and language. The fact that the Muslims of Kerala and Tamil Nadu speak Malayalam and Tamil, respectively, while their Karnataka counterparts have switched to Urdu is a testimony to his success in imposing his Islamist agenda in the region he ruled with an iron fist. Tipu ensured that Farsi and Urdu were the only permitted mediums of instruction in his kingdom.

What also goes against Tipu's 'son-of-soil' image is the fact that he, after coming to power in 1782 AD during the Second Anglo-Mysore War, rampantly changed the original names of Kannada cities and towns. So, Mangalore was called Jalalabad, Brahmapuri became Sultanpet, and Kallikote was named Farookabad; similarly, Coorg became Zafarabad, and Mysore was named Nazarabad. Tipu Sultan was often in such a hurry to change these names that he often gave the same name to different cities, causing confusion on the ground.[81]

Tipu Sultan didn't just change the names of places; he also replaced his experienced Hindu officials with incompetent coreligionists; this especially hurt the state of Mysore in the financial department. M.G. Gopal, after a detailed study of Tipu Sultan's economic policy, writes:

> The Hindus, particularly the Brahmans, had great administrative experience and had long dominated the revenue department. They had, however, not always used their position, knowledge and experience for public end, but had grown avaricious and corrupt and had shown 'gross ingratitude to Hyder'. Hyder very wisely checked them by the institution of spies and by heavy punishment. Instead of checking them by constant inspection into their conduct, by exemplary punishment when detected… and by allowing them handsome salaries to raise them above temptation, Tipu 'entirely subverted the wise and economical system

> established by his father'. He had great aversion to non-Muslims... After 1792, therefore, he placed the faithful Muslims in most of the important offices like the asofdaries and amildaries. Of the diwans or provincial revenue heads in 1792 only one was a Hindu. Of 65 asofs and deputy-asofs in 1797–98, not one was a non-Muslim and almost all principal mutsaddis even were Muslims, while of the 26 Mysore civil and military officers captured by the British in 1793 and demanded back by Tipu, six only were Hindus and even they were petty clerks...
>
> The officials so appointed to posts requiring deep knowledge and great patience, writes a Muslim historian, could scarcely read and write. In the words of another contemporary of Tipu's, the candidates 'were seldom chosen for any other reason than their being Mohamedans'. Even as early as 1785, Tipu refers to one of his asofs as 'a stranger and inexperienced in business'. Even these inexperienced men were not chosen with due deliberation.[82]

Lewin B. Bowring, who served as the chief commissioner of Mysore between 1862 and 1870, gave a detailed account of Tipu Sultan's obsession with Islam and its impact on day-to-day life. He wrote,

> Measures of distance too were amended, the kos or Indian two-miles being now defined as consisting of so many yards of twice twenty-four thumb-breadths, because the creed (Kalmah) contains twenty-four letters. The kos thus fixed was 2¾ miles, and if the letter-carriers did not travel this distance in 33 minutes they were to be flogged. All the names of weights and measures were altered. But the most wonderful of his improvements was his new method of calculating time. As is well known, the Hindus counted time in cycles of 60 years, each year having a separate name, a system which makes their chronology somewhat difficult to unravel. Tipu founded a new calendar on this basis,

> giving however fantastic names to the years, and equally strange ones to the lunar months. The year, according to his arrangement, only contained 354 days, and each month was called by some name in alphabetical order. From the year 1784, all his letters were dated according to the day of one or other of the months in this new nomenclature.[83]

Tipu Sultan's hatred for non-Muslims was clear and categorical. Though eminent distorians and the ilk often refer to his opposition to the Nizam to showcase his secular, non-communal character, the fact of the matter is that he detested the latter as an apostate and called him a barber and the 'son of a worthless mother' for siding with the Marathas and the British.[84]

One can understand the nature and extent of Tipu Sultan's fanaticism when one reads *The Dreams of Tipu Sultan*, wherein the ruler of Mysore recorded and analysed 37 of his dreams. Here Hindus are invariably referred to as 'kafirs' and the British as 'Christians'. In the dreams, Tipu Sultan goes to Mecca on a pilgrimage; Prophet Mohammad assures him that he would not enter heaven without Tipu Sultan; and that the ruler of Mysore won't rest till he converts all non-Muslims to Islam and turns Har-ul-Harb into Dar-ul-Islam.

Tipu Sultan did fight the British, but this doesn't necessarily make him a freedom fighter. Vikram Sampath, his biographer, writes:

> In his long encounters with foreigners, we have seen that he was not averse to dealing with or even allying with them. His alternative idea of the Indian nation would have been no less colonial and imperialistic than the British, as he had the French as his allies and to whom, till the very end, he kept sending emissaries and solicitations. His open invitations to the Caliph of Turkey or the Afghans to invade India and establish a religious, pan-Islamist supremacy, positing

> himself as the true torchbearer of the faith was no majorly egalitarian view of how India might have turned out to be, had by a twist of fate Tipu Sultan been victorious. Straddling between French colonialism and orthodox Islamism of the virulent kind, India would have shaped into something totally unrecognizable and toxic.[85]

There were a few instances when Tipu Sultan did make—or at least appeared to have made—some donations for a few Hindu temples and institutions. But analyzed closely, they seemed more the case of confusion, distortion and superstition. In some cases, the tradition of donation from Hyder Ali's time continued, possibly many times without Tipu Sultan's knowledge. As for distortion, Sampath mentions how Tipu 'did present gifts to some temples'. He writes,

> Seven silver cups and a silver camphor burner in the Sri Ranganathaswamy temple in Srirangapatna bear an inscription stating that they were 'gifts of Tippu Sultana Paachchha'. But interestingly, three of these cups and the camphor burner also bear additional inscriptions on them stating that those articles were presented to the deity by one Kalale Kanthaiya who was mostly a contemporary of Chikkadevaraja Wodeyar—implying that these were donated several decades preceding Tipu. From this we might conclude that they were presented initially by Kalale Kanthaiya, carried away by Tipu later, and then regranted to the temple 'at the prayer of the devotees of the temple with his inscriptions newly engraved'.[86]

Tipu did make a few grants out of superstition. He was a highly superstitious person, and some Hindus used that to their advantage. Sampath quotes scholar Melukote Araiyar Sri Rama Sharma as saying how Tipu was once advised to 'leave three types of stones (meaning idols) in Mysore unmolested':

'Yeddha Kallu (standing stone), Biddha Kallu (fallen stone), Gundu Kallu (round stone)'. He was warned that if he ever attempted to desecrate these three, his regime would end.

> The Yeddha Kallu here was the standing idol of Cheluvanarayanaswamy in Melukote, the Biddha Kallu was the supine idol of Ranganathaswamy in Srirangapatna, and the Gundu Kallu was the round Shivalinga of Srikantheshwara Swamy in Nanjanagud. Particularly, the astrologers and Brahmin priests seem to have induced this belief very strongly in Tipu's mind, along with a kind of manic fear for the very word 'Ranga' or 'Ranganatha' in his mind.[87]

This may explain Tipu Sultan's generosity in granting gifts, shawls, vessels and elephants to the three shrines in Melukote, Srirangapatna and Nanjanagud.

Writing in *The Proceedings of the Indian History Congress* in 1944, A. Subbaraya Chetty, a teacher from Madras, lists a series of donations and grants made by Tipu Sultan.[88] Sampath examines the entries provided by Chetty and reaches the following conclusion:

> When one analyses the entries provided by Chetty, a few things emerge. The sources of several of these entries are merely stated as 'L.R. (local records)' by Chetty, without giving sufficient details of what these are. Conspicuously, the number of annual grants were quite high in 1782 which was when Haidar Ali was still ruling; he died only in December that year. From 1783 onwards, which was when Tipu Sultan assumed power, the number of annual grants does see a dip.[89]

Sampath continues:

> Chetty has added to the list sundry grants of life pension and so on to individuals (astrologers and physicians), as grants to temples. Curiously, even the case of the Anjaneya temple

> of Srirangapatna being converted to the Jama Masjid has been cited as a grant by Tipu! Some entries are actually of grants made to a dargah at Penukonda and Tonnur, and these two are cited as Hindu endowments. Some are appellate entries, as in redressal of a possible unfair confiscation of lands which, when contested by the affected party, was then restored to the original grantee. These, too, have been taken up as grants made by Tipu. Many grants are not borne out of any great love or respect for the Hindu religion but driven by fear and the insecurity of retaining his throne, instilled in him by the astrologers whom he wholly depended on. Also, interestingly, the entries almost end after 1792, which marked the conclusion of the disastrous Third Anglo-Mysore War. This seems to suggest that after the war and the manner in which there was large-scale internal sabotage, Tipu gave up hope of being able to win over the trust of the Hindus.[90]

In sharp contrast, his Islamist iconoclastic tendencies had been much more dominant, pronounced and unequivocal. During his 1789 Malabar campaign, for instance, when the Chirakkal Raja tried to stop Tipu from desecrating his family temple by offering him Rs 4 lakh and plates of gold with which the temple was roofed in return for its safety, the Mysore sultan laughed it off, saying all the treasures of the earth and sea given to him could not ensure the safety of the temple[91]—reminding us of a similar offer made by the priests of the Somnath temple to Mamud of Ghazni more than 750 years ago.

One can also look at the Omkareshwara temple in Madikeri, Coorg, to understand the hardship Hindus and their religious institutions had to endure under Tipu Sultan. The local Hindu ruler, sensing trouble for the temple, replaced its dome to ensure it looked like a mosque from afar. The temple continues to retain this mosque-like appearance to this day.[92]

Mangalore, Malabar and Coorg were the epicentres of Tipu Sultan's religious cruelties. In Coorg, such has been the hatred for him that even today street dogs are contemptuously called 'Tipu'. Sandeep Balakrishna writes,

> The atrocities that he and his soldiers committed on the innocent citizens of a place he captured were truly horrifying. Apart from looting the conquered territory comprehensively, Tipu used to horribly torture and kill innocent people en masse; those who managed to survive were forcibly converted to Islam. Indeed, he had formed a separate unit of horsemen named Khazakh dedicated to this very purpose.[93]

A Portuguese missionary named Fra Paulino da San Bartolomeo, then based in Cochin, wrote about Tipu's Malabar exploits:

> That barbarian Tipu Sultan tied the naked Christians and Hindus to the legs of elephants and made the elephants to move around till the bodies of the helpless victims were torn to pieces. Temples and churches were ordered to be burned down, desecrated and destroyed. Christian and Hindu women were forced to marry Mohammadans and similarly their men were forced to marry Mohammadan women. Those Christians who refused to be honoured with Islam, were ordered to be killed by hanging immediately. These atrocities were told to me by the victims of Tipu Sultan who escaped from the clutches of his army and reached Varappuzha, which is the centre of Carmelite Christian Mission. I myself helped many victims to cross the Varappuzha River by boats.[94]

Tipu Sultan was particularly harsh on Nairs whose 'obscene' sexual mores he found 'more shameless than the beasts of the field'. In 1788, he issued a proclamation ordering the Nairs to forsake their sinful practices, with the threat that he would 'honour the whole of you with Islam' if they failed to obey him. When his threat had little or no impact, he attacked them. The result according to him was that more than four hundred thousand Hindus were converted to Islam.[95]

The numbers given by Tipu Sultan seem to be exaggerated, yet there is no denying that Nairs suffered immensely during his reign. Shashi Tharoor recalls his family history to vindicate the kind of suffering Tipu Sultan inflicted on the Hindus of Kerala. Recounting how he descended from 'two Palakkad families, one who invited Tipu Sultan to attack Palakkad (father's side of the family) and the other (mother's side) who lost their fortune' due to his attack, he writes:

> For my mother's family, the Mundaraths of Elavanchery (also in Palakkad district), suffered a different fate with Tipu. The Mundaraths were the zamindars and rulers of Elavanchery and a large part of the surrounding countryside. When news came of the imminent invasion of Tipu into Malabar, the then Mundarath karanavar loaded all the family treasures—vessels, jewels, the gold ornaments of the women—onto several carts and took them deep into the countryside to bury them for safekeeping... The Mundaraths showed great prudence and foresight, including sending off two Mundarath women to some far-flung place in the hills so that if the family was massacred by Tipu's troops, the Mundarath bloodline would continue. Unfortunately for the Mundaraths, things did not go according to plan. By the time Tipu withdrew from Malabar (and was then defeated by the British), the karanavar had breathed his last, without confiding the secret of the location of his treasure trove to anyone. A frantic search was launched the moment it was safe to do so, but the family could not recover a single item.[96]

One last line of defence for Tipu Sultan is that he was demonized by the British. The shallowness of the argument can be gauged from the fact that the British account of Hyder Ali was quite warm and laudatory even when the latter was a more dangerous and successful adversary, having defeated the East India Company in the First Anglo-Mysore War, which gave him a definite edge in the second. Tipu Sultan, in sharp contrast, had no success against the British. The Company had no reason to praise Hyder Ali and demonize Tipu Sultan.

A historian's job is to neither sanitize nor de-sanitize a historical character. As Jadunath Sarkar and R.C. Majumdar would often say, a historian's job is to present facts as they are. And in Tipu Sultan's case, there is no doubt in saying that his Islamism overshadowed his every other characteristic. His Islamism invariably made him anti-Bharat, anti-Hindu and anti-Kannadiga. And this very Islamist predisposition also made him fight the British till the end.

Tipu Sultan died fighting on 4 May 1799 after the British troops stormed Srirangapatna early that day. By afternoon, the British flag was already hoisted on the ramparts of the fort. Tipu still tried to motivate his soldiers for one last fight. But it was too late by then. He was soon hit by bullets as he fell down from his horse. He was then placed in a palanquin but couldn't evade death as he encountered British soldiers.

Bowring writes about Tipu's last moments:

> Soon afterwards some European soldiers entered the gateway, one of whom attempted to take off his richly-jewelled sword-belt, when Tipu, sorely wounded as he was, made a cut at the man, and wounded him in the knee. The enraged soldier levelled his musket and shot him in the head, causing instantaneous death.[97]

After the fall of Tipu Sultan, the East India Company, under Governor General Lord Cornwallis, did one thing right: it handed it over to the Wodeyars, the original rulers of Mysore from whom Hyder Ali had usurped the power in 1761 AD after imprisoning Krishnaraja Wodeyar II.

8

Freedom at Midnight

Gandhi, Gandhians and the Roles of Revolutionaries

I

In 1948, a year after Bharat gained independence, R.C. Majumdar, the country's foremost historian, submitted a proposal to the government to write an 'authentic' and 'truthful' history of the freedom struggle, starting with the Revolt of 1857. His letters to the education ministry of Bengal and also the Union education ministry went unheeded. A couple of years later, he wrote to Rajendra Prasad, the then president of the country, who 'heartily took up the idea and wrote a very encouraging letter' to him. Maybe it was due to Dr Prasad's intervention, the Ministry of Education, in 1952, appointed a Board of Editors.

Majumdar shares this saga in the preface to his book *The Sepoy Mutiny and the Revolt of 1857*. He writes:

> It (Board) consisted of eight or ten (or more) members at different times, about one half of whom were historians, and the other half, politicians of the Congress school, with two staunch Congressmen as its Chairman and Secretary… As the Director, I had to prepare a draft of the proposed history for the consideration of the Board… As soon as I was engaged in

> preparing the draft, I realised the difficulty of writing history on a co-operative basis in a non-academic environment… It did not take me long to find out that the Secretary held very definite views about the outbreak of 1857, and was determined to get them incorporated in the proposed history. He held that 'in 1857 an organised attempt was made by the natural leaders of India to combine themselves into a single command with the sole object of driving out the British power from India in order that a single, unified politically free and sovereign state may be established. That attempt was conscious and deliberate'. We had frequent discussions on the subject, and though I could not induce him to keep an open mind on the subject, I did not mind very much so long as it was confined to a mere opinion. But then I found that he proposed to collect only those materials which support his point of view, as otherwise it would, to use his own words again, 'thoroughly upset our purpose'.[1]

Not long after this the Board of Editors was dissolved by the government on 31 December 1955. A year later, when the project was revived, Majumdar found himself removed from the board without being informed, and his place was given to a bureaucrat named Tara Chand.

Why was Bharat's foremost historian treated so disdainfully? One finds the answer in Majumdar's other book *History of the Freedom Movement in India, Volume 1.* In its preface, he writes:

> The official history of the freedom movement starts with the premises that India lost independence only in the 18th century and had thus an experience of subjection to a foreign power for only two centuries. Real history, on the other hand, teaches us that the major part of India lost independence about five centuries before, and merely changed masters in the 18th century… Political exigencies gave rise to the slogan of Hindu–Muslim fraternity. An

> impression was sought to be deliberately created that the Hindus and Muslims had already shed so much of their individual characteristics, and there was such a complete transformation of both and a fusion of their cultures that there was no essential difference between the two. Though every true Indian must ever devoutly wish for such a consummation, it was, unfortunately, never a historical fact. Sir Syed Ahmad, M.A. Jinnah and other Muslim leaders who never believed in it entertained more realistic views in this respect than either Mahatma Gandhi or Pandit Jawaharlal Nehru. To accept as a fact what is eminently desirable but has not yet been achieved, though perhaps attainable by prolonged efforts, is not only a great historical error, but also a political blunder of the first magnitude, which often leads to tragic consequences.[2]

As we see, Majumdar had shown the moral courage and intellectual integrity to not just stand up against the Nehruvian bluff on Hindu–Muslim unity but also write matter-of-factly that the two communities 'lived in two watertight compartments', with their distinct cultures and different mental and moral characteristics.[3] Even more importantly, the historian threatened to take the lid off the Nehruvian myth that Bharat's independence was predominantly, if not solely, the handiwork of Gandhian ahimsa (non-violence) and satyagraha. Majumdar writes:

> A number of revolutionaries had joined the Non-Cooperation Movement of Gandhi, but were disillusioned after its suspension. Many of them had rejoined the revolutionary groups whose main object was to keep alive the spirit of violence leading to armed rebellion against the British for achieving independence…
>
> As a matter of fact, Gandhi fully realised the growing influence of revolutionary ideas over young men, and it is

> not without good reason that the revolutionaries claimed that they practically, though indirectly, forced Gandhi to renew the struggle for freedom, in 1930 and again in 1942; for he feared that otherwise he would lose the leadership of the country and the initiative would pass into the hands of the revolutionary young men, Gandhi himself admitted that one of his motives in undertaking non-violent Satyagraha or Civil Disobedience was to ward off the evils he apprehended from the growing strength of the revolutionary ideas. In other words, he regarded his movement as a safety-valve for youthful energy and patriotic ardour which would otherwise flow through a different channel of a violent kind.[4]

Majumdar makes three big points: one, the country's independence was not the handiwork of Gandhian ahimsa (non-violence) and satyagraha alone. Two, the revolutionaries not just worked in their revolutionary silos but also under the overarching Gandhian cover to fight for freedom. The revolutionaries would form the backbone of a Gandhian movement, such as the Non-Cooperation Movement, and when Gandhi would call it off, they would do what they did best—openly go the revolutionary way! Three, more often than not, Gandhi would start a movement to contain the growth of revolutionary fervour—a sort of 'safety-valve for youthful energy and patriotic ardour' so that it didn't 'flow through a different channel of a violent kind'.

Also, those in the thick of things just before independence saw Bharat's freedom struggle differently. For them, Gandhi's role in the freedom struggle was 'm-i-n-i-m-a-l', as former British prime minister Clement Attlee told chief justice of Calcutta High Court Justice P.B. Chakravartti, who was then Bengal's acting governor as well, at the governor's mansion in Kolkata in 1956, slowly chewing out the word to make an instant, dramatic impact.[5] 'The INA (Indian National Army) activities of Subhas Chandra Bose, which weakened the very foundation of the British empire in Bharat, and the RIN (Royal Indian Navy) mutiny which made the British realise that the armed forces could no longer be trusted to prop up the British,' Justice Chakravartti quoted Attlee as saying.[6]

B.R. Ambedkar, too, reflected the same sentiment during his interview with the BBC in 1955. He wondered, 'I don't know how Mr Attlee suddenly agreed to give Bharat independence. That is a secret that he will disclose in his autobiography. None expected that he would do that?' However, based on his 'own analysis', Ambedkar believed that the 'national army… raised by Subhas Chandra Bose' could be the reason.[7] He said:

> The British had been ruling the country in the firm belief that whatever may happen in the country or whatever the politicians do, they will never be able to change the loyalty of soldiers. That was one prop on which they were carrying on the administration. And that was completely dashed to pieces.[8]

General Claude Auchinleck, the commander-in-chief of the British armed forces in the subcontinent, too conceded on 24 November 1945, in his letter to Field Marshal Viscount Wavell, how 'the present INA trials are agitating all sections of Indian public opinion deeply'. While saying that 'any attempt to force the sentence would have led to chaos in the country at large and probably to mutiny and dissension in the army, culminating in its dissolution', he also pointed out how the INA issue provided the Congress with 'an excellent election cry'.[9]

An Intelligence Bureau report on 20 November 1946, too, admitted that 'there has seldom been a matter which has attracted so much public interest and, it is safe to say, sympathy… this particular brand of sympathy cuts across communal barriers'.[10]

The role of the Congress party and the government, however, was dubious on the INA issue. Anuj Dhar, in *India's Biggest Cover-Up*, writes about Captain Hari Badhwar, a British military intelligence mole in the Congress. Captain Badhwar first joined the INA, then switched sides and finally gave evidence against the INA men during the Red Fort trials. 'It is a great shame that Badhwar should have led a comfortable life as a general in free India', writes Dhar, exposing the Congress' duplicity that found problems with recruiting INA men in the army but had no such inhibitions with those who were in bed with the country's enemies.[11]

According to Dhar, it was Captain Badhwar's internal report, highlighting overwhelming support among the masses for the INA, which encouraged the Congress to take up the Red Fort trials. Badhwar had sourced his information to Asaf Ali, a leading Congress Working Committee member who would later become free Bharat's first ambassador to the United States. 'This inflamed feeling forced the Congress to take the line it did', Badhwar told one of his handlers in the British military.[12]

Incidentally, in a private conversation in October 1946, Asaf Ali reportedly stated that his party 'would lose much ground in the country' unless it took up the INA case, while adding in the same breath that the INA men would be removed from the army and some of them might even be put 'on trial' if the Congress came to power.[13]

Things turned out the same way as predicted by Asaf Ali. The Congress did publicly fight the INA trial case, for which Nehru donned his barrister gown after three decades to join the lawyers' team led by Tej Bahadur Shapru and Bhulabhai Desai,[14] but once it came to power, it removed all INA men from the services and even put some of them on trial. The party, which was in the forefront in 1946, as per a *New York Times* report, 'to build up Bose as the George Washington of India',[15] went on an overdrive post-Independence to wipe out his memory. Overnight, he became untouchable—someone not to be invoked, remembered and, worse, celebrated.

Interestingly, Bose and Nehru were close to each other in the early 1930s, as young, charismatic left bloc leaders within the Congress. Bose, in fact, believed that he and Nehru 'could make history together'. But Nehru 'could not see his destiny without Gandhi'.[16] No wonder, in 1939, after the Gandhi-led Congress resorted to undemocratic means to undermine Bose's party presidency, forcing him to resign, Netaji accused Nehru of betraying him while he was being viciously targeted within the Congress at Gandhi's behest. Bose wrote,

> Nobody has done more harm to me personally, and to our cause… than Pandit Nehru. If he had been with us, we would have had a majority. Even his neutrality would have probably given us a majority. But he was with the Old Guard at Tripuri.[17]

But then it was too much to expect from Nehru to give up Gandhi for Bose. Nehru might have had ideological affinity with Bose, but with Gandhi it was familial. He was a father figure, more so after the death of Motilal Nehru on 6 February 1931. Post-Independence too, Nehru would slacken his ideological rigidity when his daughter, Indira Priyadarshini, was involved.

This wasn't unexpected given the kind of sheltered, protected life the young Nehru was given.[18] In 1928, his real father (Motilal Nehru) and the one who chose to become one (Mahatma Gandhi) ensured he became the Congress president. As Motilal Nehru's term as Congress president was about to end, the buzz was that either Sardar Vallabhbhai Patel or Subhas Bose would take over the party reins. But then Jawaharlal Nehru's mother, Swarup Rani, reached out to Gandhi. She wanted to see 'a king passing on the sceptre of the throne to his logical successor'.[19] The Mahatma, by acceding to a mother's heart, unwittingly set in motion the foundation of a dynasty that was to rule the country post-Independence.

Bose can, thus, be faulted for not seeing what was obvious: that Nehru would continue 'riding two horses', as Netaji himself wrote in his 'brutally frank' letter on 28 March 1939,[20] but when push came to shove he would invariably take refuge in familial shelter rather than ideological. On the Subhas Bose saga, Minoo Masani is even more scathing in his estimation of Nehru, calling him 'an opportunist who thought about his own position first and then about everything else'.[21]

Had Bose been 'alive' post-Independence,[22] he would have seen far worse. For all his sacrifices for the nation, he failed to find a mention in Nehru's 'Tryst with Destiny' speech. When the Constituent Assembly decided to put up a portrait of Gandhi in what became the Parliament House, H.V. Kamath, a member of the august house, pleaded to get the portraits of Bal Gangadhar Tilak and Netaji Bose placed there too; he was snubbed. Such was the antagonism for Bose that the Nehru dispensation got the Intelligence Bureau to snoop upon prominent Bose family members for 20 years between 1948 and 1968.[23]

Sugata Bose sums up the reception Netaji received under the Gandhi–Nehru dynasty. He writes,

> In free India, Bose was always regarded as a great popular hero; but official recognition of his stature was somewhat muted during the prime ministership of his rival, Jawaharlal Nehru, until 1964. Nehru's daughter, Indira Gandhi, admired Netaji for his courage and his vision. Yet the Indian

> National Congress, to which he had been twice elected president, truly acknowledged him as one of its own only during the 1990s, when under Narasimha Rao it ceased to be under dynastic control.[24]

Bose wasn't the only revolutionary to be ignored, targeted and even abused. In fact, if one has to choose one who ticked all three boxes mentioned above, the name of Vinayak Damodar Savarkar will top the list. He was the foremost among revolutionaries who had already caught the nation's imagination by the time Mahatma Gandhi was starting his political journey in Bharat. It is widely believed that Gandhi had Savarkar in mind when he wrote *Hind Swaraj*. Similarly, Savarkar's 1923 treatise, *Essentials of Hindutva*, was an intellectual potshot at the Mahatma and his pacifist philosophy.

Savarkar and Gandhi share interesting similarities. Both spent significant times outside the subcontinent—Gandhi in Britain and South Africa, while Savarkar in Britain first and then over a decade in the dreaded Cellular Jail of the Andamans. They were both avowed Hindus, though their approach differed radically. In fact, Gandhi was far more orthodox and conservative than Savarkar. Both passionately favoured Hindi over other languages. Both wrote books in the same year, 1909, that were banned by the British: Gandhi's *Hind Swaraj* and Savarkar's *First War of Indian Independence* on the 1857 uprising.

Vikram Sampath, the author of a two-volume Savarkar biography, writes in detail about the first time the two giants met. When Gandhi first reached out to meet Savarkar at London's India House, the latter was busy cooking.

> Savarkar asked him to first have a meal with them. Gandhi was horrified to see the Chitpavan Brahmin, Savarkar,

> cooking prawns. Being a staunch vegetarian, Gandhi refused to partake. Savarkar apparently mocked him: 'If you cannot eat with us, how on earth are you going to work with us? Moreover, this is just boiled fish; while we want people who are ready to eat the British alive.'[25]

This was the beginning of the great rivalry,[26] which intensified during Gandhi's Khilafat movement. Confined in the infamous Cellular Jail of the Andaman and Nicobar Islands at that time, Savarkar was outraged to see Gandhi playing with the Islamist fire in the name of Khilafat. The failure of the Khilafat movement saw a series of communal clashes across the country, the worst being in Malabar where Gandhi's 'brave, God-fearing Moplahs' unleashed a pogrom on Hindu Nairs in 1921. Savarkar's Hindutva was an answer to Gandhi's Khilafat kind of experiment. Also, as Sampath recounts, his sufferings and harsh experiences at the hands of Muslim prison staff and inmates at the Cellular Jail shaped his outlook. Yet, Savarkar remained a modernist and condemned 'irrational' views and practices, religious or otherwise. His views on 2Cs—caste and cow—might offend many who adore him today. But then he had a mind of his own. And he was uncompromising and unapologetic about it.

Savarkar was Gandhi's main rival, politically and intellectually. He was a Hindutva ideologue, and yet he inspired noted communists like M.N. Roy and S.A. Dange; even Bhagat Singh was deeply influenced by a small English biography of Savarkar that he read in the Dwarkadas Library of Lahore.[27]

Yet, post-Independence, Savarkar has been pushed to the margins of the mainstream freedom struggle discourse. Worse, he is viciously criticized and called names for his 'mercy petitions' from Cellular Jail to the British government.

Journalist-author Vaibhav Purandare writes in *Savarkar: The True Story of the Father of Hindutva* that to cry 'cowardice' and 'surrender', to call him a 'traitor', or to say he was 'begging for mercy from the British while Gandhi was sleeping on the dirt floor of a jail' is unwarranted and puerile. He writes:

> [T]he most abominable, medieval ways. He was put into solitary confinement for long stretches of time. He was deprived of food and water and made to do hard labour; he would faint from exhaustion but still wasn't given reprieve from work. He was chained to a wall, hands extended above his head, for hours at a stretch on consecutive days. During these spells, he was not even allowed to go to the bathroom to relieve himself and had to stand in his own filth chained to the wall.[28]

Sampath delves in detail into the mercy petition issue and reaches two conclusions: one, it was quite normal in those days to write such petitions to the British government; and two, the move on Savarkar's part was tactical.[29] He believed that a freedom fighter was of better use outside the prison rather than inside. Sampath refers to Savarkar's own memoir, *My Transportation for Life*, written just a few years after his release in 1924, wherein he disapproved of 'the non-violent mode of struggle that was being propagated by Gandhi'. This stands in sharp contrast to his petitions where he declared his 'support for constitutionalism, non-violence, and reforms'. Explains Sampath, 'These seemingly contradicting stands lead one to believe that the petitions were a mere tactical ruse to secure a release and therefore plan a future strategy. Nothing substantial could be achieved by being holed up in jail.'[30]

Even the British saw it that way. They kept a close, watchful eye on Savarkar even a decade after his release from the jail.

Worse was still in store for him when the country got independence: Savarkar was implicated in the Gandhi assassination case, the ridiculousness of which was exposed by Ambedkar himself when he confided in Savarkar's lawyer, saying there was no case against the Hindutva leader and the latter would go scot-free. He also said that the orders to implicate Savarkar had come from the top.[31] Ambedkar was then the Union law minister, the first to occupy that post in independent Bharat.

If one thought the political divide over Savarkar would go away with the deepening of democracy in the country, and the freedom fighter would get his due, then it wasn't to be the case. In fact, over the decades, opinions on Savarkar have gotten further polarized, especially after the Bharatiya Janata Party, riding predominantly on the ideology of Hindutva, displaced the Congress to become the strongest party in the country. The Congress' distrust for the Hindutva icon, thus, became much more acute and sharper.

In a historiography manipulated by our eminent distorians, one is made to believe that Bharat's freedom struggle was all about Gandhi since his arrival in Bharat on 9 January 1915, more so after 1920, by when Tilak had passed away. The reality, however, is that, as revolutionary Sachindra Nath Sanyal, one of the founding members of the Hindustan Republican Association (or Army, HRA) in 1924, along with Ramprasad Bismil, writes in *Bandi Jeevan*,

> Mahatma Gandhi had no role to play in the freedom movement from the end of the Satyagraha in 1921 till 1930. During this decade, it was only the revolutionary movement that was announcing to the world, in no uncertain terms, that the young man of India were willing to sacrifice their lives for the liberation of the country.[32]

Gandhi called off his Non-Cooperation Movement after the Chauri Chaura incident on 12 February 1922 in which three civilians and 22 policemen were killed. There was a lull in Gandhian activities thereafter. One young revolutionary who stood out in this phase was Bhagat Singh, who emerged on the national scene after the setback of the Kakori case, which saw most prominent revolutionaries of the era either killed or imprisoned. He relaunched the HRA by adding the term 'socialist' to it, thus forming the HSRA (Hindustan Socialist Republican Association or Army).

Bhagat Singh, along with Chandrashekhar Azad and Rajguru, came to the limelight when he avenged the death of Lala Lajpat Rai by killing Saunders, a police official involved in the lathi-charge on 'Punjab Kesari' when the latter was leading a demonstration boycotting the Simon Commission in Lahore on 30 October 1928.

Bhagat Singh then decided to do something to shock the entire nation out of its status quoist slumber. He, with B.K. Dutt and Rajguru, therefore, planned to throw a bomb in the Central Legislative Assembly on 8 April 1929 against the passage of the Public Safety Bill and the Trade Disputes Bill, which would reduce the civil liberties of citizens, especially workers. The aim was not to kill, for the bombs were relatively harmless, but, as the leaflet they threw into the assembly hall proclaimed, 'to make the deaf hear'. They got arrested and were sentenced to death by hanging on 7 October 1930. Amid a lot of public clamouring for having their sentences commuted, they were hanged on 23 March 1931, a day before the scheduled hanging was supposed to take place.

The circumstances under which Bhagat Singh, B.K. Dutt and Rajguru were hanged, many people still accuse Gandhi of not doing enough to save their lives. However, if one looked dispassionately, it would appear that Gandhi did indeed try his best, raising the issue on many occasions with the Viceroy. The Gandhi–Irwin talks began on 17 February 1931 and continued till 5 March, during which time they met eight times and spent together 24 hours in negotiations.[33]

If at all, Gandhi could be charged with not being forceful enough in taking up the Bhagat Singh issue. He also seemed to have been misled by the Viceroy into believing that the hanging was not imminent.[34] What the critics of Gandhi have to understand is that he had more to gain from the commutation or suspension of death sentences. Had he succeeded in doing that, it would have only added to his special status among the pantheons of Bharat's freedom movement.[35]

Here, Netaji Bose's observation in his autobiography was significant. He wrote:

> I was reminded of a similar incident during the armistice between the Sinn Fein Party and the British government, when the strong attitude adopted by the former had secured the release of an Irish political prisoner sentenced to the gallows. But the Mahatma, who did not want to identify himself with revolutionary prisoners, would not go so far and it naturally made a great difference when the Viceroy realised that the Mahatma would not break on that question.[36]

Be that as it may, the fact of the matter is Gandhi's ahimsa and satyagraha alone didn't get Bharat its independence. The revolutionaries had played an equally important, if not bigger, role in this endeavour. According to Sanjeev Sanyal, Bharat's revolutionary movement wasn't the case of marginal, episodic and isolated heroism, more often than not misplaced in its priorities, but a well-organized phenomenon that worked incessantly for the country's independence and which had well-organized international networks and dimensions with 'nodes in Britain, France,

Thailand, Germany, Russia, Italy, Persia (now Iran), Ireland, the USA, Japan and Singapore'.[37]

Not just that, the presence of revolutionaries and their successes helped Gandhi and Gandhians bargain better with the British. The harder the revolutionaries came down upon the British, the better the Mahatma and his men were dealt with by the colonial government. The existence of revolutionaries, thus, 'made it easier for Gandhi's non-violent movement to accomplish its goals'.[38]

Looking back, it's but obvious that Gandhians had a unique advantage during the freedom struggle. While they appropriated the entire credit for the country's liberation from foreign rule thanks to the dubious role played by our eminent distorians who, with political patronage, displaced the likes of R.C. Majumdar and Jadunath Sarkar in the 1950s to hijack the country's historiography, they had it easy during the British Raj. Gandhians were handled with kid gloves by the British at a time when revolutionaries were made to go through the worst of hardships at the Cellular Jail in the Andamans and elsewhere. It also made a lot of sense for the British to handover the power to the Gandhians and Nehruvians; it helped them retain their influence over the subcontinent even after Independence. We will discuss this later in the chapter.

The story of Gaekwad ruler Sayajirao III of Baroda is apt to showcase why the British preferred those who claimed to be moderates, constitutionalists, Gandhians, et al., and not extremists and revolutionaries. For those not quite well-versed with the era and its politics, it must be told that Sayajirao had generously provided financial assistance to the likes of Ambedkar and Aurobindo Ghosh, helping them become what they ultimately did. During the 1911 Delhi Durbar, he broke the royal convention by not just refusing to wear the full regalia but also making just a single perfunctory bow, instead of the customary three, to the visiting British emperor. Worse, he turned around and walked off, showing his back to Emperor George V—much against the royal convention. This single act of defiance made him the hero of free-spirited people in this country, but Motilal Nehru, who was one of the witnesses to the event, wrote disapprovingly about the incident to his son, Jawaharlal: 'I am sorry to say that the Gaekwad had fallen from the high pedestal he once occupied in public estimation'.[39]

Now that's called eating the cake and having it too: you keep the enemy you are fighting in good humour, so as not to enrage him—and worse, accuse those who had the audacity to challenge the same adversary head-on as lesser, unsophisticated beings!

Sachindra Nath Sanyal, who was given the 'Kalapani' sentence twice—once for Ghadar (released in post-Jallianwala amnesty) and the second time for the Kakori conspiracy case—too faced this holier-than-thou attitude from no less than the Nehrus. In his memoirs, he recalled meeting Subhas Bose and the Nehrus, Motilal and Jawaharlal. While he was impressed by Netaji, he wasn't too happy after meeting the Nehrus. About his meeting with Motilal Nehru, he recalled:

> I had many thoughts, but before I could begin to enunciate them, Pandit Motilal Nehru started to laugh at my proposal. I did not have an opportunity to explain to Pandit Motilal that before the French Revolution, a lot of political clubs had been set up, especially in Paris. He did not even pay attention to what I had to say. Whenever he found some free time during the day, he would smile, look at me and ask, 'So, Mr Sanyal, any other brilliant suggestion?' To hide my embarrassment and discomfiture, I would reply, 'Everyone here is brilliant, so what brilliance

> can I display?' This was the extent of my conversation with Pandit Motilal Nehru.[40]

About Jawaharlal Nehru, this is what Sachindra Nath Sanyal had to say:

> At first, when I looked at Pandit (Jawaharlal) Nehru's face during our conversation, I felt as if I was a rather misguided young man, a simpleton who had lost his way. It was (as) if Jawaharlal Nehru was doing me a favour and wasting his time by listening to me. Something along the lines of, 'This poor chap is a lost soul and he wants to say something, so one will have to give him some time. What to do ... If it has to be done, might as well do it at breakfast.'[41]

II

Sachindra Nath Sanyal wrote *Bandi Jeevan* in the early 1920s because he feared 'the history of the revolutionaries would not be properly told or perhaps be suppressed'. He was spot on, as post-independence, they were reduced to footnotes. Revolutionaries fought for freedom very hard, but when it came to power-sharing negotiations with the British, there was no one left from their side to do the talking. The last of their giants, Subhas Bose, was mysteriously missing after World War II. The moment was seized by the Gandhians and Nehruvians to their advantage.

Interestingly, the Gandhians, who before the arrival of Mahatma Gandhi from South Africa mostly worked as moderates within the umbrella of Congress, had always had a historic advantage over others. One can find its genesis in the manner in which the Congress was founded on 28 December 1885.

As we saw in the previous chapter, the Revolt of 1857 was an epoch moment in the history of the British Raj. It marked a momentous change in the way the British ruled the country thereafter. The most obvious transformation was the British crown taking over the administration of the country directly into its hands from the East India Company. Thereafter, one thing that constantly kept the British on their feet was the fear of another armed rebellion in the country. And in the late 1870s, there were strong apprehensions of another rebellion waiting to happen. That was the time when the country saw the famine of 1876–78 consuming up to nine million people.

Amid all this, British civil servant Allan Octavian Hume reportedly received a ground report that talked about massive discontent among the masses, especially among the lower strata of society, with an 'imminent danger of a terrible outbreak'.[42] It was in this backdrop that Congress was founded by Hume and others 'under the official direction, guidance and advice of no less a person than Lord Dufferin, the Viceroy, to provide a safe, mild, peaceful, and constitutional outlet or safety valve for the rising discontent among the masses, which was inevitably leading towards a popular and violent revolution'.[43]

Lala Lajpat Rai made the mention of this safety valve theory in his 1916 book, *Young India*. He wrote:

> It is an undisputed historical fact that the idea of the Indian National Congress was a product of Lord Dufferin's brain; that he suggested it to Mr. Hume, and that the latter undertook to work it out. We have no means of knowing whether Mr. Hume communicated the fact to all the Indian leaders who joined hands with him in organising it, but in all probability he told some of them. It leaked out, however, in Lord Dufferin's lifetime, was published in the press, brought to his notice and never denied by him. Nor did Mr. Hume, who died only in 1912, ever deny it. It has since been admitted to be true by his biographer, another veteran Congress leader, Sir William Wedderburn. Sir William says on page 59 of his life of Mr. Hume: 'Indeed in initiating the National Movement,

> Mr. Hume took counsel with the viceroy, Lord Dufferin; and whereas he was himself disposed to begin his reform propaganda on the social side, it was apparently by Lord Dufferin's advice that he took up the work of political organisation as the first matter to be dealt with.' We have no hesitation in accepting the accuracy of the statement made by Sir William Wedderburn as to what Lord Dufferin told Mr. Hume, because we have no doubt of Mr. Hume's sincerity of purpose. Lord Dufferin did evidently tell Mr. Hume that 'as head of the Government, he had found the greatest difficulty in ascertaining the real wishes of the people; and that for purposes of administration it would be a public benefit, if there existed some responsible organisation through which the Government might be kept informed regarding the best Indian public opinion'.[44]

Sir William Wedderburn, in his book on Hume, writes how Lord Dufferin 'further observed that, owing to the wide differences in caste, race, and religion, social reform in India required local treatment, rather than the guidance of a national organization'. He adds,

> Indeed, so cordial were the relations, that Lord Dufferin was approached with a view to the first Congress being held under the presidency of Lord Reay, then Governor of Bombay. Lord Dufferin welcomed the proposal, as showing the desire of the Congress to work in complete harmony with the Government, but he considered that many difficulties would be involved if a high official presided over such an assembly. The idea was therefore abandoned, but none the less the first Congress was opened with the friendly sympathy of the highest authorities.[45]

One further gets an inkling of the initial Congress–British connection from the fact that prominent Bengali leaders such as Surendranath Banerjee, who would often be critical of the Raj, were not invited to participate in the inaugural session of the Congress on 28 December 1885. Banerjee had set up the National Conference in 1883. Interestingly, the National Conference's demands found themselves replicated two years later in the first Congress session.

Amales Tripathi writes in his 1990 Bengali book, *Swadhinata Sangrame Bharater Jatiya Congress*, translated into English by Amitava Tripathi in 2014:

> Very surprisingly, on his Calcutta mission (March 1885), Hume discussed the proposed Indian National Union, not with Anandamohan Basu or Surendranath, but with Narendranath Sen and Umeshchandra Bandopadhyay, and scheduled the Poona session at a time when Surendranath would be busy planning the second session of the National Conference. A conspiracy to sideline Surendranath, featuring Narendranath, Umeshchandra, and even Manmohan Ghosh, cannot be ruled out.[46]

No wonder the earlier Congress sessions were thus more of a 'talking club for the Westernised elite of Bombay, Calcutta and Madras, not a real political'.[47] Rabindranath Tagore, too, found the early Congress sessions to be more about hospitality and chatter rather than socio-economic and political reforms. As one of the characters, a swadeshi movement leader, of Tagore's novel *The Home and the World*, written in 1915–16, says,

> When I was attached to the Congress party never hesitated to dilute 10 per cent of truth with 90 per cent of untruth. And now, merely because I have ceased to belong to that party, I have not forgotten the basic fact man's goal is not truth but success.[48]

With no fixed source of income, the Congress' membership dropped considerably to 472 in the 1902 Ahmedabad session, with one leader calling such meetings 'a three-day farce'.[49]

Such was the state of affairs that Lord Curzon, then viceroy, in his letter to the secretary of state on 18 November 1900, predicted that the Congress was 'on the verge of dissolution and my endeavour will be to give it a peaceful demise'.[50]

Incidentally, it was Curzon, through his hard-line policy, especially the decision to partition Bengal in 1905, who gave the Congress a new lease of life, with the extremist wing coming into prominence under the leadership of 'Lal–Bal–Pal' (Lala Lajpat Rai, Bal Gangadhar Tilak, and Bipin Chandra Pal). They mocked the moderates for their 'petition politics' and launched with great intensity the swadeshi movement.

The Congress, however, couldn't sustain the revolutionary fervour for long, as the party was formally divided into moderate and extremist sections in the Surat session in 1907. It took the wind out of the Congress' sail, more so after the government launched a massive attack on the extremists. The extremist newspapers were banned; Tilak, their tallest leader, was sent to the Mandalay jail for six years. Aurobindo Ghose was arrested in a revolutionary conspiracy case, and though he was later acquitted, he gave up politics for spirituality as he shifted his base to Pondicherry. Bipin Chandra Pal retired temporarily from politics, and Lajpat Rai left for Britain for a year in 1908.

Aurobindo Ghose summed up the sentiment aptly as he wrote:

> When I went to jail the whole country was alive with the cry of Bande Mataram, alive with the hope of a nation, the hope of millions of men who had newly risen out of degradation. When I came out of jail I listened for that cry, but there was instead a silence. A hush had fallen on the country and men seemed bewildered... No man seemed to know which way to move.[51]

The stage was set for Mahatma Gandhi, who came to Bharat in January 1915 after a successful sojourn in South Africa.

III

Mahatma Gandhi completely changed the character of the Congress from being an elitist party confined to the educated few to a mass-oriented one. It was evident at the Kanpur Congress session in 1925 where 8,000 people converged. V.S. Naipaul writes about the Kanpur session thus:

> They were in a tent about a hundred yards long and 60 yards wide, with a light roof of brown canvas, and they were all seated on matting on the ground. Whereas earlier in the century (according to Nehru) there would have been delegates in morning coats and striped trousers, now they were all in Indian dress and many were wearing the boat-shaped white cotton cap which was already known as Gandhi cap. The meeting went on for three days, six hours the first day, seven hours the second day, and finally nine hours, speeches all the time, and no food.[52]

It was Gandhi who connected the Congress with the masses. Even the move by Gandhi to shun the Western dress was a well-calibrated decision to dress and look like the poor. His experiments with his clothes began in South Africa, where he stayed between 1893 and 1914. He started wearing 'a shirt, a *dhoti*, a white cloak and scarf, all of cheap Indian mill cloth'. When he returned to Bharat in 1915, 'because he intended to travel third class on the railways, he got rid of the cloak and the scarf as being too showy'.[53]

Gandhi began his political innings in Bharat by travelling in trains across the country to see and understand the country first-hand. Once he grasped the grim realities of Bharat, he decided to put his satyagraha experiment to the test in Champaran, north Bihar, in 1917. The movement was a massive success for Gandhi. He became the talk of the country for doing the impossible—making the mighty British Empire surrender without the use of any arms. This novel way of protest, coupled with his saint-like appearance and subtle and not-so-subtle usage of religio-cultural idioms, metamorphosed him into much more than just a political leader: he became the 'Mahatma', for whom people of all classes and genders would go out of their way to have a '*darshan*'.

Dinanath Gopal Tendulkar writes about one of Gandhi's travels in Bihar in 1921 and the mass hysteria it created. He writes:

> Remarkable scenes were witnessed. In a Bihar village when Gandhi and his party were stranded in the train, an old woman came seeking out Gandhi. 'Sire. I am now one hundred and four,' she said, 'and my sight has grown dim. I have visited the various holy places. In my own home I have dedicated two temples. Just as we had Rama and Krishna as avatars, so also Mahatma Gandhi has appeared as an avatar, I hear. Until I have seen him death will not appear.' This simple faith moved India's millions who greeted him everywhere with the cry, 'Mahatma Gandhi-ki-jai'. Prostitutes of Barisal, the Marwari merchants of Calcutta, Oriya coolies, railway strikers, Santals eager to present khadi chaddars, all claimed his attention. From Aligarh to Dibrugarh and then as far as Tinnevelly he went from village to village, from town to town, sometimes speaking in temples and mosques. Wherever he went he had to endure the tyranny of love.[54]

Even Gandhi's own secretary, Mahadev Desai, writes in his tour diary about the 'Boundless Love' that the masses gave to the Mahatma:

> It is impossible to put in language the exuberance of love which Gandhiji and Shaukat Ali experienced in Bihar. Our train on the B.N.W. Railway line stopped at all stations and there was not a single station which was not crowded with hundreds of people at that time. Even women, who never stir

> out of their homes, did not fail to present themselves so that they could see and hear him. A huge concourse of students would everywhere smother Gandhiji with their enthusiasm. If at some place a sister would take off her coral necklace and tell him, 'I give this specially for you to wear', at some other, *sanyasis* would come and leave their rosaries on his lap. If beautiful sheets or handspun and hand-woven cloth, many yards long, would be presented at one place, at some other place would turn up a loving villager from the woods, boastful of his trophy, saying, 'Maharaj (an address of reverence) this is my feat of strength. The tiger was a terror to our people: I am giving the skin to you.' At some places, guns normally used as fog-signals were fired in his honour. At some others, we came across railway officers who would not give the green flag, when our train came within their jurisdiction, in order to have and let others have Gandhiji's *darshan*... We have met with even policemen who had the courage to approach Gandhiji to salute him or touch his hand, and… say: 'We have taken to this dirty work for the sake of the sinning flesh, but please do accept these five rupees.'[55]

The *Pioneer* newspaper, in its editorial, too talked about Gandhi's 'magical' powers. It wrote in the spring of 1921:

> In the *Swadesh*, a paper published in Gorakhpur, four miracles were quoted last month as being popularly attributable to Mr Gandhi. Smoke was seen coming from wells and, when water was drunk, it had the fragrance of keora (*pandanus odaratissimus*) an aloe-like plant which is used in the manufacture of perfume: a copy of the Holy *Quran* was found in a room which had not been opened for a year; an Ahir who refused alms to a *Sadhu* begging in Mahatma Gandhi's name, had his gur and two buffaloes destroyed by fire; and a sceptical Brahmin, who defied Mr Gandhi's authority, went mad and was only cured three days afterwards by the invocation of the saintly name![56]

Interestingly, Gandhi's inspiration to become a 'Mahatma' largely came from non-Indic sources. It was this tendency to pick up things from 'foreign' sources that made Sri Aurobindo call Gandhi 'a European… in an Indian body'.[57] A 'bits-and-pieces man', in Naipaul's words, he adopted things from sources as different as his mother's love for fasting and Leo Tolstoy's religious belief, John Ruskin's ideas on labour, and South Africa's jail code. Naipaul explains this further:

> His (Gandhi's) ascetic ideas drew from many sources. He went to jail for the first time in 1908; this was in Johannesburg. Africans and Indians were not given tea or coffee and their last meal in jail had to be finished before sunset. This was hard, but Gandhi grew to think it was something he might add to his own daily discipline. Prisoners could use salt to season their food, but nothing else. Gandhi, pushing at the laws, as always, asked the jail medical officer for curry powder and also to be allowed to put salt in the food while it was cooking. (He knew, or had found out, the form: he knew who to ask.) The officer refused. He said, 'You are not here for satisfying your palate.' Gandhi played with that idea, of not satisfying the palate, and was pleased with it. When he left jail he adopted two of the jail restrictions: eating dinner before sunset, and doing without tea and coffee.[58]

Such has been the impact of South Africa in the making of the Mahatma that author Joseph Lelyveld left out Gandhi's childhood and student years while writing the latter's biography *Great Soul*—a decision he made because he believed that the 23-year-old law clerk, when he arrived in South Africa in 1893, had little in him of the man he would finally become.[59]

If Gandhi's South African experience made him the Mahatma, it also, in a way, unmade him. His Khilafat movement, which was a protest against the British government's policies towards Turkey and the planned dismemberment of the Ottoman Empire after World War I, can be said to be the result of his African learning. Ramachandra Guha explains,

> Gandhi's first struggles against racial discrimination [in South Africa] had largely been funded and staffed by Muslims. In the diaspora such trans-religious solidarity was easier, since Hindus, Muslims, Christians and Parsis from India all faced the same disabilities. In the homeland, however, the different communities were established in their particular ways of life.[60]

It was a 'fundamental mistake' on Gandhi's part to 'insist on treating India as if it were South Africa'.[61] Just as in South Africa, where he befriended prominent Muslim leaders, during the Khilafat movement he cultivated close ties with the Ali brothers, who were 'the eyes of the Muslims'. Gandhi hoped that just like in Africa, his amicable relations with the Ali brothers would manifest in bringing Hindus and Muslims together. It was a blunder of Himalayan proportions.

The Khilafat movement resulted in a number of Hindu–Muslim riots across the country, the most prominent being the 1921 Moplah pogrom in Malabar and the 1924 Kohat riots in the then North-West Frontier Province. While these riots, especially the one led by the Moplahs, are projected as 'peasant rebellion against Hindu landlords' by eminent distorians, this was largely the result of pan-Islamism getting a kick out of Gandhi's Khilafatism. John J. Banninga, in his 1923 article 'The Moplah Rebellion of 1921' wondered, '[S]ince the Hindu tenants and labourers admittedly suffered quite as much, if not more, from the great power of the big *jenani* (landlords), why were outbreaks confined to the Muslim community?'[62]

Gandhi failed to understand the nature of Islam and Islamism, which was manifested by the conduct of Maulana Mohammed Ali. The learned Maulana, 'who had been kissing Gandhiji's feet, who had been falling at his feet, who had been shedding tears in such profusion, who had hailed him as "the most Christ-like man of our times"', declared first in Aligarh and again in Ajmer: 'However pure Mr. Gandhi's character may be, he must appear to me from the point of religion inferior to any Mussalman though he be without character.'[63]

Later, in Lucknow, when asked if the above statement attributed to him was true, Mohammed Ali reiterated: 'Yes, according to my religion and creed, I do hold an adulterous and a fallen Mussalman to be better than Mr. Gandhi.'[64]

If the Khilafat movement ended up in riots across the country, his Non-Cooperation Movement, which he launched as a protest against the Rowlatt Act[65] and the Jallianwala killings[66] in 1919, was largely successful in arousing people for the cause of the nation. However, he had to suddenly call off the movement after it turned violent at Chauri Chaura in the Gorakhpur district of today's Uttar Pradesh in 1922; three civilians and 22 policemen were killed in the incident.

Gandhi's next big movement came eight years later, in the form of the Civil Disobedience Movement. In 1930, he began this with his Dandi March that created excitement across the country. While 'the officials on the spot' were worried, Lord Irwin, the viceroy, was unruffled by the turn of events. Even when the march was in its third week, Irwin wrote to Cosmo Gordon Lang, the archbishop of Canterbury and also his spiritual preceptor: 'Gandhi is continuing his theatrical march to the coast, but so far is arousing a good deal less excitement than he had anticipated. And I am quite certain that we have been right not to arrest him so far.'[67]

The day after Gandhi broke the salt law in Dandi, Lord Irwin wrote a private letter to the editor of the *Times*, again defending his policy of non-interference. He claimed that Gandhi himself hoped to be arrested early in his march for two reasons: it would have, one, led to 'the shedding of a great lustre about his name and cause'; two, his arrest would have spared 'an elderly man the disagreeable duty of walking 12 miles a day for three weeks through dust in order to get to a hot sea-side in the end'.[68]

Ramachandra Guha is right in assessing that for Irwin, Gandhi was 'an object of curiosity, a subject of study, but not—or at least not yet—a political threat'.[69] But as things unfolded later, Irwin was wrong in his assessment. Gandhi's presence galvanized the movement, which resonated across the country.

The British, however, had learnt their lesson hard: from now onwards, they would come down hard on the Congress leadership just before the launch of any movement. As we saw in the 1942 Quit India Movement, Gandhi and his lieutenants were put behind bars well before the launch. Quit India had initially galvanized the masses to come out on the streets in large numbers, but being leaderless, it lost its steam. The British had cracked the code of dealing with Gandhi and his satyagraha.

IV

As Bharat moved towards the 1940s, Gandhi seemed to have lost the kind of grip he had over the country's politics in the last two decades. He, for instance, wanted the Congress to unconditionally support the British government during World War II but had to give in to the demands of others in the party who wanted to bargain with Britain at this hour of crisis. Moreover, the 1940s was the decade of Mohammed Ali Jinnah, who outclassed and outwitted the Congress leadership, especially Gandhi, as he managed to carve almost single-handedly a separate nation, Pakistan, out of Bharat in the name of Islam.

Rajmohan Gandhi explains the historic consequences of Congress' decision to go against Gandhi. He writes:

> Gandhi's proposal of unconditional non-violent support was shot down by the Working Committee. No one agreed with him. For the first time in 19 years his younger colleagues banded together to vote him down. Though anticipated and accepted by Gandhi, the outcome was a milestone that he and everyone else registered, and he regretted, for more than most he understood the cards the British held in India, and the risks in antagonising Britain at war. Nehru's resolution declaring opposition to fascism but asking Britain to spell out her war aim and their application to India was easily passed. Jawaharlal was expressing the national opinion when he said that friendship between India and England was 'possible but only on equal terms'.[70]

M.J. Akbar writes how

> by 1942, the British had already given a firm commitment to Jinnah, who offered full support. 'Ifs' are the bane of history, but if the Congress had accepted Gandhi's advice in 1939, Jinnah space for manoeuvre would have been blocked and Pakistan might have remained a fantasist's dream.[71]

Sardar Vallabhbhai Patel, if an entry in his daughter Maniben Patel's diary is to be believed, regretted his opposition to Gandhi on the issue.[72] K.M. Munshi, too, conceded the Congress' mistake of not accepting the Cripps' proposals. The failure of the Cripps Mission paved the way for the Quit India Movement in August 1942. Munshi wrote in 1951, 'Today, we realise that if the first (Cripps) proposal had been accepted, there would have been no Partition, no refugees, and no Kashmir problem.'[73]

The timing of the Quit India Movement was disastrous. Today, a section of the intelligentsia accuses Savarkar of being 'unpatriotic' for not supporting the 1942 movement. But wasn't Savarkar sagacious enough to foresee the consequences of the Quit India Movement?

In fact, Savarkar wasn't an exception in opposing the 1942 movement. Sri Aurobindo, too, had strong reservations about it. He, in fact, wanted the Congress to accept the Cripps Mission proposals, which among others promised to grant Bharat dominion status after the big war and not full-fledged independence, the failure of which made Gandhi launch the Quit India Movement.

Sir Stafford Cripps, on arriving in the subcontinent, issued the following Draft Declaration on behalf of the British government:

> His Majesty's Government, having considered the anxieties expressed in this country and in India as to the fulfilment of promises made in regard to the future of India, have decided to lay down in precise and clear terms the steps which they propose shall be taken for the earliest possible realisation of self-government in India. The object is the creation of a new Indian Union which shall constitute a Dominion associated with the United Kingdom and other Dominions by a common allegiance to the Crown but equal to them in every respect, in no way subordinate in any aspect of its domestic and external affairs.[74]

On 31 March 1942, Aurobindo sent a telegram to Sir Stafford:

> I have heard your broadcast. As one who has been a nationalist leader and worker for India's independence, though now my activity is no longer in the political but in the spiritual field, I wish to express my appreciation of all you have done to bring about this offer. I welcome it as an opportunity given

> to India to determine for herself and organize in all liberty of choice her freedom and unity and take an effective place among the world's free nations.[75]

Louis Fischer mentions in detail the meeting between Gandhi and Cripps. Fischer writes:

> On 27 March, at 2.15 pm, Gandhi arrived at 3 Queen Victoria Road and remained with Cripps until 2.45 pm. Sir Stafford showed the Mahatma the as-yet-unpublished proposals of His Majesty's Government. 'After a brief study,' Gandhi told me in Sevagram, 'I said to Cripps, "Why did you come if this is what you have to offer? If this is your entire proposal to India, I would advise you to take the next flight home." 'I will consider that,' Cripps replied.[76]

When Aurobindo realized that the negotiations with the Congress were not going well, he reached out to Gandhi and Nehru, saying that Cripps' offer should be accepted unconditionally. He also sent a telegram to C. Rajagopalachari on 2 April 1942.

Winston Churchill, when he heard that the Congress had rejected the Cripps proposal, 'sighed in relief'. He was against the offer from the beginning but 'had gone through the motions to satisfy US President Franklin D. Roosevelt, who had been pressing him to grant more self-government to India'.[77] Not just Churchill, even Lord Linlithgow, then viceroy, personally hated Cripps, referring to Sir Stafford Cripps as 'Sir Stifford Crapps'![78] Another reason for the Congress leadership to have engaged with Cripps more seriously.

Peter Heehs writes,

> What would have happened if the Cripps proposal had been accepted? Many believe that the Partition of India might

> have been averted if the various parties had learned to work together in a wartime national government. Another view is that Congress leaders squandered a once in a lifetime 'opportunity of entrenching themselves in the seats of power and also the chance of smothering the Muslim League before it was too late'.[79]

Despite the obvious pitfalls of 'what-if' history, it can safely be said that the Congress could have handled the 1940s better. There must have been something good for this country in the Cripps proposal that Churchill heaved 'a sigh of relief' when the Congress rejected it. The Quit India Movement, a result of the Cripps Mission failure, was not just ill-timed, strategically or otherwise, but also an extremely lacklustre movement. The British government defused it by placing almost all of the top Congress leadership in jail, but the damage was done: the British distrust for the Congress was absolute, which gave the Muslim League the opportunity to bring itself closer to the Raj, though Churchill and Jinnah were in touch with each other for a much longer time. Such has been Churchill's role in the creation of Pakistan that author Alex von Tunzelmann goes to the extent of calling him the 'uncle' of Pakistan. She writes, 'If Jinnah is regarded as the father of Pakistan, Churchill must qualify as its uncle; and, therefore, as a pivotal figure in the resurgence of political Islam.'[80]

Narendra Singh Sarila, who was aide-de-camp to Lord Mountbatten and served in the country's foreign service between 1948 and 1985, in his book *The Shadow of the Great Game: The Untold Story of India's Partition*, establishes a crucial link between Bharat's Partition and British fears about the erstwhile Soviet Union gaining ground in the region at the cost of the US-led Western powers.[81] Fearing that the country's leadership led by Nehru would not be the West's ally in the 'Great Game' against the Russians, the British settled for the one willing to do so—Jinnah. In fact if the memos of then British foreign secretary Earnest Bevin, dated 14 June 1946, are to be believed, the Pentagon had already begun asking the British about gaining 'access to air bases in northwest India, from which US bombers could attack Soviet industrial centres in the Urals'.[82]

Britain, thus, did what Churchill had advised Lord Wavell in a parting message on 31 August 1945: 'Keep a bit of India'.[83] The idea of Pakistan, thus, was as much the result of the naked Islamist ambition[84] as it was the outcome of the sinister British agenda. It was sheer British ingenuity—complemented by Congress' stupidity—that despite playing a proactive role in Bharat's partition, the 'British left India with dignity'.[85]

The British could leave Bharat 'with dignity'—despite the sinister Pakistan project, despite the monumental mishandling of the country's partition leading to lakhs of people losing their lives—because they launched a very effective PR exercise under the charismatic Mountbattens—Dickie and Edwina. What further helped them was that by then Subhas Bose was reportedly dead in an air crash outside Bharat. Gandhi was missing from action in Delhi, stuck in riot-hit areas. And Sardar Patel was bogged down by the onerousness of the crisis, with the prospect of Bharat ending up in 565 different parts. The Mountbattens, thus, had to just deal with Nehru. Which they did commendably well.

Shahid Hamid, Field Marshal Sir Claude Auchinleck's private secretary, recalled how Lord Mountbatten 'established close contact with Nehru knowing that he would one day become the Prime Minister of India'. He added:

> It was the efforts of Krishna Menon which further cemented their (Nehru-Mountbatten) friendship… According to common gossip, Mountbatten has come to partition India

> as quickly as possible, irrespective of the consequences—sort out the Princes; take all possible measures to keep the two countries in the Commonwealth; ensure that Britain's strategic and mercantile interests in South Asia are not jeopardized; and finally, keep the Indian leaders under pressure and give them no time to think.[86]

When one looks back, all the points raised by Hamid turned out to be true. Mountbatten, indeed, was in a hurry to divide the country. Tunzelmann's argument that Dickie was pushing the plan at the 'unrealistic pace'[87] because Edwina was anxious to leave the subcontinent, and by doing that, 'he might still save his marriage',[88] seems simplistic. Their marriage was already dead when they came to Bharat; they were more like friends with no strings attached, but they continued to look after each other's interests. This explains why, 'seeing the strong emotional bond between' Nehru and Edwina, 'Dickie and Pamela discreetly withdrew to give them time together'.[89]

Mountbatten's unholy haste in partitioning the country resulted in a man-made catastrophe in which at least 20 million people were displaced and about a million lost their lives. While the Churchillian conspiracy to divide Bharat was accomplished amid monumental chaos, costs and casualties, the Mountbattens still 'saved India for Britain'[90] by posing as its friend. They were able to do so by successfully wooing Nehru and his friends.

Nehru not only continued the services of Lord Mountbatten, British-ruled Bharat's last viceroy, as the first governor-general of independent Bharat, but also retained the country's Commonwealth connection. Worse, to Britain's strategic advantage, Mountbatten worked towards aggravating Nehru's distrust for America. The feeling in the UK in the late 1940s, as former foreign secretary Vijay Gokhale writes in *Crosswinds*, was that 'far from trying to create a joint

Anglo-American policy on China, the US was paying scant attention to British interests when crafting its China policy'.[91] Britain played both ways: to the Americans, it said that Nehru was too tied up internally to play any role in Asia, especially vis-à-vis China. And to the Indians, it said that China was largely an American problem with which India should not get involved. Mountbatten used his influence on Nehru to 'raise his suspicion about the US motives in Asia'.[92]

Tunzelmann sums up the success of the Mountbattens with her depiction of the situation on 15 August 1947. She writes:

> Everyone had expected that such a day would be glorious in India's history; but, thanks to Mountbatten, it had somehow been made glorious in Britain's as well. Thanks to his impressive gift for public relations, the end of Empire was presented as the purpose of Empire—India was as a well-nurtured and fattened chick, raised to fly from the imperial nest while Britain, the indulgent parent, looked on with pride. And so the British were able to celebrate their loss alongside the Indians who celebrated their victory. Comforting fictions were established that happy night: that the British left India with dignity, having seen the error of their ways through Gandhi's soft but compelling per-suasion; that the Indian independence campaign won its prize by non-violence and civil disobedience; that the departure of the British was completed with enough goodwill to pave the way for genuine friendship between India and the west, and separately between Pakistan and the west; that the end of the British Empire in India was a triumph for freedom.[93]

While Jinnah resurrected the Islamist djinn to divide Bharat and the British dirtied their hands by giving it a covering fire, the Congress' splendid short-sightedness gave a cakewalk to the proponents of Pakistan. This was the time when Gandhi not just found himself sidelined but also villainized. A section of society, outraged by his perceived pro-Pakistan/Muslim stand, wanted him dead. The Mahatma, too, was desperately seeking his own 'martyrdom'. Worse, the Congress began seeing him as a liability. Amid all this came Nathuram Godse with his Beretta M1934 semi-automatic pistol.

V

Godse murdered Gandhi at Delhi's Birla House on 30 January 1948. Author Makarand Paranjape, however, believes it was the Mahatma who 'martyred himself'. Gandhi saw it as 'an offering, as he himself put it, a last and desperate *yajna*—sacrifice, oblation, sacred rite—to save India'.[94]

Gandhi, who worked all his life for Hindu–Muslim unity, could see his life-long project vanish in thin air with Partition. In December 1947, about a month before his assassination, Pyarelal Nayyar, the Mahatma's secretary, could sense that Gandhi 'was literally praying that God should gather him into his bosom and deliver him from the agony which life had become'.[95]

Gandhi, however, had always had the predisposition for his dramatic death. His old comrade, Henry Polak, thought the same about him, albeit in private. In 1934, when Polak heard about Gandhi planning a fresh fast, he wrote to a friend: 'He (Gandhi) has a chronic tendency to offer himself as a public sacrifice, and I can never feel any sense of certainty that he will in the normal course of events pass away in any but the most dramatic circumstances'.[96]

On 29 January 1948, just a day before his assassination, Gandhi told Manuben, his grandniece:

> If I were to die of a lingering disease, or even from a pimple, then you must shout from the housetops to the whole world that I was a false Mahatma... And if an explosion took place, as

> it did last week, or someone shot at me and I received his bullet on my bare chest, without a sigh and with Rama's name on my lips, only then should you say that I was a true Mahatma.[97]

Gandhi died in the most tragic circumstances on 30 January 1948, when Godse shot point-blank, pumping three bullets into his chest. But as Paranjape raises a pertinent question in his book, *The Death and Afterlife of Mahatma Gandhi*, 'Did Godse really succeed? Or, did the Mahatma, even in his own death, turn the tables on his assassin?'[98]

When one looks back at what happened on 30 January 1948, it's startling to see how Gandhi was so easily assassinated just 10 days after a failed bomb attack on the same venue—and that too by the same set of people. Had Gandhi become an inconvenience for a lot more people than just Godse and his men? On 18 December 1947, just a month and a half before he was assassinated, Gandhi himself had confessed: 'I know that today I irritate everyone… What irks me is that people deceive me. They should tell me frankly that I have become old, that I am no longer of any use and that I should not be in their way.'[99]

While Gandhi was desperately seeking 'martyrdom', especially at a time when there were enough people with grievances against him, the state administration seemed callous and indifferent. With a section of the public so angry and with credible intelligence about threats to the Mahatma's life, it's inconceivable why the police failed to beef up Gandhi's security. If British historian Robert Payne is to be believed, on the day Gandhi was killed, there were only one assistant sub-inspector, two head constables, and 16 foot constables.[100]

Tushar Gandhi, the Mahatma's grandson, goes a step further and blames the Congress government for his death, accusing the Congress of finding it easier to live with a martyred Mahatma than the alive one.

> The Congress government and at least some of the members of the cabinet were fed up with the interventions of the meddlesome old man… The way the investigation was carried out, and the lackadaisical approach of the police in trying to protect Gandhi's life, leads one to believe that the investigation was meant to hide more than it was meant to reveal. The measures taken by the police between 20th and 30th January 1948 were more to ensure the smooth progress of the murderers, than to try to prevent his murder.[101]

In this context, Dr B.R. Ambedkar made a pertinent observation. Writing to Sharada Krishnarao Kabir, who would later become his wife, Ambedkar said: 'Great men are of great service to their country, but they are also at certain times a great hindrance to the progress of their country… Mr Gandhi had become a positive danger to his country.'[102]

Had Gandhi become a 'great hindrance' and a 'positive danger' to the country and its progress? At least a section of the ruling party seemed to have shared this sentiment.

The Gandhi assassination saga had deep implications for everyone: to Gandhi, it gave him 'martyrdom', saving him, as some saw, from 'the dustbin of history', for which he was headed after the creation of Pakistan.[103] To the Nehruvian establishment, it gave the much-needed freedom from Gandhian 'tantrums', protests, fasts—and, of course, the emerging Opposition under the Hindu Mahasabha, which collapsed like a pack of cards after the assassination. The only sore losers in all this were Hindus: they were left licking their wounds, feeling guilty for the assassination of 'the most famous and the most popular Indian since Buddha'.[104] It took them more than three decades to come out of their self-imposed sense of culpability, often heightened by the Nehruvian ecosystem that patronized and pampered a class of intellectuals, including our eminent distorians, who took pride in Hindu bashing.

VI

It was the best of times, it was the worst of times. As Bharat gathered to celebrate its independence, it also witnessed a tragedy of epic proportions with the Partition woes. Delhi epitomized these two contrasting scenarios, hosting a large number of bemoaning refugees from what became West Pakistan, while at the same time gearing up for the fervour of freedom.

Journalist D.F. Karaka reminisces about the festive mood in Delhi that was suddenly marked by an upsurge of 'religious spirit'. It was the rise of Hindu spirit that the author erroneously, and in sync with the Nehruvian consensus, called 'superstitious'. He writes:

> In Delhi, as the great day approached, the enthusiasm and excitement grew. Then, for some inexplicable reason, a religious spirit spread over the capital. Time magazine in its report said: 'As the great day approached, the Indians thanked their various gods and rejoiced with prayers, poems, hymns and songs.' Even Pandit Nehru, who had never been known to frequent the temples or to indulge in much religious ceremony, consented to have the blessings of the religious pandits. From Tanjore there came emissaries of the head priest the Sanyasis, an order of Hindu ascetics. It was traditional in ancient India to derive power and authority from the holy men. Pandit Nehru yielded to all this religious ceremony. ... The mood of New Delhi had become almost superstitious.[105]

Karaka continues:

> In the evening the priests walked ahead of these religious processions. They carried the sceptre, the holy water which they had brought with them from Tanjore, and rice. They

> laid their gifts at the feet of the Prime Minister. Holy ash was marked on the Pandit's forehead and the priests gave him their blessings. Later, at the house of the President of the Constituent Assembly, Dr. Rajendra Prasad, who was also President of the Congress, Pandit Nehru sat round a holy fire; around it the women of the house were chanting hymns. The oldest woman among them made an auspicious till mark on the forehead of all the ministers and Constitution makers.[106]

What sealed the Hindu-ness of independent Bharat was the manner in which the transfer of power was formalized. Before the transfer of power on 15 August 1947, Lord Mountbatten reportedly asked Nehru about the rituals needed to mark the occasion. Nehru reached out to Rajaji, who recommended him to follow the Chola model of power transfer, wherein a priest would present a sceptre (Sengol) to the new ruler to convey the idea of power transition.

Rajaji, in fact, took the lead in approaching Thiruvavaduthurai Adheenam, a Shaivite *mutt* based in the town of Thiruvavaduthurai in Tamil Nadu's Mayiladuthurai district, to assist in the making of a Sengol. The 5-ft long intricately carved, gold-plated silver sceptre, with a finial of a bull (a symbol of dharma) on top, was made before the transfer of power.

On 10 August 1947, two *sannyasis* from the Thiruvavaduthurai *mutt* left for New Delhi. Just like the ancient Hindu kings, Nehru was handed over the Sengol right before his historic 'Tryst with Destiny' speech in the Constituent Assembly that marked the birth of the nation freed from British rule.

Dominique Lapierre and Larry Collins capture this moment as they write: 'As once Hindu holy men had conferred upon ancient India's kings their symbols of power, so the *sannyasin* had come to York Road to bestow their antique emblems of authority on the man about to assume the leadership of a modern Indian nation.'[107]

They mention how Nehru, 'who had never ceased to proclaim the horror the word "religion" inspired in him, their rite was a tiresome manifestation of all he deplored in his nation, … submitted to it with almost cheerful humility'. They write:

> No arsonist's hands had lit the little fire burning in the New Delhi garden of Dr. Rajendra Prasad, the president of India's Constituent Assembly. It was a Sacred Fire, consecrated and purified according to Vedic rite by the Brahmin priest who sat beside it rhythmically chanting his mantras. … As he repeated his atonal chant, the learned men and women who would shortly become the first ministers of an independent India, filed past the fire. A second Brahmin sprinkled each with a few drops of water. Then they stepped over to a woman waiting with a copper vessel, its exterior white-washed, its lip covered with palm leaves. As the ministers paused before her, she dipped her right forefinger into the vessel, then, with the liquid on her fingertip, pressed a bright vermilion dot on their foreheads.[108]

The free nation that was born in 1947 was unapologetically Hindu. This was also evident from the look of the original Constitution. The book includes 22 illustrations, made under the guidance of Nandlal Bose, within its main body. While the illustrations from the ancient era ranged from a Mohenjodaro seal to a scene of a Vedic *ashram*, from Rama's victory over Ravan to Krishna propounding the Gita to Arjun, and Buddha delivering a sermon, the illustrations chosen to represent the mediaeval era were a Hindu sculpture from Odisha, the image of Nataraj, a Mahabalipuram scene depicting the penance of Bhagiratha, and the descent of Ganga. Among Muslim themes, only the portrait of Akbar found space. The other two individuals included in the mediaeval era list were Shivaji and Guru Gobind Singh. In the modern era, Gandhi's Dandi March and his visit to riot-hit Noakhali, and Subhas Chandra Bose and his INA, found space, indicating that revolutionaries had not yet been pushed to the margins.[109]

Bharat, thus, was born as a Hindu state in 1947. It was the Nehruvian conspiracy in the 1950s that saw further ascendency in the 1960s and 1970s, which pushed the country towards a socialist, secular order, much against the civilization grain of this land. And in all this, our eminent distorians played a prominent role. How Bharat lost its Hindu-ness, within a few years of regaining it, soon after Independence, is another sordid saga, for another book.

Epilogue

In *The Book of Laughter and Forgetting*, Czech author Milan Kundera, while exploring the theme of societal and personal amnesia in a communist setting, writes,

> You begin to liquidate a people by taking away its memory. You destroy its books, its culture, its history. And then others write other books for it, give another culture to it, invent another history for it. Then the people slowly begins to forget what it is and what it was. The world at large forgets it still faster.[1]

Post-Independence, especially since the late 1960s, Bharat too has been seeing a similar endeavour of enforced liquidation of the nation's memory by distorting its history and denigrating its culture. It began with the hijacking of history in the name of writing it from the people's perspective. Romila Thapar wrote about this in 1969: 'Perhaps the greatest advantage of archaeological data is that it forces the historian to move from what has now become an arid study of dynasties and events relating to royalty, to the more purposeful study of society as a whole.'[2]

Thapar had talked about this in an article in 1962 in which she promised to come up with a new way of history writing to let the readers know 'what the elephant-keeper of the emperor Ashoka thought of his edicts' or what the lives and thoughts of the masons who built the Taj Mahal were.[3]

More than six decades later, Thapar's grand promise remains unfulfilled. The left-dominated history of Bharat is today stuck in a soulless, ideologically obsessed mindscape, telling neither the story of kings nor the 'lives and thoughts' of the masses. It's become a tool to forward a particular ideology that projects violent revolutions as the panacea for all ills.

Our eminent historians—err distorians—who have been pastmasters in misrepresenting the history of Bharat to suit their dubious ideological agenda, could retain their pre-eminence not through intellectual heft but through political patronage and networking. In the late 1960s and the early 1970s, when communists infiltrated the country's academic institutions and think tanks en masse through political patronage and interference, the offices of P.N. Haksar and Nurul Hasan, the two leftist stalwarts who should be credited for this turn of events, would look like 'the durbars of old except that conversation would be mouthed in Marxist jargon even though it could not hide the grovelling and cringing overtones which clung tenaciously to words and gestures'.[4]

These distorians retained their monopolistic hold over Bharat's mindscape not through the supremacy of their ideas but through the sustainability of the political power that chose to patronise them. Since the 1990s, when the hold of the grand old party, the biggest benefactor of the communist ecosystem, slackened considerably, leftist historiography, quite predictably, suffered a setback.

Apart from the lack of political patronage, what further made history writing a level playing field, especially in the last decade and a half, was the emergence of social media, which democratized the world of ideas and opinions as never before. Younger writers and historians led by Sanjeev Sanyal, Prof. Lavanya Vemsani, Vikram Sampath, J. Sai Deepak, Amish Tripathi, Ashwin Sanghi, and Sandeep Balakrishna, among others, have enviable mass following and acceptance thanks to social media. 'Right-wing' scholars of yore, such as Ram Swarup, Sita Ram Goel, Koenraad Elst, Michel Danino, Shrikant S. Talageri, and N.S. Rajaram, among others—Arun Shourie and, to an extent, Swapan Dasgupta and Chandan Mitra were exceptions as they could write in newspapers and magazines, defying the left-imposed intellectual curfew—were confined to the margins despite their monumental contributions to the making of the non-left, dharmic history of Bharat. (The usage of the term 'right wing' is not right in the Indic context, but it is being used to keep things simpler and easy to understand.) This new breed of intellectuals could not be sidestepped. In fact, several right-wing scholars of the previous generation, such as David Frawley, Subhash Kak, and Meenakshi Jain, have adapted themselves to the needs of the social media generation and have done well.

Interestingly, the younger writers and historians are not just competing with the left-'liberals'; they are also beating them squarely on what was till the other day the exclusive communist turf. They aren't camera shy and are equally articulate with a pen. They rule the TV and social media shows and write bestsellers much more consistently than eminent distorians. Also, what separates the new right wing from the old is that while the previous generation largely operated within the parameters defined by their intellectual adversaries, the current ones are redefining and rewriting their own path.

The hold of the left scholars may have slackened, especially since 2014, but they still call the shots, especially in the field of publishing. Today, the likes of Sanyal and Sampath, Amish and Ashwin get published by mainstream publishers, but the right still finds itself on the wrong side of the publishing world. This is largely because the endeavour to intellectually dislodge the left in Bharat is individual-oriented rather than institutional or governmental. Unlike how the left piggybacked on Indira Gandhi's shoulders to infiltrate the country's academic world, the new right isn't the direct byproduct of political patronage, though there is no denying that the political development in the country has a spillover effect on the overall intellectual sphere.

The ongoing assault against the left is, thus, a less organized but more organic response from the intellectual right. This may explain why one finds an eclectic range of books coming up from individual efforts challenging the old, statist, leftist worldview, but the same doesn't get reflected spontaneously in the sarkari NCERT books of the day.

The gravity of the situation demands the right to get it right institutionally as well. Individual efforts are fine, but the change won't be durable without creating a strong, vibrant academic ecosystem. Bharat still has miles to go.

Notes

Introduction

1 https://economictimes.indiatimes.com/news/politics-and-nation/no-information-on-time-capsule-buried-during-indira-gandhis-tenure-pmo/articleshow/18716334.cms?from=mdr (accessed 30 October 2024).
2 Harishankar Parsai, *Aisa Bhi Socha Jata Hai*, Vani Prakashan, New Delhi, 2013.
3 Shankar Sharan, *Marxism and the Writing of Indian History*, India First Foundation, New Delhi, 2007.
4 Harishankar Parsai, *Aisa Bhi Socha Jata Hai*, Vani Prakashan, New Delhi, 2013.
5 Ibid.
6 Shankar Sharan, *Marxism and the Writing of Indian History*, India First Foundation, New Delhi, 2007.
7 Ibid.
8 Sarvepalli Gopal, *Jawaharlal Nehru: A Biography, Volume I*, Oxford University Press, Bombay, 1976.
9 Ibid.
10 Shankar Sharan, *Marxism and the Writing of Indian History*, India First Foundation, New Delhi, 2007.
11 Raj Thapar, *All These Years,* Penguin, New Delhi, 1991.
12 Bipan Chandra, Mridula Mukherjee and Aditya Mukherjee, *India After Independence 1947–2000*, Penguin, New Delhi, 2000.
13 Ibid.
14 Ibid.
15 Ibid.

16 Radha Rajadhyaksha, 'Liberals Battle against Siege of Minds', *The Times of India*, 18 May 2003.

17 https://www.loc.gov/programs/john-w-kluge-center/kluge-prize/past-winners/item/n50007613/romila-thapar-1931/ (accessed 30 October 2024).

18 Edward Luce, 'A Troubling Empire', FT.com, 30 May 2003.

19 Ram Puniyani, 'Did Bakhtiyar Khilji Destroy Nalanda University?', *The Wire*, 25 June 2024, https://thewire.in/history/did-bakhtiyar-khilji-destroy-nalanda-university (accessed 30 October 2024).

20 Minhaj al-Siraj, *Tabakat-i-Nasiri, Volume I*, translated from original Persian by Major H.G. Raverty, 1881.

21 Arun Shourie, *Eminent Historians: Their Technology, Their Line, Their Fraud*, HarperCollins, New Delhi, 1998.

22 Romila Thapar, Harbans Mukhia and Bipan Chandra, *Communalism and the Writing of Indian History*, People's Publishing House, New Delhi, 1969. The book contains three papers that were originally presented at an All India Radio seminar in October 1968.

23 Shankar Sharan, *Marxism and the Writing of Indian History*, India First Foundation, New Delhi, 2007.

24 Meenakshi Jain, *Flight of Deities and Rebirth of Temples*, Aryan Books, New Delhi, 2019.

25 R.C. Majumdar, *The History of Bengal, Volume I, Hindu Period*, University of Dacca, Dacca, 1943.

26 M.A. Stein, *Kalhana's Rajatarangini: A Chronicle of the Kings of Kashmir, Volume I*, Motilal Banarasidass, New Delhi, 2017.

27 Prof. Mohammad Habib, 'Introduction', *Elliot and Dowson's History of India As Told by Its Own Historians, Volume II*, Cosmopolitan Publishers, Aligarh, 1952.

28 Ibid.

29 Ibid.

30 Ibid.

31 K.A. Nizami, *Religion and Politics in India During the 13th Century*, Oxford University Press, New Delhi, 2002.

32 R.C. Majumdar (ed.), *The Delhi Sultanate, Volume VI*, Bharatiya Vidya Bhavan, New Delhi, 2017.

33 A.B.M. Habibullah, 'The Foundation of Muslim Rule in India', Doctoral Dissertation, Sh. Muhammad Ashraf Kashmiri Bazaar, Lahore, 1945.

34 Dr Edward C. Sachau, *Alberuni's India,* Rupa Publications, New Delhi, 2016.

35 K.S. Lal, *Growth of Scheduled Tribes and Castes in Medieval India*, Aditya Prakashan, New Delhi, 1995.

36 Ibid.

37 Ibid.

38 Ibid.

39 Ibid.

40 Wheeler M. Thackston (translator, editor and annotation), *The Baburnama: Memoirs of Babur, Prince and Emperor* (Introduction by Salman Rushdie), Modern Library, New York, 2002.

41 H.A.R. Gibb, *The Travels of Ibn Babttuta*, Goodword Books, New Delhi, 2012.

42 Dharampal, *The Beautiful Tree: Indigenous Indian Education in the 18th Century*, Society for Integrated Development of Himalayas, Mussoorie, 2007.

43 Ibid.

44 Ibid.

45 Ibid.

46 Arvind Sharma, *The Ruler's Gaze: A Study of British Rule over India from a Saidian Perspective*, HarperCollins, New Delhi, 2017.

47 Dipesh Chakrabarty, *The Calling of History: Sir Jadunath Sarkar and His Empire of Truth*, Permanent Black, New Delhi, 2017.

48 Ibid.

49 T.C.A. Raghavan, *History Men: Jadunath Sarkar, G.S. Sardesai, Raghubir Sinh and Their Quest for India's Past,* HarperCollins, New Delhi, 2020.

50 Ibid.

51 D.N. Jha, 'Grist to the reactionary mill', *The Indian Express*, 9 July 2014, https://indianexpress.com/article/opinion/columns/grist-to-the-reactionary-mill/ (accessed 31 October 2024).

52 Sarkar acknowledged the statesmanship and the legacy of Shivaji. According to him, Shivaji was 'not only the maker of the Maratha nation but also the greatest constructive genius of medieval India'. He writes, 'States fall, empires break up, dynasties become extinct, but the memory of a true "hero as king" like Shivaji remains an imperishable historical legacy for the entire human race'. But all this did not stop him from recording not-so-savoury episodes of Shivaji's life. Sarkar, for instance, refused to see the murder of Chandrarao More in 1655 to be 'undertaken in the interest of Shivaji's larger project of founding a Hindu *swaraj* when More, an agent of the Muslim ruler of Bijapur, simply stood in the way'. The sultan of Bijapur had made the Mores the jagirdar of the state of Javli in the 16th century, and Sarkar believed that the acquisition of this territory was central to the founding of Shivaji's kingdom. Further, as Dipesh Chakrabarty writes in *The Calling of History*, 'Furthermore, it hurts the Maratha intellectuals' regional pride that Sarkar's book on Shivaji (1919) should refer to the Maratha king in the diminutive form "Shiva". A review published in the *Mahratta* found this way of referring to "Shivaji Maharaj"—"following perhaps his Persian authorities"—disrespectful.'

53 Jadunath Sarkar (ed.), *The History of Bengal, Volume II: Muslim Period*, BR Publishing, New Delhi, 1943.

54 T.C.A. Raghavan, *History Men: Jadunath Sarkar, G.S. Sardesai, Raghubir Sinh and Their Quest for India's Past*, HarperCollins, New Delhi, 2020.

55 Ibid.

56 Ibid.

57 Ibid.

58 Satish Chandra, 'Mythifying History', *Seminar*, New Delhi, 1989.

59 Audrey Truschke, *Aurangzeb: The Man and the Myth*, Penguin, New Delhi, 2017.

60 Ibid.

61 Bryan Rigg, *Hitler's Jewish Soldiers: The Untold Story of Nazi Racial Laws and Men of Jewish Descent in the German Military*, University Press of Kansas, Kansas, 2002.

62 Audrey Truschke, *Aurangzeb: The Man and the Myth*, Penguin, New Delhi, 2017.

Chapter 1: Saraswati Sutra

1 Nirad C. Chaudhuri, *The Continent of Circe: An Essay on the Peoples of India*, Jaico, Bombay, 1966.

2 Ibid.

3 Shrikant G. Talageri, *Genetics and the Aryan Debate*, Voice of India, New Delhi, 2019.

4 Michel Danino, *The Lost River: On the Trail of the Sarasvati*, Penguin, New Delhi, 2010.

5 Ibid.

6 The basic problem with the Aryan invasion/migration theory is that it is premised on the assumption that the world was created, as per the Biblical time frame, in 4004 BC. So, after squeezing the millennia-old Indic civilization within this time frame, it became obvious that the so-called Aryan invasion couldn't have taken place before 1500–1200 BC. It was a tough job, but Max Muller was up to the task. In fact, he was so satisfied with his efforts that he smugly told his wife in a letter that any Hindu reading his translated Vedas would refuse to be a Hindu. Is it any surprise that the East India Company paid him £200 annually, quite a handsome payment in those times?

7 Shrikant G. Talageri, *Genetics and the Aryan Debate*, Voice of India, New Delhi, 2019.

8 Ibid.

9 Arun Shourie, *Eminent Historians: Their Technology, Their Line, Their Fraud*, HarperCollins, Gurgaon, 2014.

10 Throughout the earth's history, landmasses have often come together to form a supercontinent and then broken away, as is the case right now—each episode roughly taking place at the gap of 500 million years. As biochemist Pranay Lal writes in *Indica:*

A Deep Natural History of the Indian Subcontinent, 'Most often, continents break along pre-existing lines of weakness which were created during earlier continental collisions. Scientists call the clumping of all continents into one big landmass the "supercontinent cycle". We are witnessing a super slow-motion version of this cycle of collision even now. Africa, Arabia and Australia are slowly pressing into Eurasia. Scientists predict that in a couple of hundred million years, barring the Americas and Antarctica, most of these landmasses will fuse together again.'

11 Yuval Noah Harari, *Sapiens: A Brief History of Humankind*, Vintage, 2011.

12 Adam Rutherford, *A Brief History of Everyone Who Ever Lived*, W&N, 2017.

13 Yuval Noah Harari, *Sapiens: A Brief History of Humankind*, Vintage, 2011.

14 The jury is still out on whether the Agricultural Revolution was a boon or 'history's biggest fraud', as Harari argues in *Sapiens*. No doubt, the foundation of human civilization, as we know it today, is based primarily on the successes of the Agricultural Revolution. But then Harari has a point when he says that the 'Agriculture Revolution left farmers with lives generally more difficult and less satisfying than those of foragers'. He explains, 'The Agriculture Revolution certainly enlarged the sum total of food at the disposal of humankind, but the extra food did not translate into better diet or more leisure. Rather, it translated into population explosions and pampered elites. The average farmers worked harder than average foragers, and got a worse diet in return.'

Author James Suzman adds to this narrative in *Work: A History of How We Spend Our Time* (Bloomsbury, 2021). He tells the story of Richard Borshay Lee, who had researched one of the world's last few isolated hunting and gathering societies—the northern Ju/'hoansi, or the '!Kung Bushmen', as he referred to them at the time. Lee's research in 1963 coincided with a massive drought in the region. To his amazement, while 'most of rural Botswana's farming population only survived courtesy of emergency food-aid drops, the Ju/'hoansi needed no external assistance and sustained themselves easily on wild foods and hunting'. He also found that 'each individual in the band he followed consumed on an average 2,140 calories per day, a figure close to 10 per cent higher than the recommended daily intake for people of their stature'. Significantly, they would get the food they needed through 'a modest effort', so that they have far more leisure time than the 'modern' man!

15 Shrikant G. Talageri, *Genetics and the Aryan Debate*, Voice of India, New Delhi, 2019.

16 Michel Danino, *The Lost River: On the Trail of the Sarasvati,* Penguin, New Delhi, 2010.

17 Ibid.

18 Romila Thapar, Michael Witzel, Jaya Menon, Kai Friese and Razib Khan, *Which of Us Are Aryans?*, Aleph, New Delhi, 2019.

19 Michael Witzel, 'Autochthonous Aryans? The Evidence from Old Indian and Iranian Texts', *Electronic Journal of Vedic Studies*, Vol. 7 (2001), Issue 3.

20 Shrikant G. Talageri, *Genetics and the Aryan Debate,* Voice of India, New Delhi, 2019.

21 David Frawley, *Gods, Sages and Kings: Vedic Secrets of Ancient Civilization*, Motilal Banarsidass Publishing House, New Delhi, 1999.

22 Sri Aurobindo, *The Secret of Veda,* Sri Aurobindo Ashram Trust, Pondicherry, 1956.

23 B.R. Ambedkar, 'Caste in India: Their Genesis, Mechanism and Development', in Narendra Jadhav, *Ambedkar Writes*, Vol. 2, Konark Publications, New Delhi, 2013.

24 B.R. Ambedkar, 'Who Were the Shudras? How They Came to Be the Fourth Varna in the Indo-Aryan Society', in Narendra Jadhav, *Ambedkar Writes*, Vol. 2, Konark Publications, New Delhi, 2013.

25 B.R. Ambedkar, 'The Untouchables: Who Were They and Why They Became Untouchables?', in Narendra Jadhav, *Ambedkar Writes*, Vol. 2, Konark Publications, New Delhi, 2013.

26 Ancient Hindu literature, both secular and religious, is full of stories that showcase the flexibility of the caste system. So,

Mahidasa, a Chandala, could become a *rishi* associated with the *Aitareya Brahman*. Rishi Matanga was also a Chandala. There is mention of persons like Sharyati, Nahusha, Mandhata, and Prithu, who were *rishis* as well as kings. Nabhag, the son of King Dishta, became a Vaishya. His son, Bhalandan, again became a Kshatriya and established an empire. Vishwamitra was born a Kshatriya but later became a prominent Brahmin *rishi*. In fact, Bharat's most celebrated authors—Valmiki and Vyasa—hailed from lower castes. My personal favourite is the story of Satyakama Jabala, son of an unwed mother, whose truthfulness on his origins made his guru say he was a Brahmin. For, the guru explains, a Brahmin alone could have said nonchalantly such inconvenient truths.

27 Subhash Kak, *The Idea of India: Bharat as a Civilisation*, Garuda Prakashan, New Delhi, 2023.

28 The *Rig Veda* contains about a hundred references to the ocean (*samudra*), besides dozens of references to ships and to rivers flowing into the sea. Some of the most prominent Vedic figures like Manu, Turvasha, Yadu, et al., are flood figures, saved from across the sea. Varuna, the Vedic god of the sea, is the father of several Vedic *rishis*, including Vasishtha, the main architect behind Sudas' victory against a confederacy of 10 kings in the Battle of the Ten Kings, and Bhrigu, the second most important seer family.

29 Sanjeev Sanyal, *Land of the Seven Rivers: A Brief History of India's Geography*, Penguin, New Delhi, 2013.

30 Navaratna S. Rajaram and David Frawley, *Vedic Aryans and the Origins of Civilisation,* Voice of India, New Delhi, 2014.

31 R.C. Majumdar (ed.), *History and Culture of Indian People, Volume 1: The Vedic Age*, George Allen & Unwin, London, 1951.

32 P.L. Bhargava, *India in the Vedic Age: A History of Aryan Expansion in India*, DK Printworld, New Delhi, 2001.

33 Shrikant G. Talageri, *Aryan Invasion Theory and Indian Nationalism*, Voice of India, New Delhi, 1993.

34 K.D. Sethna, *The Problem of Aryan Origins*, Aditya Prakashan, New Delhi, 1980.

Chapter 2: Epics and Empires

1 Romila Thapar, Valmik Thapar and Yusuf Ansari, *Exotic Aliens: The Lion and the Cheetah in India,* Aleph Book Company, New Delhi, 2013.
2 Ibid.
3 Romila Thapar, *Early India: From the Origins to AD 1300,* Penguin, New Delhi, 2003.
4 Romila Thapar, Valmik Thapar and Yusuf Ansari, *Exotic Aliens: The Lion and the Cheetah in India,* Aleph, New Delhi, 2013.
5 Ibid.
6 Ibid.
7 Divyabhanusinh Chavda, *The Story of Asia's Lions,* Marg publications, New Delhi, 2006.
8 Charles Allen, *Ashoka: The Search for India's Lost Emperor*, Abacus, London, 2013.
9 Patrick Olivelle, *Ashoka: Portrait of a Philosopher King*, HarperCollins, New Delhi, 2023.
10 Upinder Singh, *Political Violence in Ancient India*, Harvard, New Delhi, 2021.
11 Sanjeev Sanyal, *Land of the Seven Rivers*, Penguin, New Delhi, 2012.
12 Romila Thapar, *Asoka and the Decline of the Mauryas*, Oxford University Press`, New Delhi, 2023.
13 Romila Thapar, *A History of India, Volume 1*, Penguin, New Delhi, 1996.
14 Yoshita Srivastava, 'Romila Thapar's "Ashoka-Yudhisthira" Reference Sparks Controversy', *The Quint*, 21 September 2019.
15 Romila Thapar, *Early India: From the Origins to AD 1300*, Penguin, New Delhi, 2002.
16 Romila Thapar, *A History of India, Volume 1*, Penguin, New Delhi, 1996.
17 Subhash Kak, *The Idea of India: Bharat as a Civilisation*, Garuda Prakashan, New Delhi, 2023.
18 Ibid.

19 R.C. Majumdar, (ed.), *History and Culture of Indian People, Volume 1: The Vedic Age*, Allen & Unwin, London, 1951.
20 Ibid.
21 John Keay, *India: A History*, William Collins publications, London, 2000.
22 Romila Thapar, *A History of India, Volume 1*, Penguin, New Delhi, 1996.
23 Sri Aurobindo writes in *The Secret of the Veda*, 'The ritual system recognised by Sayana may, in its externalities, stand; the naturalistic sense discovered by European scholarship may, in its general conceptions, be accepted; but behind them there is always the true and hidden secret of the Veda—the secret words, *ninya vacamsi*, which were spoken for the purified in soul and the awakened in knowledge… Finally, the incoherencies of the Vedic texts will at once be explained and disappear. They exist in appearance only, because the thread of the sense is to be found in an inner meaning. That thread found, the hymns appear as logical and organic wholes and the expression, though alien in type to our modern ways of thinking and speaking, becomes, in its own style, just and precise and sins rather by economy of phrase than by excess, by over-pregnancy rather than by poverty of sense. The Veda ceases to be merely an interesting remnant of barbarism and takes rank among the most important of the world's early Scriptures.'
24 A.L. Basham, *The Wonder That Was India*, Pan Macmillan, New Delhi, 2019.
25 The term *Upanishad* literally means 'a session', sitting at the feet of a master who imparts esoteric doctrines. There are said to be 108 Upanishads altogether, though many of them were compiled much later and are of little importance. The earlier Upanishads, like the great *Brihadaranyaka* and the *Chandogya*, are in prose and consist of a series of short expositions of some aspect of the new doctrines, often in the form of question and answer. The Upanishads of somewhat later compositions, like the *Kaṭha* and the *Svetasvatara*, are in verse, and their contents are more closely integrated.

26 A.L. Basham, The Wonder That Was India, Pan Macmillan, New Delhi, 2019.

27 Ibid.

28 Ananda Coomaraswamy, *The Dance of Shiva*, Rupa, New Delhi, 2019.

29 Sri Aurobindo, *The Secret of the Veda,* Sri Aurobindo Ashram Trust, Pondicherry, 2020.

30 A.L. Basham, *The Wonder That Was India*, Rupa, New Delhi, 1995.

31 Ibid.

32 While most contemporary historians, under the Marxist or colonial influence, regard the Puranas as a make-believe, superstitious work, the Indic tradition gives it a Veda-like importance. F.E. Pargiter writes in *Ancient Indian Historical Tradition*, 'The Brahmin, who may know the four *Vedas* with the *Angas* and *Upanishads*, should not really be (regarded as) having attained proficiency, if he should not thoroughly know the *Purana*.'

33 A.L. Basham, *The Wonder That Was India*, Rupa, New Delhi, 1995.

34 Subhash Kak, *The Idea of India: Bharat as a Civilisation*, Garuda Prakashan, New Delhi, 2023.

35 D.N. Jha, *Ancient India: An Introductory Outline*, People's Publication House, New Delhi, 1995.

36 John Zubrzycki, *The Shortest History of India*, Picador, New Delhi, 2022.

37 Ibid.

38 Arundhati Roy, *The Doctor and the Saint*, Penguin, New Delhi, 2017.

39 Ambedkar bemoaned in his letter of resignation from Nehru's Cabinet: 'Many ministers have been given two or three portfolios so that they have been overburdened… I was not even appointed to be a member of the main Committees of the Cabinet such as the Foreign Affairs Committee, or the Defence Committee. When the Economics Affairs Committee was formed, I expected, in view of the fact that I was primarily a student of Economics and Finance, to be appointed to this Committee. But I was left out.'

40 https://www.thehindubusinessline.com/companies/ambedkar-voted-greatest-indian-in-poll/article23082947.ece (accesssed 30 October 2024).
41 Arun Shourie, *Worshipping False God: Ambedkar and the Facts Which Have Been Erased*, HarperCollins, New Delhi, 2017.
42 *Dr Babasaheb Ambedkar: Writings and Speeches, Volume 9*, New Delhi, 1991.
43 Arun Shourie, *Worshipping False God: Ambedkar and the Facts Which Have Been Erased*, HarperCollins, New Delhi, 2017.
44 Ibid.
45 B.R. Ambedkar, 'Pakistan or the Partition of India', 1940, in Narendra Jadhav, *Ambedkar Writes*, Vol. 3, Konark Publications, New Delhi, 2013.
46 Ibid.
47 Shashi Tharoor, *Ambedkar: A Life*, Aleph, New Delhi, 2022.
48 Romila Thapar, *A History of India, Volume 1: From the Discovery of India to 1526*, Penguin, New Delhi, 1996.
49 According to Indologist T.W. Rhys-Davids, Buddha ate mushrooms. In *Buddhism: Being a Sketch of the Life and Teachings of Gautama* (Gyan Publishing, New Delhi, 2020), he writes, 'On reaching Pava he is entertained by a goldsmith of that place named Chunda (a man therefore not of high social standing), who prepares for him a meal of rice and mushrooms. (The Pali word used is *sukaramaddava*. This has been rendered "tender pork". But for the reasons given in my "Milinda", I. 244, I now think it means mushrooms.).'
50 T.W. Rhys-Davids, *Buddhism: Being a Sketch of the Life and Teachings of Gautama*, Gyan Publishing, New Delhi, 2020.
51 Romila Thapar, *Asoka and the Decline of the Mauryas*, Oxford India Perennials, New Delhi, 2023.
52 Charles Allen, *Ashoka: The Search for India's Lost Emperor*, Abacus, London, 2013.
53 Sanjeev Sanyal, *Land of the Seven Rivers*, Penguin, New Delhi, 2012.

54 Romila Thapar, *Asoka and the Decline of the Mauryas*, Oxford University Press, New Delhi, 2023.
55 Ibid.

Chapter 3: Invasion to Affluence

1 Romila Thapar, *Early India: From the Origins to AD 1300*, Penguin, New Delhi, 2003.
2 B.B. Kumar, *India and Central Asia: A Shared Past*, Concept publications, New Delhi, 2015.
3 B.B. Kumar, *Lord Shiva: In India and Abroad*, Motilal Banarasidass publications in collaboration with ICSSR, New Delhi, 2024.
4 Elsworth Huntington, *The Pulse of Asia: A Journey in Central Asia Illustrating the Geographic Basis of History*, Houghton, Mifflin, New York, 1907.
5 Bibek Debroy (trans.), *The Brahma Purana· Volume 1*, Penguin, New Delhi, 2021.
6 Bibek Debroy (trans.), *The Markandeya Purana*, Penguin, New Delhi, 2019.
7 S.M. Ali, *The Geography of the Puranas*, People's Publishing House, New Delhi, 1966.
8 Valmiki, The Ramayana, Kishkindha Kand, 43.55.60.
9 Ved Vyas, The Mahabharata, Sabha Parva, 52. 13–17·
10 Ved Vyas, The Mahabharata, Ugyog Parva, 4.15.
11 Ved Vyas, The Mahabharata, Bhishma Parva, by 75.21.
12 Ved Vyas, The Mahabharata, Sabha Parva, 28.11–15, 52. 13–17.
13 Subhash Kak, *The Idea of India: Bharat as a Civilisation*, Garuda Prakashan, New Delhi, 2023.
14 Ibid.
15 *Bhagavad Purana*, 9.8.4–7; *Vishnu Purana*, 4.3.42–48.
16 The story of Buddhist scholar Kumarajiva (344–413 AD), born to a Kashmiri father, probably a minister in the Takshashila royal court, and a Kuchean mother, is a reminder of India's deep connections with the Central Asian region—and also how much its civilizational/cultural spread has shrunk in the

last two millennia. Kumarajiva, after all, studied Buddhism in Kashmir, but for Vedas he chose to visit Kashgar in today's Xinjiang region. It's pertinent to note that the land where Kumarajiva went to study Vedas was the hub of Buddhism, disputing the predominant Hindu–Buddhist conflict narrative put forward by colonial-leftist historiography.

Kucha, in the northern Tarim basin, for instance, was a centre of Buddhist learning, and from here Indian music spread to China. Similarly, Yarkand and Khotan (which tradition says was built by King Ashoka's son Kutsan in 240 BC) in northern Tarim valley were centres of Mahayana Buddhism, while Kashgar, Kucha and Turfan were the hubs of Hinayana Buddhism. What further manifests the Hindu–Buddhist cultural continuum in the region is that 'not very far' from a monastery in Miran, as William Dalrymple writes in his 2024 book, *The Golden Road*, 'some of the very earliest surviving fragments of the text of the *Mahabharata* have recently been dug up'.

17 B.B. Kumar, *Lord Shiva: In India and Abroad,* Motilal Banarasidass publications in collaboration with ICSSR, New Delhi, 2024.

18 Berthold Laufer, 'Inspirational Dreams in Eastern Asia', *Journal of American Folklore*, April 1931.

19 B.B. Kumar, *Lord Shiva: In India and Abroad,* Motilal Banarasidass publications in collaboration with ICSSR, New Delhi, 2024.

20 Subhash Kak, *The Idea of India: Bharat as a Civilisation*, Garuda Prakashan, New Delhi, 2023.

21 Kalidasa, *Malavikagnimitram*, Srinivas Reddy (trans.), Penguin, New Delhi, 2014.

22 Sanjeev Sanyal, *The Ocean of Churn: How the Indian Ocean Shaped Human History*, Penguin, New Delhi, 2016.

23 D.R. Bhandarkar, *Corpus Inscriptionum Indicarum, Volume III: Inscriptions of the Early Gupta Kings*, Archaeological Survey of India, New Delhi, 1981.

24 Vishakhadatta was a Sanskrit poet who lived somewhere between the fourth and the sixth century AD. He is known for

two of his plays, the *Mudrarakshasa* and the *Devichandraguptam. Mudrarakshasa* narrates the rise of Chandragupta Maurya to power with the help of his guru, Chanakya.

25 Author Peter Frankopan, in his book *The Silk Roads: A New History of the World*, writes how 'Rome's eyes were opened by the world it encountered in the east'. He writes, 'Asia had already acquired a reputation for lazy luxury and fine living. It was indescribably wealthy, wrote Cicero, its harvests the stuff of legend, the variety of its produce incredible, and the size of its herds and flocks simply amazing. Its exports were colossal. Such was Asia's wealth that Romans opined that its inhabitants could afford to dedicate themselves to idle pleasure. Little wonder that it was in the east that Roman soldiers came of age, wrote the poet Sallust: this was where Roman soldiers learnt how to make love, to be drunk, to enjoy statues, pictures and art.'

26 Angus Maddison, *The World Economy, Volume 2: Historical Statistics*, Academic Foundation, New Delhi, 2007.

27 Wilfred H. Schoff, *The Periplus of the Erythraean Sea: Travel and Trade in the Indian Ocean by a Merchant of the First Century*, Kessinger Publications, USA, 2007.

28 Sanjeev Sanyal, *Land of the Seven Rivers: A Brief History of India's Geography*, Penguin, New Delhi, 2012.

29 Kanakalatha Mukund, *Merchants of Tamilakam: Pioneers of International Trade*, Penguin, New Delhi, 2012.

30 Subhash Kak, *The Idea of India: Bharat as a Civilisation*, Garuda Prakashan, New Delhi, 2023. In this book, Kak also quotes British traveller Abraham Parsons to showcase the sophistication of Bharat's ships vis-à-vis the Western. Parsons writes, 'Ship building at Bombay are not only as strong, but as handsome, are as well finished as ships built in any part of Europe; the timber and plank, of which they are built, so far exceeds any in Europe for durability that it is usual for ships to last 50 to 60 years'.

31 William Dalrymple, *The Golden Road: How Ancient India Transformed the World*, Bloomsbury, London, 2024.

32 Rahul Sankrityayan, *Madhya Asia Ka Itihas (Vol. 1)*, Bihar Rashtrabhasha Parishad, Patna, 1956.

33 Bertil Lintner, *The End of the Chinese Century?*, HarperCollins, New Delhi, 2024.
34 Valerie Hansen, *Silk Road: A New History*, Oxford University Press, New Delhi, 2012.
35 The term 'Silk Road' is a 19th-century invention, first coined by German geographer Ferdinand von Richthofen in 1877. In the English language world, it became a buzzword after E.P. Dutton came up with *The Silk Road*, an English translation of a Swedish book by Sven Hedin, one of von Richthofen's students. Dutton's 1936 book became a bestseller, and the rest is history.
36 Valerie Hansen, *Silk Road: A New History*, Oxford University Press, New Delhi, 2012.
37 Ibid.
38 Ibid.
39 Tamilakam was ruled by the 'three kings' or *muvendar*. The Pandyas had their capital at Madurai, the Cholas at Uraiyur (Tiruchi), and Cheras as Vanji (Karur). According to *Silappadikaram*, a Tamil epic attributed to a prince-turned-monk, Ilanko Atikal: 'The Tamil region extends from the hills of Vishnu (Tirupati) in the north to the oceans at the cape in the south. In this region of cool waters were the four great cities of Madurai with its towers; Uraiyur which was famous; tumultuous Kanchi; and Puhar with the roaring waters (of the river Kaveri and the ocean.'
40 Sanjeev Sanyal, *The Ocean of Churn: How the Indian Ocean Shaped Human History*, Penguin, New Delhi, 2016.
41 Kanakalatha Mukund, *Merchants of Tamilakam: Pioneers of International Trade*, Penguin, New Delhi, 2012.
42 *Naturalis Historia* by Pliny the Elder is the largest single work to have survived from the Roman Empire to this day.
43 Francois Bernier, *Travels in the Mogul Empire: 1656 to 1668*, Manohar Publishers & Distributors, New Delhi, 2023.
44 D.N. Jha, *Ancient India: An Introductory Outline*, People's Publishing House, New Delhi, 1977.
45 Ibid.
46 In *Das Kapital*, German philosopher Karl Marx propounds the theory of historical materialism, according to which human

societies pass through six stages of development: primitive communism, slave society, feudalism, capitalism, socialism and global, and stateless communism. In the last stage, according to Marx, the exploitation of one class by another would end as the society would be classless, without private ownership of the means of production.

47 Fa Hien, a Chinese scholar who visited Bharat in the early fifth century AD, left a fascinating account of his life and times in the country. Although his writings are focused primarily on Buddhism and Buddhist sites, institutions and people, it does leave behind an impression of a rich, prosperous country under the Guptas.

48 Vatsyayana, *Kama Sutra*, translated by A.N.D. Haksar, Penguin, New Delhi, 2011.

49 The journey of *Kama Sutra,* too, reveals Bharat's civilizational journey as a consolidated effort of one generation after another. The writers of ancient texts would invariably recall the contribution of past *rishis* in the making of a text. Just like Kautilya, who credits previous lawmakers for the making of *Arthashastra*, Vatsyayana doesn't claim the ownership of the *Kama Sutra*. He gives credit to the lord of beings for first enunciating in one hundred thousand chapters the means for pursuing the aforementioned three ends of life in this world. He then credits 'great God's servant Nandi' for separating Kama Sutra and 'put them forth in 1,000 chapters'. Shvetaketu, the son of Uddalaka, compresses it into 500 chapters. And Babhravya of Panchala abridged them into 150 chapters. Vatsyayana further condensed them to what we read today as *Kama Sutra*.

50 Vatsyayana, *Kama Sutra*, translated by A.N.D. Haksar, Penguin, New Delhi, 2011.

Chapter 4: The Age of Extremes

1 R.S. Sharma, *Indian Feudalism*, MacMillan, New Delhi, 1990.

2 Peter Jackson, *The Delhi Sultanate: A Political and Military History*, Cambridge University Press, New York, 2003.

3 According to *Advaita Vedanta*, there is no duality between the creator and the created universe; everything in the experienced world has its root in Brahman, which is unchanging consciousness.
4 Sudhakshina Rangaswami (ed.), *The Roots of Vedanta: Selections from Shankara's Writings*, Penguin, New Delhi, 2012.
5 Ibid.
6 Pavan K. Varma, *Adi Shankaracharya: Hinduism's Greatest Thinker*, Tranquebar Press, Chennai, 2018.
7 Nayanjot Lahiri, *Time Pieces: A Whistle-Stop Tour of Ancient India*, Hachette, New Delhi, 2022.
8 Ibid.
9 R.C. Majumdar, H.C. Raychaudhuri and Kalikinkar Datta, *An Advanced History of India*, Macmillan, Madras (Chennai), 1986.
10 John Keay, *India: A History*, William Collins, London, 1986.
11 In the Mahabharata, Karkota sought—and received—help from King Nala when there was a wildfire in the forest where he resided.
12 Samuel Beal, *Si-Yu-Ki: Buddhist Record of the Western World, Volume I*, Trubner & Co., London, 1906.
13 R.C. Majumdar (ed.), *The History and Culture of the Indian People, Volume 3: The Classical Age*, Bharatiya Vidya Bhavan, New Delhi, 2018.
14 Kashmiri historian Prithivi Nath Kaul Bamzai in his book, *Cultural and Political History of Kashmir*, states that the victory over the Tibetans was so significant that they 'were celebrated not only during the time of Lalitaditya but even long afterwards. Kalhana records that in his time the victories were annually celebrated and Alberuni mentions that the Kashmiris observed the second of Chitra as a day of Lalitaditya's victory over the Tibetans.'
15 R.C. Majumdar (ed.), *The History and Culture of the Indian People, Volume 3: The Classical Age*, Bharatiya Vidya Bhavan, New Delhi, 2018.
16 Hermann Gaetz, *Studies in the History of Art in Kashmir and the Indian Himalaya*, Otto Harrassowitz publications, Wiesebaden (Germany), 1969.

17 Vikram Sampath, *Bravehearts of Bharat: Vignettes From Indian History*, Penguin, New Delhi, 2022.
18 R.C. Majumdar, H.C. Raychaudhuri and Kalikinkar Datta, *An Advanced History of India*, Macmillan, Madras (Chennai), 1986.
19 R.C. Majumdar (ed.), *The History and Culture of the Indian People, Volume 4: The Age of Imperial Kanauj*, Bharatiya Vidya Bhavan, New Delhi, 2018.
20 Ibid.
21 R.C. Majumdar (ed.), *The History and Culture of the Indian People, Volume 4: The Age of Imperial Kanauj*, Bharatiya Vidya Bhavan, New Delhi, 2018.
22 Ibid.
23 Ibid.
24 Anirudh Kanisetti, *Lord of the Deccan: Southern India from the Chalukyas to the Cholas*, Juggernaut, New Delhi, 2022.
25 R.C. Majumdar (ed.), *The History and Culture of the Indian People, Volume 4: The Age of Imperial Kanauj*, Bharatiya Vidya Bhavan, New Delhi, 2018.
26 Romila Thapar, *A History of India, Volume I: From the Discovery of India to 1526*, Penguin, New Delhi, 1996.
27 Anirudh Kanisetti, *Lord of the Deccan: Southern India from the Chalukyas to the Cholas*, Juggernaut, New Delhi, 2022.
28 Major H.G. Raverty, *Tabakat-i-Nasiri: A General History of the Muhammadan Dynasties of Asia, Including Hindustan, Volume I*, Gilbert & Rivington, London, 1881.
29 Sandeep Balakrishna, *Invaders and Infidels, Book 2: The Khilji Devastation of Infidel Devagiri*, BluOne Ink, New Delhi, 2023.
30 Richard M. Eaton, *The Rise of Islam and the Bengal Frontier: 1204-1760*, Oxford University Press, New Delhi, 1997.
31 Sanjeev Sanyal, *The Ocean of Churn: How the Indian Ocean Shaped Human History*, Penguin, New Delhi, 2016.
32 Romila Thapar, *A History of India, Volume I: From the Discovery of India to 1526*, Penguin, New Delhi, 1996.
33 R.C. Majumdar (ed.), *The History and Culture of the Indian People, Volume 3: The Classical Age*, Bharatiya Vidya Bhavan, New Delhi, 2018.

34 One can gauge the prosperity and opulence of the Cholas from their temples, especially the Brihadishvara temple of Thanjavur, built by Rajaraja I between 1003 and 1010 AD. This temple structure is so huge that it contains almost 40 times as much stone as the average Chola temple. The temple is 208 feet tall, and yet it doesn't cast a shadow on the ground. This is because of the ingenuity of the architect who placed stones in such a manner that it prevented the formation of a shadow on the ground. As the story goes, when the temple was completed, Rajaraja I questioned the architect about its strength and stability, to which the latter replied, 'Even its shadow will not fall, Raja!'

35 Romila Thapar, *Early Indians: From the Origins to AD 1300*, Penguin, New Delhi, 2003.

36 Anirudh Kanisetti, *Lord of the Deccan: Southern India from the Chalukyas to the Cholas*, Juggernaut, New Delhi, 2022.

37 K.A. Nilakanta Sastri, *The Cholas*, University of Madras, Madras (Chennai), 1955.

38 Ibid.

Chapter 5: Of Invaders and Infidels

1 Mohammad Habib, who taught at the Aligarh Muslim University, wrote his book *Sultan Mahmud of Ghazni: A Study* in 1927.

2 *Tarikh-i-Yamini*, by Abu Nasr al-Utbi.

3 Ibid.

4 Ibid.

5 Ibid.

6 Arab geographer Zakariya al-Qazwini writes in his 13th-century book, *Athar al-Bilad wa Akhbar al-'ibad*: 'Somnath is a celebrated city of India, situated on the shore of the sea, and washed by its waves. Among the wonders of that place was the temple in which was placed the idol called Somnath. This idol was in the middle of the temple without anything to support it from below, or to suspend it from above. It was held in the highest honour among

the Hindus, and whoever beheld it floating in the air was struck with amazement, whether he was a Musulman or an infidel.'

7 Zakariyya' al-Qazwini of Persia, in his book *Athar al-Bilad wa Akhbar al-'ibad* (1263 AD), wrote about the 1025 AD Somnath incident, thus: 'The Indians made a desperate resistance. They would go weeping and crying for help into the temple, and the issue forth and fight till all were killed. The number of the slain exceeded 50,000.'

8 John Briggs, *History of the Rise of the Mahomedan Power in India till the Year AD 1612, Volume I*, Atlantic Publishers, New Delhi, 2023.

9 Romila Thapar, *Somnatha: The Many Voices of a History*, Penguin, New Delhi, 2004.

10 Jawaharlal Nehru, *Discovery of India*, Penguin, New Delhi, 2008.

11 R.C. Majumdar (ed.), *The History and Culture of the Indian People, Volume 3: The Classical Age*, Bharatiya Vidya Bhavan, New Delhi, 2018.

12 Ram Gopal Misra, *Indian Resistance to Muslim Invaders up to 1206 AD*, Anu Books, Meerut, 1992.

13 Will Durant, *The Story of Civilisation, Volume I: Our Oriental Heritage*, Simon and Schuster, New York, 1964.

14 R.C. Majumdar (ed.), *The History and Culture of the Indian People, Volume 3: The Classical Age*, Bharatiya Vidya Bhavan, New Delhi, 2018.

15 H.M. Elliot and John Dawson, *The History of India as Told by Its Own Historians, Volume I*, Trrubner & Co, London, 1867.

16 Mirza Kalichbeg Fredunbeg, *The Chachnamah: An Ancient History of Sindh*, Commissioner's Press, Karachi, 1900.

17 R.C. Majumdar (ed.), *The History and Culture of the Indian People, Volume 3: The Classical Age*, Bharatiya Vidya Bhavan, New Delhi, 2018.

18 Ibid.

19 Mirza Kalichbeg Fredunbeg, *The Chachnamah: An Ancient History of Sindh*, Commissioner's Press, Karachi, 1900.

20 The *Chachnama* says that King Dahar had 500 Arab troops in his service. They were Muslims and were said to have fled to

Bharat to evade punishment by the caliph. Yet, when the Arabs attacked Sind, they refused to fight on Dahar's behalf against their co-religionists.

21 R.C. Majumdar (ed.), *The History and Culture of the Indian People, Volume 3: The Classical Age*, Bharatiya Vidya Bhavan, New Delhi, 2018.

22 Sandeep Balakrishna, *Invaders and Infidels: From Sindh to Delhi, Book I*, Bloomsbury, New Delhi, 2021.

23 Ram Gopal Misra, *Indian Resistance to Muslim Invaders up to 1206 AD*, Anu Books, Meerut, 1992.

24 Vikram Sampath, *Bravehearts of Bharat: Vignettes from Indian History*, Penguin, New Delhi, 2022.

25 In 1000 AD, Mahmud of Ghazni began his Bharat attacks and three generations of Hindu Shahi kings sacrificed themselves trying to stem the tide of the Muslim invasion. Jayapala could not bear the indignity of defeat and committed suicide in 1001 AD. Anandapala died fighting in 1009 AD, and Trilochanapala died around 1019 AD in a similar manner. They managed to organize a confederacy of Hindu rulers against Muslims twice in two decades. In the first case, Jayapala managed to get the support of Tomaras, Chahamanas and Chandelas, but lost in a close battle. In the second case, Anandapala had gained the initial advantage over Mahmud, who then assigned his best archers to target the Shahi king, who could easily be recognized in the battlefield as he was sitting on an elephant (another incident where a Hindu ruler's elephant obsession let him down).

26 R.C. Majumdar (ed.), *The History and Culture of the Indian People, Volume 5: The Struggle for Empire*, Bharatiya Vidya Bhavan, New Delhi, 2018.

27 Vikram Sampath, *Bravehearts of Bharat: Vignettes from Indian History*, Penguin, New Delhi, 2022.

28 Jadunath Sarkar, *Military History of India*, Gyan Publishers, New Delhi, 2022.

29 Ibid.

30 K.M. Munshi, *Somanatha: The Shrine Eternal*, Bharatiya Vidya Bhavan, Bombay, 1965.

31 Jadunath Sarkar, *Military History of India*, Gyan Publishers, New Delhi, 2022.

32 Ibid.

33 Sandeep Balakrishna, *Invaders and Infidels: The Khalji Devastation of Infidel Devagiri, Book 2*, BluOne Ink, New Delhi, 2023.

34 In Book 1 of *Invaders and Infidels*, published by Bloomsbury in 2021, author Sandeep Balakrishna, writes how 'Lahore was the gateway to infidel India. It was also the city that Ghiyath al-Din Muhammad had gifted to his more famous younger brother Muhammad of Ghori to launch his incursions into mainland India. Which is why the latter had made it the capital of his dominions in India. At the height of the Ghaznavid and Ghurid power, Muslim chroniclers had declared Lahore as "the centre of Islam in India"… It (Lahore) was where Persian poetry originated and then blossomed and spread to Indian soil as Muslim rule spread deeper in the country'.

35 John Briggs, *History of the Rise of the Mahomedan Power in India till the Year* AD *1612, Volume I*, Atlantic Publishers, New Delhi, 2023.

36 Abraham Eraly, *The Age of Wrath: A History of the Delhi Sultanate*, Penguin, New Delhi, 2014.

37 As quoted by Sita Ram Goel in his book, *The Story of Islamic Imperialism in India*, Voice of India, New Delhi, 1994.

38 K.S. Lal, in *History of Khaljis*, writes about Jalaluddin Khilji: 'The new king's character is clearly reflected in an incident which occurred early in his reign. After Jalal has been firmly seated on the throne, writes Barani, he rode one day into Delhi and visited the Red Palace of Balban. The old memories of how he had stood before the throne in years gone by filled his eyes with tears. He got down from his horse at the outer gate of the palace and bowed in obeisance. When Malik Ahmad Chap reminded him that the palace now belonged to him and he should not behave in the way he did, Jalaluddin burst into tears and remonstrated: "You know that nobody among my ancestors has been a king, so that the pride and dignity of kingship might have been inherited by me. Sultan Balban sat here on the throne and I served him.

The awe and dignity of that monarch have not left my breast. ... This palace had been built by Balban during his Khanship and it is his property and that of his sons and relatives." The old King could not think of sitting on the throne while his colleagues, who, like himself, had served under Balban, remained standing before him. He only took his seat among the nobles and putting his turban to his eyes wept bitterly.'

39 H.M. Elliot and John Dawson, *The History of India as Told by Its Own Historians, Volume III*, Trrubner & Co., London, 1871.

40 Sandeep Balakrishna, *Invaders and Infidels: The Khalji Devastation of Infidel Devagiri, Book 2*, BluOne Ink, New Delhi, 2023.

41 K.S. Lal, *History of the Khiljis,* Munshiram Manoharlal Publishers, New Delhi, 1980.

42 Ibid.

43 Ibid.

44 Sita Ram Goel, *The Story of Islamic Imperialism in India*, Voice of India, New Delhi, 1994.

45 Ramdhari Singh Dinkar, *Sanskriti Ke Char Adhyay*, Lokbharati Prakashan, Allahabad (Prayagraj), 2009.

46 M.N. Roy 'Historic Role of Islam', https://www.marxists.org/archive/roy/1939/historical-role-islam/ch05.htm#:~:text=Islam%20as%20the%20most%20rigorous,the%20foundation%20of%20modern%20rationalism (accessed 2 November 2024).

47 R.C. Majumdar (ed.), *The History and Culture of the Indian People, Volume III: The Classical Age*, Bharatiya Vidya Bhavan, New Delhi, 2018.

48 Ibid.

49 Ibid.

50 A.L. Srivastava, *The Sultanate of Delhi,* Shiva Lal Agarwala & Company, Agra, 1966.

51 Sita Ram Goel, *The Story of Islamic Imperialism in India*, Voice of India, New Delhi, 1994.

52 V.S. Naipaul, *Beyond Belief: Islamic Excursions Among the Converted Peoples,* Penguin, New Delhi, 1998.

53 While Alauddin Khilji attacked Devagiri in south Bharat in 1295 AD, Malik Kafur led a series of expeditions in the south, against the Yadavas (1308), the Kakatiyas (1310), the Hoysalas (1311), and the Pandyas (1311). As for Mohammed bin Tughlaq, he attacked the south in the 1320s.

54 The four Hindu rulers of the south—Yadavas, Kakatiyas, Hoysalas, and Pandyas—were busy fighting against themselves even when the Muslim invasion was just a matter of time. In fact, when Alauddin Khilji attacked Devagiri, the crown prince was busy settling scores with his southern neighbour. Worse, the Yadava king of Devagiri, Ramachandra, actually assisted against Hindu rulers in the south.

55 K.A. Nilakanta Sastri, *A History of South India: From Prehistoric Times to the Fall of Vijayanagar,* Oxford University Press, New Delhi, 2023.

56 In her poem, *Madhuravijayam*, Gangadevi poignantly describes the situation in Madurai after the attack of Muslims. She was the wife of Kumara Kampana, son of Bukka. She writes (as quoted by Sandeep Balakrishna in his 2024 book, *Reclaiming Bharatavarsha*):

'O King! The city, which is called Madhurapuri for its honeyed loveliness, has now become the city of cruel beasts; it now lives up to its earlier name of Vyaghrapuri, the city of tigers because humans don't dwell there (anymore).

Those temples of Gods, which used to reverberate with the sacred melody of the mridangam, now echo the dreadful howls of jackals. In the Agraharams of our city, huge columns of smoke emanating from the scared yagnas used to rise up and reach the skies amid the sacred Vedic chants but alas, today those self-same quarters send up wretched stenches of meat roasted by the Turushkas; the Vedic chants are today replaced by the beastly cacophonies of drunken hoodlums.

During the days of Pandyas, our women used to bathe in (river) Taamraparni, whose waters turned white from the sandal-paste applied to their breasts. My lord! Now she's coloured only in red from the currents of blood flowing into her from all the cows slaughtered by its wicked occupiers all over the country.

King! I cannot bear to look at the countenance of those Dravida ladies who were bounteously endowed with beauty. Ravished horribly by the scourging Turushkas, these delicate women now sport lifeless lips and exhale hot breaths, and their abundant tresses that have come undone are painful to the eyes. I don't have the words to describe the suffering and dishonour painted on their faces, which know neither redemption nor protection.'

57 There has been a tendency to portray Sage Vidyaranya's role as marginal so as to negate the importance of Hinduism in the making of the Vijayanagar empire. The fact of the matter is that the vow of '*Hindu dharma rakhsna*' taken by Harihara and Bukka was the result of the influence Vidyaranya had on the Sangama brothers—just the same way Samarth Ramdas played a great role in the making of Shivaji three centuries later.

58 V.S. Naipaul, *India: A Wounded Civilisation,* Penguin, New Delhi, 1979.

59 Ibid.

60 Ibid.

61 Robert Sewell, *A Forgotten Empire Vijayanagar*, Master Mind Books, Bengaluru, 2022.

62 Ibid.

63 K.A. Nilakanta Sastri, *A History of South India: From Prehistoric Times to the Fall of Vijayanagar,* Oxford University Press, New Delhi, 2023.

64 Robert Sewell, *A Forgotten Empire Vijayanagar,* Master Mind Books, Bengaluru, 2022.

65 Several eminent distorians invoke the title, 'Sultan among Hindu kings', used by the Vijayanagar emperors, to challenge the notion of the empire being a 'Hindu state'. This is a fallacious argument because titles are largely dictated by contemporary styles, and one should avoid reading too much into it.

66 K.A. Nilakanta Sastri, *A History of South India: From Prehistoric Times to the Fall of Vijayanagar,* Oxford University Press, New Delhi, 2023.

67 Robert Sewell, *A Forgotten Empire Vijayanagar*, Master Mind Books, Bengaluru, 2022.

Chapter 6: The M Factor

1 Karan Thapar, 'Why Yogi Is Wrong about the Mughals', *Hindustan Times*, 20 September 2020, https://www.hindustantimes.com/columns/why-yogi-is-wrong-about-the-mughals/story-kQsbMlqIEf4NuWq9baILdP.html (accessed 4 November 2024).

2 Ibid.

3 J.L. Mehta, *Advanced Study in the History of Medieval India, Vol II (1526–1707): Mughal Empire*, Sterling Publishers, New Delhi, 1995.

4 H. Beveridge, *The Akbar Nama of Abul Fazl, Vol II*, Asiatic Society, Calcutta, 1907.

5 Aabhas Maldahiyar, *Babur: The Chessboard King*, Penguin, New Delhi, 2024.

6 John Zubrzycki, *The Shortest History of India*, Picador, New Delhi, 2022.

7 Jawaharlal Nehru, *The Discovery of India*, Penguin, New Delhi, 2004.

8 Listing the native powers in Bharat, Babur placed first the 'Raja of Bijanagar'. This was Krishnadevaraya, the greatest of the Vijayanagar kings. Since the Vijayanagar empire was more than 1,000 km from Delhi, it posed no direct threat to Babur. The second ruler named by Babur was Rana Sangha of Mewar who 'in those days had grown great by his own valour and sword'.

9 Wheeler M. Thackston, 'Introduction' by Salman Rushdie, *The Baburnama: Memoirs of Babur, Prince and Emperor*, The Modern Library, New York, 2002.

10 Ibid.

11 Ibid.

12 Jadunath Sarkar, *Military History of India*, Gyan Publications, New Delhi, 2022.

13 Ibid.

14 Wheeler M. Thackston, 'Introduction' by Salman Rushdie, *The Baburnama: Memoirs of Babur, Prince and Emperor*, The Modern Library, New York, 2002.

15 Andrew Robinson, *India: A Short History*, Thames & Hudson, London, 2014.

16 Alexander Rogers (trans.), Henry Beveridge (ed.), *The Tazuk-i-Jahangiri or Memoirs of Jahangir*, London Royal Asiatic Society, London, 1909.

17 Jadunath Sarkar, *Shivaji and His Times*, Longmans, Green and Co., London, 1920.

18 Jadunath Sarkar, *A Short History of Aurangzib*, Orient BlackSwan, Hyderabad, 2009.

19 Ibid.

20 The Hindus of Delhi and the suburbs gathered together and sought the withdrawal of the decree. But the emperor turned a deaf ear. Next Friday, Sarkar writes in *A Short History of Aurangzib*, '[T]he whole road from the gate of the fort to the Jama Masjid was blocked by a crowd of Hindu supplicants. They did not disperse in spite of warning; and the Emperor, after waiting vainly for an hour to go to the public prayer, ordered elephants to be driven through the mass of men, trampling them down and clearing a way for him. A temperate and reasoned letter from Shivaji urging the impolicy of the new impost and appealing to Aurangzib to think of the common Father of mankind and the equality of all sincere beliefs in God's eyes, met with no better success.'

21 Dennis Kincaid, *Shivaji: The Grand Rebel*, Rupa, New Delhi, 2015.

22 Vincent A. Smith, *The Oxford History of India: From the Earliest Times to the End of 1911*, Clarendon Press, London, 1923.

23 Abdul Hamid Lahori, *Badshahnama,* https://archive.org/details/badshahnamaabdulhamidlahori/page/n7/mode/2up (accessed 10 November 2024).

24 Ibid.

25 A.L. Srivastava, *A Short History of Akbar the Great (1542–1605),* Shiva Lal Agarwala & Co., Agra, 1957.

26 K.S. Lal, *The Mughal Harem,* Aditya Prakashan, New Delhi, 1988.

27 Ibid.

28 Ibid.

29 William Dalrymple, *The Anarchy: The East India Company, Corporate Violence, and the Pillage of an Empire,* Bloomsbury, New Delhi, 2019.

30 Dara Shikoh was an interesting phenomenon. Several historians and commentators have bemoaned the fact that Shah Jahan was succeeded by Aurangzeb, and not Dara Shikoh. Philosopher Jonardon Ganeri, in *The Lost Age of Reason*, audaciously chooses 1656 ad as a seminal year for the flowering of a culture of syncretism in Bharat. He writes, 'In India, this was the year in which a long-running process of religious isomorphism, pioneered by Akbar's chronicler Abu-i-Fazl and orchestrated around the idea of Ibn al-Arabi, the Sufi mystic and philosopher, of "unity in being" (*wahdat al-wujud*), reached fulfillment in Dara Shikoh's grand project to translate 52 Upanishads in Persian, a project for the sake of which he assembled in Varanasi a large team of bilingual scholars. Dara believed that he could establish that the differences between Hinduism and Islam were largely terminological, and even that the Upanishads can be read as a sort of commentary upon the Qur'an.'

In the eagerness to see this grand project of cultural amalgamation of Hinduism and Islam reach a logical conclusion, two fundamental aspects are ignored. One, this attempt to see the Upanishads as 'a sort of commentary upon the Quran' was based on an absolute falsehood, for there was nothing in common between the Quran and the Upanishads; also, it does elevate the status of Upanishads from being a heathen's book worthy of being burnt, but the Quran retains an incontestable, unchallengeable status, with Hindu text playing the role of a subsidiary. Two, the attempt was destined to fail as the very nature of Islam denies such compromises, even if it was largely favourable for the Abrahamic religion. In Islam, it's my way or the highway; there is no middle path.

History shows how any attempt to find a middle path has failed miserably, as we have seen in Bharat, Iran and Turkey.

31 Jadunath Sarkar, *Studies in Aurangzib's Reign,* M.C. Sarkar & Sons, Calcutta, 1933.

32 Aurangzeb used Hindu generals to either fight his Hindu enemies or to conquer some of the most treacherous terrains of the subcontinent. Read the history of Raja Jai Singh of Amber, who fought Shivaji, or Maharaja Jaswant Singh of Jodhpur, who was sent to fight the ferocious Afghans in the northwestern frontier—and Aurangzeb's deception becomes evident. Historian J.L. Mehta writes in *Advanced Study in the History of Medieval India, Vol II (1526-1707): Mughal Empire*, 'He (Aurangzeb) did not declare his open hostility towards the Hindus as such so long as powerful and influential Rajput nobles of Shah Jahan's times adorned the imperial court. Aurangzeb taxed their energies and exploited their resources in men and material to the maximum. They were made to carry out the most arduous military assignments until they were totally exhausted and finished. Raja Jai Singh of Amber, the grandson of Raja Man Singh, carried fire and sword into the Maratha territories and brought Shivaji to his knees at Purandhar in 1665; thereafter, he was deputed on the Bijapur front to extirpate the Shia kingdom. Worn out by age and totally exhausted, he was recalled to the court from Aurangabad in May l667; and he died a broken hearted man at Burhanpur on July 2, 1667. (According to Manucci, he was poisoned to death by the orders of Aurangzeb.) Likewise, Maharaja Jaswant Singh of Jodhpur had been sent to fight the turbulent Pathan tribes of the northwestern frontier with the hope that he might end his career there. Two of his sons, who were on his own staff, died fighting the tribesmen for the Mughal throne. The state of Jodhpur had been left under the charge of his heir apparent Prithvi Singh. It is said that Aurangzeb called him to the court where 'at the end of a flattering entertainment' he was presented by the emperor with a poisoned dress of honour; he wore the dress and died of poison that very day. The old and grief-stricken Maharaja Jaswant Singh died at Jamrud on December 10, 1678.

On the receipt of intelligence, Aurangzeb forthwith despatched the Mughal troops for the annexation of Jodhpur (Marwar), and he himself shifted his court to Ajmer to facilitate the task.'

33 Jadunath Sarkar, *Studies in Aurangzib's Reign,* M.C. Sarkar & Sons, Calcutta, 1933.

34 Jadunath Sarkar, *A Short History of Aurangzib,* Orient BlackSwan, Hyderabad, 2009.

35 Ibid.

36 Dennis Kincaid, *Shivaji: The Grand Rebel,* Rupa, New Delhi, 2015.

37 Jadunath Sarkar, *Shivaji and His Times,* Longmans, Green & Co., London, 1920.

38 Thomas Watters, *On Yuan Chwang's Travels in India,* Royal Asiatic Society, London, 1904.

39 Jadunath Sarkar, *Shivaji and His Times,* Longmans, Green & Co., London, 1920.

40 Ibid.

41 Gajanan Bhaskar Mehendale, *Shivaji: His Life and Times,* Param Mitra Publications, Thane, Maharashtra, 2011.

42 Jadunath Sarkar, *Shivaji and His Times,* Longmans, Green & Co., London, 1920.

43 Gajanan Bhaskar Mehendale, *Shivaji: His Life and Times,* Param Mitra Publications, Thane, Maharashtra, 2011.

44 H.M. Elliot, *The History of India, As Told by Its Own Historians, Volume VII,* Trubner & Co., London, 1877.

45 Jadunath Sarkar, *Shivaji and His Times,* Longmans, Green & Co., London, 1920.

46 Uday S. Kulkarni, *The Maratha Century: Vignettes & Anecdotes of the Maratha Empire,* Mula Mutha Publishers, Pune, 2021.

47 Ibid.

48 Ibid.

49 R.C. Majumdar, H.C. Raychaudhuri and Kalikinkar Datta, *An Advanced History of India,* Macmillan, Madras, 1978.

50 Ahmed Shah Abdali invaded Bharat eight times between 1748 and 1767.

51 R.C. Majumdar (ed.), *History and Culture of the Indian People, Volume 7, The Mughul Empire,* Bharatiya Vidya Bhavan, Bombay, 1974.
52 Vikram Sampath, *Bravehearts of Bharat: Vignettes from Indian History,* Penguin, New Delhi, 2022.
53 Kesri Singh, *Maharana Pratap: The Hero of Haldighati,* Books Treasure, Jodhpur, 2010.
54 Rima Hooja, *Maharana Pratap: The Invincible Warrior,* Juggernaut, New Delhi, 2018.
55 Sri Ram Sharma, *Maharana Pratap,* Hope India Publication, Gurgaon, 2002.
56 Kesri Singh, *Maharana Pratap: The Hero of Haldighati,* Books Treasure, Jodhpur, 2010.
57 R.C. Majumdar (ed.), *History and Culture of the Indian People, Volume 7, The Mughul Empire,* Bharatiya Vidya Bhavan, Bombay, 1974.
58 James Tod, *Annals and Antiquities of Rajasthan, or The Central and Western Rajpoot States of India*, Gyan Publications, New Delhi, 2020.
59 Rima Hooja, *Maharana Pratap: The Invincible Warrior,* Juggernaut, New Delhi, 2018.
60 Gajanan Bhasker Mehendale writes in his book *Shivaji: His Life and Times*, 'On 20th August 1666, Trimbakpant, Raghunathpant Korde and three other followers of Shivaji were arrested by Fulad Khan in the house of Kishan Rai, a petty mansabdar who was son-in-law of Pratit Rai, the chief of spies! Faulad Khan (kotwal of Shahjahanabad under *Aurangzeb*) reported to the Emperor that the prisoners were saying that Jai Singh had written to his son Ram Singh to extricate Shivaji in any way he could and that Pratit Rai knew about it. Most probably either Faulad Khan or the prisoners were trying to falsely implicate Jai Singh in Shivaji's escape. Perhaps the Emperor perceived this fact and his reaction was mild. He dismissed Kishanrai from service, removed Pratit Rai from his post and demoted him, and appointed Itimad Khan in his place. Ram Singh was dismissed from service

and Jai Singh's agent at the court was forbidden to come to the antechamber. On the same day, the following *farman* was dispatched to Jai Singh: 'With great effort and exertion you had subdued Shivaji and sent him to our presence. And we, considering Ram Singh to be trustworthy and a well-wisher, placed Shivaji in his custody. But he, digressing from good wishes and service, favoured Shivaji and, with deceit and deception, let him escape. Therefore we wanted to punish Ram Singh, remove him from our presence and parade him through the city (in disgrace). But because of you, who are firm and constant in service, we granted him his life and dismissed him from service. Tender thanks to god because your son received such a small punishment for his offence.'

61 S.K. Bhuyan, *Lachit Barphukan and His Times: A History of Assam-Mogul Conflicts of the Period 1667 to 1671 AD*, Department of Historical and Antiquarian Studies, Government of Assam, Guwahati, 1947.

62 Manuscript 'Assam Buranji', which is a collection of 192 letters exchanged between the kings and officers of Assam, and the courts of Delhi, Dacca, Cooch Behar, Cachar, Sylhet, Jayanta, *et al.*, from the earliest times to the death of King Swargadeo Rudra Singha in 1714 AD (DHAS, Guwahati).

63 Suniti Kumar Chatterji, *The Place of Assam in the History and Civilisation of India*, Department of Publication, University of Gauhati, Guwahati, 1970.

64 Vikram Sampath, *Bravehearts of Bharat: Vignettes from Indian History*, Penguin, New Delhi, 2022.

65 B.B. Kumar, *The Tribal Societies of India*, Omsons Publications, New Delhi, 1999.

66 Sir Herbert Risley, *The People of India*, Thacker, Spink & Co., Calcutta, 1915.

67 B.B. Kumar, *Folklores and Folklore Motifs*, Omsons Publications, New Delhi, 1993.

68 Ibid.

69 Ibid.

70 Suniti Kumar Chatterji, *The Place of Assam in the History and Civilisation of India*, Department of Publication, University of Gauhati, Guwahati, 1970.
71 Ibid.
72 Sir Jadunath Sarkar writes in *History of Aurangzib, Volume 3*, 'Indeed, there is reason to believe that Ram Singh wets sent to Assam as a punishment for his having secretly helped Shivaji to escape from captivity at Agra. He had only 8,000 troopers round his standards, and his losses were seldom replenished. The Ahoms, being a nation in arms, mustered one hundred thousand when mobilised. Unlike the time of Mir Jumla's invasion, the mastery of the water now belonged to the Ahoms, and the Mughals could do little with their 40 war-vessels on the Brahmaputra.'
73 Arup Kumar Dutta, *The Ahoms: A Reimagined History*, HarperCollins, New Delhi, 2022.
74 Ibid.
75 Ibid.
76 S.K. Bhuyan, *Lachit Barphukan and His Times: A History of Assam-Mogul Conflicts of the Period 1667 to 1871 AD*, Department of Historical and Antiquarian Studies, Government of Assam, Gauhati, 1947.

Chapter 7: White Mischief

1 Nassim Nicholas Taleb, *The Black Swan: The Impact of the Highly Improbable*, Penguin, New Delhi, 2008.
2 Ibid.
3 Jon Wilson, *India Conquered: Britain's Raj and the Chaos of Empire*, Simon & Schuster, London, 2016.
4 Manohar Malgonkar, *Kanhoji Angrey, Maratha Admiral: An Account of His Life and His Battles with the British*, Asia Publishing House, Bombay, 1959.
5 Ibid.
6 Clement Downing, *A History of the Indian Wars*, Oxford University Press, London, 1924.

7 Manohar Malgonkar, *Kanhoji Angrey, Maratha Admiral: An Account of His Life and His Battles with the British*, Asia Publishing House, Bombay, 1959.

8 Uday S. Kulkarni, *The Maratha Century: Vignettes & Anecdotes of the Maratha Empire*, Mula Mutha Publishers, Pune, 2021.

9 The *Ajnapatra,* a royal edict on the principles of Maratha policy, was written by the formidable Amatya Ramachandra Pant who served as Shivaji's finance minister. Written in the Marathi Modi script, it is regarded as the formal documentation of Shivaji's ideals and policies of administration. Pant composed the *Ajnapatra* in 1715, both as a theoretical and practical manual or guide for Shivaji's grandson, Sambhaji II, who ruled as the raja of Kolhapur.

10 Amatya Ramachandra Pant, *Ajnapatra,* (https://archive.org/details/Adnyapatra/page/82/mode/2up (accessed 10 November 2024).

11 Ibid.

12 Dr B.K. Apte, *A History of Maratha Navy and Merchant Ships*, State Board for Literature and Culture, Bombay, 1973.

13 Dylan Sullivan and Jason Hickel, 'How British Colonialism Killed 100 Million Indians in 40 Years', *Al Jazeera*, 2 December 2022, https://www.aljazeera.com/opinions/2022/12/2/how-british-colonial-policy-killed-100-million-indians (accessed 12 November 2024).

14 The Arab scholar, Alberuni, who wrote an account of Bharat during Mahmud of Ghazni's time, said that due to the sultan's raids 'the Hindus became like the atoms of dust scattered in all directions'.

15 K.S. Lal, *Growth of Scheduled Tribes and Castes in Medieval India*, Aditya Prakahan, New Delhi, 1995.

16 Ibid.

17 The British presence in Bharat can be roughly divided into three phases: the first phase was when Captain William Hawkins set foot on Bharat's soil in 1608 AD. This was the era (roughly corresponding to the 17th century) when Bharat had a population of 150 million people, which was about a fifth of the world's total, and was the world's industrial powerhouse, producing about a

fourth of the global manufacturing. Britain, in sharp contrast, was a minnow with just 5 per cent of Bharat's population and was producing about 3 per cent of the world's manufactured goods. Bharat had everything at its disposal and was just not interested in trading with Britain. No wonder Captain Hawkins and later Sir Thomas Roe found themselves ignored by the Timurid officials and nobility; even Emperor Jahangir was only interested in British wines and 'expects great presents and jewels and regards no trade but what feeds his insatiable appetite after stones, riches and rare pieces of art'. The second phase (largely the 18th century) saw quite a few British officials behaving 'like a Native, and with great propriety', as was the case with James Kirkpatrick, the British resident of Hyderabad. They would ride in a palanquin, attend nautches, keep several concubines, and even smoke hookah. In fact, as Dalrymple writes in *White Mughals*, that was the time when the British 'showed no particular enthusiasm for cleanliness', and it were desi women who 'introduced' them 'to the delights of regular bathing'. This was also the time when the British promoted the study of Bharat's ancient past, often seeking common connections with Sanskrit and the Indic civilization. The third phase (roughly from the beginning of the 19th century till the end of the Raj) saw the British taking up the role of a progressive, civilizing force that alone could pull Bharat out of its darkness and depravity.

18 William Dalrymple begins his book, *The Anarchy*, by saying that 'one of the first Indian words to enter the English language was the Hindustani slang for plunder: *loot*'. Dalrymple then explains how, according to the *Oxford English Dictionary*, the word loot 'was rarely heard outside the plains of north India until the late 18th century, when it suddenly became a common term across Britain'. Shashi Tharoor takes this forward as he writes in *An Area of Darkness*: '"Loot" being a Hindustani word they (British) took into their dictionaries as well as their habits'.

19 William Dalrymple, *The Anarchy: The East India Company, Corporate Violence, and the Pillage of an Empire*, Bloomsbury, London, 2019.

20 W.W. Hunter, *Famine Aspects of Bengal Districts*, Trubner & Co., London, 1874.
21 John Fiske, *The Unseen World, and Other Essays*, Houghton, Mifflin and Company, Boston, 1876.
22 Roy Moxham, *The Theft of India: The European Conquests of India (1498–1765)*, HarperCollins, New Delhi, 2016.
23 Ibid.
24 Ibid.
25 John Keay, *The Honourable Company: A History of the English East India Company*, HarperCollins, New Delhi, 1993.
26 Sudeep Chakravarti quoting W.W. Wilson in his book, *Plassey: The Battle That Changed the Course of Indian History*, Aleph Book Company, New Delhi, 2020.
27 Tibetan diplomat George Bogle, after meeting Hastings, described him as 'a man who is in every way fitted for the station he holds'.
28 M.J. Akbar, *Doolally Sahib and the Black Zamindar: Racism and Revenge in the British Raj*, Bloomsbury, New Delhi, 2022.
29 Nick Robins, *The Corporation That Changed the World: How the East India Company Shaped the Modern Multinational*, Pluto Press, London, 2012.
30 Philip Mason, *The Men Who Ruled India*, Rupa, New Delhi, 1985.
31 Sumanta Banerjee, *Crime and Urbanisation: Calcutta in the Nineteenth Century*, Tulika Books, New Delhi, 2006.
32 Amartya Sen, who as a nine-year-old boy had witnessed the 1943 Bengal famine, believed that the death of over three million people could have been prevented by a responsive government as there was adequate food supply at the time. In his milestone book, *Poverty and Famines: An Essay on Entitlement and Deprivation*, he revealed that in many cases of famine, food supplies were not significantly reduced. Instead, what aggravated the crisis were socio-economic factors such as declining wages, unemployment, rising food prices, and poor food-distribution systems. According to Sen, thus, famines do

not occur in functioning democracies because their leaders are more responsive to the demands of the citizens.

33 Madhusree Mukerjee, *Churchill's Secret War*, Tranquebar Press, New Delhi, 2010.

34 Nick Robins, *The Corporation That Changed the World: How the East India Company Shaped the Modern Multinational*, Pluto Press, London, 2012.

35 As quoted in Mike Davis, *Late Victorian Holocausts: El Nino Famines and the Making of the Third World*, Verso, London, 2001.

36 As quoted in Shashi Tharoor, *An Area of Darkness: The British Empire in India*, Aleph Book Company, New Delhi, 2016.

37 Ibid.

38 Ibid.

39 Angus Maddison, *The World Economy*, Academic Foundation, New Delhi, 2007.

40 William Dalrymple, *The Last Mughal: The Fall of a Dynasty, Delhi, 1857*, Penguin, New Delhi, 2007.

41 R.C. Majumdar (ed.), *The History and Culture of the Indian People Vol 9: British Paramountcy and Indian Renaissance Part 1*, Bharatiya Vidya Bhavan, Bombay, 1988.

42 Ibid.

43 Mahmood Farooqui, in his book *Besieged Voices from Delhi 1857*, finds Zafar to be an indispensable symbol and a moral authority of the rebellion.

44 William Dalrymple, *The Last Mughal: The Fall of a Dynasty, Delhi, 1857*, Penguin, New Delhi, 2007.

45 R.C. Majumdar, *The Sepoy Mutiny and the Revolt of 1857*, Firma K.L. Mukhopadhyay, Calcutta, 1957.

46 Ibid.

47 Jon Wilson, *India Conquered: Britain's Raj and the Chaos of Empire*, Simon & Schuster, London, 2016.

48 Catherine Hall, *Macaulay and Son: Architects of Imperial Britain*, Yale University Press, New Haven, 2012.

49 Jon Wilson, *India Conquered: Britain's Raj and the Chaos of Empire*, Simon & Schuster, London, 2016.

50 Rosie Llewellyn-Jones, *The Great Uprising in India, 1857-58*, Boydell & Brewer, Woodbridge, 2007.

51 Andrew Ward, *Our Bones Are Scattered: The Cawnpore Massacres and the Indian Mutiny of 1857*, John Murray, London, 2004.

52 R.C. Majumdar, *The Sepoy Mutiny and the Revolt of 1857*, Firma K.L. Mukhopadhyay, Calcutta, 1957.

53 Amaresh Misra, *War of Civilisations: India* AD *1857*, Rupa, New Delhi, 2007.

54 Shubhra Chakrabarti and Utsa Patnaik (ed.), *Agrarian and Other Histories: Essays for Binay Bhushan Chaudhuri*, Tulika Books, New Delhi, 2019.

55 V.S. Naipaul, *India: A Million Mutinies*, Vintage, London, 1998.

56 William Howard Russell, *My Diary in India: In the Year 1858–59*, Routledge, Warne, and Routledge, London, 1860.

57 V.S. Naipaul, *India: A Million Mutinies*, Vintage, London, 1998.

58 Khushwant Singh, *The Fall of the Kingdom of the Punjab*, Penguin Viking, New Delhi, 2014.

59 Ibid.

60 General Sir John J.H. Gordon, *The Sikhs*, William Blackwood & Sons, Edinburg and London, 1904.

61 Sikhism was founded by Guru Nanak in the late 15th century with a focus on promoting equality, social justice and tolerance for other religions. It remained a pacifist, non-violent religion till Jahangir got Guru Arjan Dev, the fifth guru, killed on 30 May 1606 AD. After the martyrdom of Guru Tegh Bahadur, the ninth guru, on 24 November 1675, the Sikhs were on the warpath with the Timurids. It completely changed the character of Sikhism.

62 V.S. Naipaul, *India: A Million Mutinies*, Vintage, London, 1998.

63 Khushwant Singh, *A History of the Sikhs, Vol 1: 1469–1839*, Oxford University Press, New Delhi, 2015.

64 Amandeep Sandhu, *Panjab: Journeys through Fault Lines*, Westland, Chennai, 2019.

65 Khushwant Singh, *A History of the Sikhs, Vol 1: 1469–1839*, Oxford University Press, New Delhi, 2015.
66 Ibid.
67 M.A. Macauliffe, *The Sikh Religion: Its Gurus, Sacred Writings and Authors, Volume IV*, Oxford, 1909.
68 Khushwant Singh, *A History of the Sikhs, Vol 1: 1469–1839*, Oxford University Press, New Delhi, 2015.
69 As quoted by Khushwant Singh from *Dabistan-e Mazahib*, written by Muhsin Fani, a 17th-century Persian historian.
70 Khushwant Singh, *A History of the Sikhs, Vol 1: 1469–1839*, Oxford University Press, New Delhi, 2015.
71 William Irvine, *Later Mughals: 1707–1720, Vol. 1*, edited by Jadunath Sarkar, M.C. Sarkar & Sons, Calcutta, 1922.
72 Ibid.
73 Khushwant Singh, *A History of the Sikhs, Vol 1: 1469–1839*, Oxford University Press, New Delhi, 2015.
74 As quoted by Ganda Singh in his book *Life of Banda Singh Bahadur: Based on Contemporary and Original Records*, Sikh History Research Department, Khalsa College, Amritsar, 1935.
75 Ibid.
76 Gokul Chand Narang, *Transformation of Sikhism*, New Book Society, Lahore, 1912.
77 Pathi Venkata Thadhagath, 'Congress MLA Promises 100-ft Statue of Tipu Sultan in Mysuru', *Hindustan Times*, 12 November 2022, https://www.hindustantimes.com/cities/bengaluru-news/congress-mla-promises-100-ft-statue-of-tipu-sultan-in-mysuru-101668257389536.html (accessed 12 November 2024).
78 Bhagwan S. Gidwani, *The Sword of Tipu Sultan,* Rupa, New Delhi, 2009.
79 Charles Allen, *Coromandel: A Personal History of South India*, Little, Brown and Company, London, 2017.
80 Vikram Sampath, *Tipu Sultan: The Saga of Mysore's Interregnum (1760-1799),* Penguin, New Delhi, 2024.

81 Sandeep Balakrishna, *Tipu Sultan: The Tyrant of Mysore*, Rare Publications, Chennai, 2013.

82 M.G. Gopal, *The Sultan's Mysore: An Economic Study*, Popular Prakashan, Bombay, 1971.

83 Lewin B. Bowring, *Hyder Ali and Tipu Sultan*, Pharos Books, New Delhi, 2022.

84 Sandeep Balakrishna, *Tipu Sultan: The Tyrant of Mysore*, Rare Publications, Chennai, 2013.

85 Vikram Sampath, *Tipu Sultan: The Saga of Mysore's Interregnum (1760-1799),* Penguin, New Delhi, 2024.

86 Ibid.

87 Ibid.

88 Ibid.

89 Ibid.

90 Ibid.

91 K.M. Panikkar, *Malabar and the Mysore: Being the History of Expansion of Mysore in South*, Life Span Publishers, New Delhi, 2020.

92 Utpal Kumar, 'Tipu Sultan was inherently anti-India, anti-Hindu and anti-Kannadiga—still Congress won't stop batting for him', *Firstpost*, 16 November 2022, https://www.firstpost.com/opinion-news-expert-views-news-analysis-firstpost-viewpoint/tipu-sultan-was-inherently-anti-india-anti-hindu-and-anti-kannadiga-still-congress-wont-stop-betting-for-him-11633191.html (accessed 4 December 2024).

93 Sandeep Balakrishna, *Tipu Sultan: The Tyrant of Mysore*, Rare Publications, Chennai, 2013.

94 As quoted by Charles Allen in his book, *Coromandel: A Personal History of South India*, Little Brown & Co., London, 2017.

95 Ibid.

96 Shashi Tharoor, *The Battle of Belonging: On Nationalism, Patriotism, and What It Means to be Indian*, Aleph, New Delhi, 2020.

97 Lewin B. Bowring, *Hyder Ali and Tipu Sultan*, Pharos Books, New Delhi, 2022.

Chapter 8: Freedom at Midnight

1 R.C. Majumdar, *The Sepoy Mutiny and the Revolt of 1857*, Firma K.L. Mukhopadhyay, Calcutta, 1957.
2 R.C. Majumdar, *History of the Freedom Movement in India, Volume 1*, Firma K.L. Mukhopadhyay, Calcutta, 1971.
3 Ibid.
4 R.C. Majumdar, *History of the Freedom Movement in India, Volume 3*, Firma K.L. Mukhopadhyay, Calcutta, 1971.
5 It took Justice Chakravartti two decades to reveal his 1956 interactions with Attlee in a letter dated 30 March 1976 to Sureshchandra Das, who was the publisher of eminent historian R.C. Majumdar.
6 Chandrachur Ghose, *Bose: The Untold Story of an Inconvenient Nationalist*, Penguin, New Delhi, 2022.
7 Ibid.
8 Ibid.
9 Ibid.
10 Note prepared by the director, Intelligence Bureau, on the INA situation, *Transfer of Power, Volume VI*, Her Majesty's Stationery Office, London.
11 Anuj Dhar, *India's Biggest Cover-Up*, Vitasta, New Delhi, 2012.
12 Ibid.
13 Sumit Sarkar, *Modern India: 1885–1947*, Macmillan, New Delhi, 1983.
14 Sanjeev Sanyal, *Revolutionaries: The Other Side of How India Won Its Freedom*, HarperCollins, New Delhi, 2023.
15 Sugata Bose, *His Majesty's Opponent: Subhas Chandra Bose and India's Struggle Against Empire*, Penguin, New Delhi, 2011.
16 Rudrangshu Mukherjee, *Nehru & Bose: Parallel Lives*, Penguin Viking, New Delhi, 2014.
17 Letter to Amiya Bose, 17 April 1939, as quoted in *Netaji: Collected Works, Volume 9*.
18 B.K. Nehru, Jawaharlal's first cousin, in his memoirs *Nice Guys Finish Second*, published by Penguin in 1997, writes: 'He (Motilal Nehru) used to say that men like Jawaharlal were

born once in a century. It was a pity that he had been born in a country like India; anywhere else he would have been ruling his nation and leading it to even greater glory. He said that if Jawaharlal lived for another ten years he would revolutionise this country of ours into something unrecognisable. But he feared that he would not live that long. Such men, he said, burnt themselves out.'

He further informs that Motilal Nehru was always plagued by the fear that his son would somehow or the other be done to death by the British government. He writes: 'He did not think they would have him assassinated but he feared they would involve him in some case of violent conspiracy of which at that time two very serious ones—the Kakori dacoity case and the Meerut conspiracy case—were going on. Or they would treat him so badly in prison that he would lose his health and die young. Or they would find some other way to end his life… Sir Alexander Mudiman, who was Home Member in those days, had assured him that there was no such intention but he did not believe this assurance. The day Bhagat Singh threw a bomb into the Legislative Assembly chamber Dadaji (Motilal) rang up Anand Bhavan and asked in what seemed to be panic where Jawaharlal was. I told him Jawaharlal was not in town and I did not know where he had gone. This only increased his anxiety. He was afraid that either Jawaharlal might have been actually involved in the conspiracy with Bhagat Singh or would be falsely implicated in it by the police.'

19 Rajmohan Gandhi, *The Good Boatman: A Portrait of Gandhi*, Penguin, New Delhi, 2000.

20 Sugata Bose, *His Majesty's Opponent: Subhas Chandra Bose and India's Struggle Against Empire*, Penguin, New Delhi, 2011.

21 Minoo Masani, *Bliss Was It in That Dawn: A Political Memoir up to Independence*, Arnold-Heinemann Publishers, New Delhi, 1977.

22 There are controversies—and question marks—surrounding the death of Netaji Bose in a plane crash in Taipei on 18 August

1945. Critics believe the Nehruvian government hurried in giving legitimacy to the Taiwan crash theory, despite several glaring loopholes—from reports saying that there was no plane crash in Taiwan in that month to the need for Bose to get into a crowded plane when his personal 12-seater with the INA insignia was very much available.

23 Sandeep Unnithan, 'Jawaharlal Nehru Spied on Subhas Chandra Bose's Family for 20 Years', *India Today*, 10 April 2015, https://www.indiatoday.in/india/story/jawaharlal-nehru-netaji-subash-chandra-bose-spy-exclusive-247945-2015-04-09 (accessed 16 November 2024).

24 Sugata Bose, *His Majesty's Opponent: Subhas Chandra Bose and India's Struggle Against Empire*, Penguin, New Delhi, 2011.

25 Vikram Sampath, *Savarkar: Echoes from a Forgotten Past 1883–1924*, Penguin, New Delhi, 2019.

26 Sampath writes, in *Savarkar: Echoes from a Forgotten Past*, how Gandhi and Savarkar met on 24 October 1909, exactly three years after their first meeting in October 1906. 'Nearly seventy Indians participated. Gandhi was invited to preside over the meeting. He agreed on the condition that "no controversial politics were to be touched upon" and that he would rather speak on the greatness of the Ramayana.' When Savarkar's turn for speaking came, he indirectly took on Gandhi as he said, 'It would be worthwhile to remember that Vijayadashami is preceded by a nine-day fast to propitiate Goddess Durga, who is symbol of war and annihilation of evil'. He further reminded the audience to remember that even Rama 'could not establish Rama Rajya (his kingdom) without slaying Ravana who symbolized tyranny, aggression, and injustice. If Ramachandra had merely sat on a fast, it was unlikely that his kingdom could have been established.' Similarly, when Gandhi attributed the massive 1934 Bihar earthquake to God's punishment for 'the barbaric caste system', Savarkar couldn't stop himself from reminding him about the Quetta quake!

27 Vikram Sampath, *Savarkar: Echoes from a Forgotten Past 1883–1924*, Penguin, New Delhi, 2019.

28 Vaibhav Purandare, *Savarkar: The True Story of the Father of Hindutva,* Juggernaut, New Delhi, 2019.
29 Vikram Sampath, *Savarkar: A Contested Legacy 1924–1966*, Penguin, New Delhi, 2021.
30 Ibid.
31 Vikram Sampath, *Savarkar: A Contested Legacy 1924–1966*, Penguin, New Delhi, 2021.
32 Sachindra Nath Sanyal, *Bandi Jeevan: A Life in Chains*, Rupa, New Delhi, 2023.
33 D.G. Tendulkar, *Mahatma: Life of Mohandas Karamchand Gandhi, Vol. 3*, Publications Division, New Delhi, 2016.
34 Chander Pal Singh, *Bhagat Singh Revisited: Historiography, Biography and Ideology of the Great Martyr*, Originals, New Delhi, 2011.
35 Ibid.
36 Subhas Chandra Bose, *The Indian Struggle*, Abhishek publications, New Delhi, 2019 (1935).
37 Sanjeev Sanyal, *Revolutionaries: The Other Side of How India Won Its Freedom*, HarperCollins, New Delhi, 2023.
38 Peter Heehs, 'Terrorism in India During the Freedom Struggle', *Historian*, Vol. 55 (1993), Issue 3.
39 Sunil Raman and Rohit Agarwal, *Delhi Durbar 1911: The Complete Story*, Roli Books, New Delhi, 2011.
40 Sachindra Nath Sanyal, *Bandi Jeevan: A Life in Chains*, Rupa, New Delhi, 2023.
41 Ibid.
42 R.C. Majumdar (ed.), *British Paramountcy and the Indian Renaissance, Volume 2*, Bharatiya Vidya Bhavan, Bombay, 1965.
43 Bipan Chandra, Mridula Mukherjee, Aditya Mukherjee, K.N. Panikkar, and Sucheta Mahajan, *India's Struggle for Independence*, Penguin, New Delhi, 1988.
44 Lala Lajpat Rai, *Young India: An Interpretation and a History of the Nationalist Movement From Within*, BW Huebsch, New York, 1916.
45 Sir William Wedderburn, *Allan Octavian Hume, C.B.: Father of the Indian National Congress*, T. Fisher Unwin, London, 1913.

46 Amales Tripathi, *Indian National Congress and the Struggle for Freedom*, translated by Amitava Tripathi, Oxford University Press, New Delhi, 2014.
47 Andrew Robinson, *India: A Short History*, Thames & Hudson, London, 2014.
48 Rabindranath Tagore, *The Home and the World*, Macmillan, London, 1919.
49 Amales Tripathi, *Indian National Congress and the Struggle for Freedom*, translated by Amitava Tripathi, Oxford University Press, New Delhi, 2014.
50 Ibid.
51 Sri Aurobindo, *Uttarpara Speech*, Sri Aurobindo Ashram Publications Department, Auroville, 2000.
52 V.S. Naipaul, *A Writer's People: Ways of Looking and Feeling*, Picador, New Delhi, 2007.
53 Ibid.
54 D.G. Tendulkar, *Mahatma: Life of Mohandas Karamchand Gandhi, Volume 2*, Publication Division, New Delhi, 1951.
55 Shahid Amin, 'Gandhi as Mahatma', in Ranjt Guha (ed.), *Subaltern Studies III: Writings on South Asian History and Society*, Oxford University Press, New York, 1984.
56 Ibid.
57 Ibid.
58 Ibid.
59 Joseph Lelyveld, *Great Soul: Mahatma Gandhi and His Struggle with India*, HarperCollins, New Delhi, 2011.
60 Ramachandra Guha, *Gandhi: The Years That Changed the World (1914–1948)*, Penguin, New Delhi, 2018.
61 Faisal Devji, *The Impossible Indian: Gandhi and the Temptation of Violence*, Harvard University Press, Cambridge, Massachusetts, 2012.
62 As quoted by J. Sai Deepak in *India, Bharat and Pakistan: The Constitutional Journey of a Sandwiched Civilisation*, Bloomsbury, New Delhi, 2022.
63 Arun Shourie, *The World of Fatwas or the Shariah in Action*, Rupa, New Delhi, 2002.

64 As quoted by B.R. Ambedkar in *Thoughts on Pakistan*, Thacker & Co., Bombay, 1941.

65 As per the Rowlatt Act, a person could be arrested by the police without any reason.

66 The British Indian Army, at Colonel Reginald Dyer's behest, fired indiscriminately—almost at point-blank range—on the unarmed and largely peaceful crowd at the Jallianwala Bagh in Amritsar on 13 April 1919. When the firing finally ended, the Bagh had turned into a garden of the dead and even kids as young as three weren't spared. The official number was 379 dead and 1,100 wounded, but an inquiry carried out by Madan Mohan Malaviya and Motilal Nehru that very year put the number at 1,000 dead and 1,500 wounded. Kim A. Wagner, in his new book *Jallianwala Bagh: An Empire of Fear and the Making of the Amritsar Massacre*, writes about how Dyer nonchalantly defended his action as he claimed that he shot 'to save the British Raj—to preserve India for the Empire, and to protect Englishmen and Englishwomen'. 'I had to shoot. I had 30 seconds to make up my mind what action to take, and I did it,' Dyer said, reminding rather unconvincingly that had he not shot, he and his 'little force would have been swept away like chaff'.

67 As quoted in Ramachandra Guha, *Gandhi: The Years That Changed the World (1914–1948)*, Penguin, New Delhi, 2018.

68 Ibid.

69 Ibid.

70 Rajmohan Gandhi, *Mohandas: A True Story of a Man, His People, and an Empire*, Penguin, New Delhi, 2007.

71 M.J. Akbar, *Gandhi: A Life in Three Campaigns*, Bloomsbury, New Delhi, 2023.

72 P.N. Chopra and Prabha Chopra (eds), *Inside Story of Sardar Patel: The Diary of Maniben Patel (1936–50)*, Vision Books, New Delhi, 2001.

73 Peter Heehs, *The Lives of Sri Aurobindo*, Columbia University Press, New York, 2008.

74 Ibid.

75 Ibid.

76 Louis Fischer, *The Life of Mahatma Gandhi*, HarperCollins, New Delhi, 2012.
77 Ibid.
78 Walter Reid, *Keeping the Jewel in the Crown: The British Betrayal of India*, Penguin Viking, New Delhi, 2016.
79 Peter Heehs, *The Lives of Sri Aurobindo*, Columbia University Press, New York, 2008.
80 Alex von Tunzelmann, *Indian Summer: The Secret History of the End of an Empire,* Simon & Schuster, London, 2007.
81 Narendra Singh Sarila, *The Shadow of the Great Game: The Untold Story of India's Partition,* HarperCollins, New Delhi, 2005.
82 Nisid Hajari, *Midnight's Furies: The Deadly Legacy of India's Partition*, Penguin Viking, New Delhi, 2015.
83 Sandeep Bamzai, *Princestan*, Rupa, New Delhi, 2020.
84 In the 1946 provincial elections, the Muslim League got over 89 per cent of Muslim votes, winning 425 out of 476 seats reserved for Muslims, on a policy of creating the independent state of Pakistan, while the Congress could get 4.5 per cent Muslim votes. Nine out of 10 Muslims at the time of Independence voted for a separate nation.
85 Alex von Tunzelmann, *Indian Summer: The Secret History of the End of an Empire,* Simon & Schuster, London, 2007.
86 Shahid Hamid, *Disastrous Twilight: A Personal Record of the Partition of India*, Pen & Sword Books, Barnsley, 1993.
87 Ibid.
88 Alex von Tunzelmann, *Indian Summer: The Secret History of the End of an Empire,* Simon & Schuster, London, 2007.
89 Andrew Lownie, *The Mountbattens: Their Lives and Loves*, Blink Publishing, London, 2019.
90 Alex von Tunzelmann, *Indian Summer: The Secret History of the End of an Empire,* Simon & Schuster, London, 2007.
91 Vijay Gokhale, *Crosswinds: Nehru, Zhou and the Anglo-American Competition Over China,* Penguin, New Delhi, 2024.
92 Narendra Singh Sarila, *The Shadow of the Great Game: The Untold Story of India's Partition,* HarperCollins, New Delhi, 2005.

93 Alex von Tunzelmann, *Indian Summer: The Secret History of the End of an Empire,* Simon & Schuster, London, 2007.
94 Makarand R. Paranjape, *The Death and Afterlife of Mahatma Gandhi*, Random House, New Delhi, 2015.
95 Pyarelal Nayyar, *Mahatma Gandhi: The Last Phase, Volume 2*, Navajivan Press, Ahmedabad, 1958.
96 Ramachandra Guha, *Gandhi: The Years That Changed the World (1914–1948)*, Penguin, New Delhi, 2018.
97 Manuben Gandhi, *Last Glimpses of Bapu*, Shiva Lal Agarwala, New Delhi, 1962.
98 Makarand R. Paranjape, *The Death and Afterlife of Mahatma Gandhi*, Random House, New Delhi, 2015.
99 *The Collected Works of Mahatma Gandhi*, Volume 98.
100 Robert Payne, *The Life and Death of Mahatma Gandhi*, Rupa, New Delhi, 1997 (1969).
101 Tushar Gandhi, *Let's Kill Gandhi*, Rupa, New Delhi, 2010.
102 Ramachandra Guha, *Gandhi: The Years That Changed the World (1914–1948)*, Penguin, New Delhi, 2018.
103 Koenraad Elst quotes Jana Sangh leader Balraj Madhok as saying in his book, *Why I Killed the Mahatma: Uncovering Godse's Defence*, Rupa, New Delhi, 2018.
104 Alex von Tunzelmann, *Indian Summer: The Secret History of the End of an Empire*, Simon & Schuster, New Delhi, 2007.
105 D.F. Karaka, *Betrayal in India*, Victor Gollancz, London, 1950 (distributed in Bharat by Allied Publishers).
106 Ibid.
107 Dominique Lapierre and Larry Collins, *Freedom at Midnight*, Vikas Publishing, New Delhi, 1997.
108 Ibid.
109 S. Gurumurthy, *Eternal India and the Constitution*, India First Foundation, New Delhi, 2005.

Epilogue

1 Milan Kundera, *The Book of Laughter and Forgetting*, Faber & Faber, London, 1996.

2 Romila Thapar, Harbans Mukhia and Bipan Chandra, *Communalism and the Writing of Indian History*, People's Publishing House, New Delhi, 1969.
3 Shankar Sharan, *Marxism and the Writing of Indian History*, India First Foundation, New Delhi, 2007.
4 Raj Thapar, *All These Years*, Penguin, New Delhi, 1991.

About the Author

Credit: Ahaan Kumar.

Utpal Kumar is the opinion editor at News18 and Firstpost. During more than two decades of his journalistic experience, he has worked with several media houses in the country. He started his career at the *Pioneer* and went on to work at the *Hindustan Times*, *Mail Today* (India Today Group) and the *Sunday Guardian*. Kumar has written hundreds of articles for reputed newspapers and magazines. As the books editor of most of the organizations he has worked at, he reviewed hundreds of books and interviewed preeminent authors. He is among the most trenchant nationalist voices in the mainstream media. *Eminent Distorians: Twists and Truths in Bharat's History* is his second book. His debut, *Bharat Rising: Dharma, Democracy, Diplomacy*, published in January 2024, is a bestseller.

About the Author

[illegible]

[illegible]